Voluntary Agen

Gambling, Public and Voluntary Agen...

WITHDRAWN

WITHDRAWN

Also by David Billis

Organising Public and Voluntary Agencies

Voluntary Agencies

Challenges of Organisation and Management

Edited by

David Billis

and

Margaret Harris

MACMILLAN

First published 1996 by
MACMILLAN PRESS LTD
Houndmills, Basingstoke, Hampshire RG21 6XS
and London
Companies and representatives
throughout the world

ISBN 0–333–62950–7 hardcover
ISBN 0–333–62951–5 paperback

A catalogue record for this book is available
from the British Library.

This book is printed on paper suitable for recycling and
made from fully managed and sustained forest sources.

10   9   8   7   6   5
05   04   03   02   01

Printed in Malaysia

Contents

List of Tables

Acknowledgements

This book is the outcome of a conference held in March 1994 to celebrate the 15th anniversary of the London School of Economics Centre for Voluntary Organisation (CVO). In addition to the researchers whose papers appear in this book, the conference was attended by several experienced voluntary sector practitioners: Julian Ashby, Ian Bruce, Melvyn Carlowe, Tim Cook, Stuart Etherington, Sally Greengross, Richard Gutch, Stephen Hatch, Janet Novak, Jane Skinner, Peter Tihanyi, Winifred Tumin and Mike Whitlam. This distinguished group of practitioners not only contributed to the success of the conference by engaging over the two days in discussions with the academics, they also took time prior to the conference to prepare written comments on the research papers. In this way, they facilitated an event in which the legendary theory/practice gap was positively bridged.

Our thanks are due also to the Home Office and the Third Sector Trust who helped with funding for the conference, and to Romayne Hutchison who worked with us cheerfully and meticulously in preparing this book for publication. Finally, we must pay tribute to the enthusiasm and commitment of the CVO team who worked so hard on the planning and organisation of the Anniversary Conference: Helen Cameron, Colin Rochester, Sue Roebuck and Jane Schiemann.

DAVID BILLIS
MARGARET HARRIS

Notes on the Contributors

David Billis is Director of the London School of Economics Centre for Voluntary Organisation (CVO). After graduating from the LSE, he spent ten years in a kibbutz, and was eventually responsible for financial and cost accounting. He returned to obtain a doctorate at the LSE and took up a post at Brunel University, where in 1978 he founded PORTVAC, the first university-based programme working with voluntary agencies. In 1987 he was appointed Director of the CVO, which incorporates and builds on the work of PORTVAC. In 1990 he co-founded and is International Editor of the journal *Nonprofit Management and Leadership*. In the past twenty years he has also worked as a researcher and consultant in the public, private and voluntary sectors in Europe, India, Africa and North and South America. In addition to numerous papers, he is the author or co-author of a number of books, including *Organising Public and Voluntary Agencies*.

Justin Davis Smith is Head of Research and Information at the Volunteer Centre UK, a post he has held since 1988. He was previously political assistant to the Rt Hon. Sir James Callaghan MP (now Lord Callaghan). He obtained a first class honours degree in modern history from the University of Loughborough in 1982, and a doctorate on the history of industrial relations after the Second World War in 1986. He is author of *The Attlee and Churchill Administrations and Industrial Unrest 1945–55* (1990) and co-editor of *Volunteering and Society* (1992) and *An Introduction to the Voluntary Sector* (1994). He is co-founder of the Voluntary Action History Society.

Nicholas Deakin has been Professor of Social Policy and Administration at Birmingham University since 1980. Previously, he worked in central and local government and at an independent research institute. He has held numerous research grants and written widely on urban policy, race relations and the voluntary sector. His most recent publications include *The Enterprise Culture and the Inner City* (with John Edwards, 1993), *The Costs of Welfare* (edited with Robert Page, 1993) and a new edition of his text *The Politics of Welfare* (1994).

Margaret Harris is Assistant Director of the London School of Economics Centre for Voluntary Organisation. Before moving into academia she worked in local government administration and research and as a volunteer adviser and trainer for the Citizens Advice Bureau service. She has researched and published numerous articles in the practitioner and academic press on voluntary sector management, governing bodies and religious-based organisations.

Richard Kay is Director of the Rainer Foundation. He has worked in the voluntary sector in senior management positions for the last eighteen years, following a period in the public sector. Papers based on his research into chief executives in the voluntary sector have been published in the Cranfield School of Management Working Papers (1992), *The Future of Services Management* (co-author with Professor Colin Fletcher), *The Cranfield Management Series* (ed. Colin Armistead, 1994) and in *Nonprofit Management and Leadership*, no. 3, vol. 4 (1994).

Martin Knapp is Professor of the Economics of Social Care, Personal Social Services Research Unit, University of Kent at Canterbury, where he has been employed since 1975. Since 1993 he has also been Professor of Health Economics and Director of the Centre for the Economics of Mental Health, Institute of Psychiatry, University of London. He has written ten books and published over a hundred journal articles in the areas of health and social policy. He was co-editor of *Voluntas* from 1990 to 1994.

Diana Leat is Visiting Senior Research Fellow at VOLPROF, City University Business School. She has held research and teaching posts in a number of universities and national voluntary organisations.

Diana has written extensively on the voluntary sector and on social policy. Her most recent publications include: *Managing Across Sectors: Similarities and Differences Between For-Profit and Voluntary Non-Profit Organisations*, VOLPROF, City University Business School, London; *Trusts in Transition: the Policy and Practice of Grant-Giving Trusts*, Joseph Rowntree Foundation, York (with I. Bruce); *Management for Tomorrow*, VOLPROF, City University Business School, London; *The Development of Community Care by the Independent Sector*, Policy Studies Institute, London.

Jane Lewis is a Professor of Social Policy at the London School of Economics. She is currently engaged in research on the implementation of the 1990 community care legislation. Her publications include *The Voluntary Sector, the State and Social Work in Britain, 1869–1994* (1995) and (with David Clark and David Morgan) *Whom God Hath Joined Together: Marriage Guidance, 1920–1990* (1992).

Tony Marshall gained his MA degree in Social Anthropology at Cambridge University. He is Principal Research Officer in the Research and Planning Unit at the Home Office and is currently responsible for research on the voluntary sector, refugees, partnership between agencies and mediation. He has carried out research on many aspects of criminal justice, community, social policy and voluntary organisations. He was the first Director of Mediation UK, a national voluntary organisation, for two years, and later acted as Chair of its Trustees. His publications include *Counselling and School Social Work*; *Bringing People Together*; *Alternatives to Criminal Courts*; *Crime and Accountability* and *Community Disorders and Policing*.

Stephen Osborne is a lecturer in Public Services Management at Aston Business School, Aston University, which he joined in 1990. He is also Joint Director of the Voluntary and Non-profit Research Unit at Aston University. He is a qualified social worker, with twelve years' experience as a social work practitioner and manager. He has directed a number of recent research projects about voluntary organisations, including studies of their role in innovation in social services, and of the income and expenditure of the voluntary sector in the UK. He has spoken extensively at international conferences as a result of this research. He is co-author (with Sandra Nutley) of the mainstream textbook *The Public Sector Management Handbook*.

Rob Paton is a Senior Lecturer in Management at the Open University. His early research was on employee buy-outs, co-ops and local employment initiatives. Subsequently he set up and directed the Voluntary Sector Management Programme, which attracts more than 500 students a year. He currently chairs the MBA foundation course at the Business School. His publications include *Reluctant Entrepreneurs*, (with Carolyn Hooker) *Developing Managers in Voluntary Organizations: a Handbook* and (as co-editor) *Issues in Voluntary and Non-profit Management*.

Marilyn Taylor joined the School for Advanced Urban Studies at the University of Bristol in 1990 after twenty-one years working in the voluntary and community sectors. She has written widely on community development and voluntary sector issues and published a series of *State of the Sector* reports for the National Council for Voluntary Organisations. Her most recent publication, with colleagues, is *Encouraging Diversity: Voluntary and Private Organisations in Community Care* (1995).

David Wilson is Professor of Organization Studies at Aston University, Birmingham. He was previously at Warwick Business School, Bradford Management Centre and the University of Uppsala, Sweden. He is Vice-Chairman of the British Academy of Management. He is the author of five books and over fifty articles on strategic decision-making and managing organisational diversity and change. His current research includes work on strategic performance and the financial income and expenditure national survey of voluntary organisations.

1

Introduction: Enduring Challenges of Research and Practice

David Billis and Margaret Harris

Towards the end of March 1994 an invited group of academics and practitioners took part in a conference to celebrate the 15th anniversary of the London School of Economics Centre for Voluntary Organisation (CVO). Conferences are hardly novel in the academic world, and as the Director of the LSE put it when welcoming the guests to the celebratory dinner: 'how else would academics celebrate other than by holding a conference?' Nevertheless, the traditional format disguised a rather different sort of event. This was an unconventional conference based on a distinctive approach to organisation, management and leadership in the voluntary sector.

The unconventional nature of the conference had been signalled several months earlier after the academics had prepared their papers, each of which was then subject to a written response from a leading practitioner. For two days papers and responses were presented and discussed within this mixed group. In fact, several of the participants wore both hats ('academic' and 'practitioner') with comfort, and some had moved with distinction from one side of the fence to the other. Yet, in the main, this was intended to be, and was, a rare opportunity for the two sides to meet without the usual hurly-burly of university or agency life. The participants in the conference shared a number of common interests.

First, all had a long history of involvement as scholars or practitioners in what we in the UK generally call the 'voluntary sector'. All had demonstrated through their writings and actions an interest and concern for the sector which usually stretched back many years.

A second unifying factor was a common desire to address important organisational and management issues facing leaders of voluntary agencies. Although the original agenda was set by the academic organisers, it drew on a detailed knowledge of the practical challenges of running voluntary agencies.

A final common factor was linked to the concern about practical problems. The participants in the conference were colleagues invited by the staff of the CVO to celebrate the Centre's 15th anniversary. The mixed nature of the group thus reflected the mission of the CVO itself, which was founded with the intention of bridging the theory–practice divide.

This book reflects the spirit of that original conference and, in these opening comments, we wish to set the scene by offering some personal reflections on three themes:

the attempt to bridge theory and practice;
the changing times for practitioners and academics;
the enduring challenges facing sector managers and leaders.

A distinctive approach to the field: bridging theory and practice

Academics who venture into the production of ideas that are intended to respond to real organisational problems need to be very sure of the relevance of their work. It is a most daunting experience to subject ideas to critical examination by a group of spirited practitioners. Yet the risks must be faced since the alternative is that the notorious gap between academe and the world of practice will grow ever wider.

Concern about this gap is not confined to this country. It is high on the agenda of the non-profit (voluntary) sector in the United States. Some of the potential dangers were highlighted in the report of a conference of more than 200 academics, private consultants, trustees and staff (Independent Sector, 1988, p. 29–30). It suggested that 'if the majority of innovation is to be found in the arena of practice, then academia is in a reactive mode. Coalitions across and on the boundaries of the "turf" become crucial'. The report continued by exhorting academics to 'stay close to real problems, and to get in contact with real dilemmas'.

A few years later the same theme provoked a major discussion at the annual conference of the leading scholarly association, the Association for Research on Nonprofit Organizations and Voluntary Action (ARNOVA). In the conference edition of *Nonprofit and Voluntary Sector Quarterly* Peter Dobkin Hall took the opportunity to warn that:

> despite the best of intentions and some very considerable commitments of money and energy, the gap remains. At its most basic level, scholars scoff at the practitioner literature as hopelessly superficial, and practitioners regard scholarly work either as trivial or incomprehensible (Hall, 1993, p. 259–60).

There are a number of reasons why academics need to forge coalitions with practitioners. It is not just a matter of pragmatic necessity; it may help, for example, to secure research grants from funders increasingly looking for evidence of contact with the real world. Unless we cross the 'turf' and engage in real debate with those who work in the sector we shall end up talking primarily to ourselves through the medium of scholarly journals; or, increasingly and even more remotely, on the 'electronic highway'.

Forging links is also essential for the directors, chairpersons and other leaders of voluntary agencies – these we have for simplicity called 'practitioners'. They need usable organisational ideas. This was made clear to us fifteen years ago by the practitioners who took part in our earliest workshops and collaborative research projects. The message we received was that planned change – or at the very least a better idea of where voluntary organisations had come from and where they might be going in the future – would require better theories. To develop those theories requires not only academics who are interested in real problems; it requires also agencies that are willing to allow academics (in an appropriate professional relationship) access to deep and often sensitive organisational problems.

Our 1994 conference stands testimony to the constructive dialogue that can take place between academics and practitioners. One of the striking aspects of that conference was that the participants did not see themselves as starry-eyed advocates for the voluntary sector. Nor are we ourselves apologists for the sector. However, we do believe that our experience of the past fifteen years amply demonstrates that voluntary organisations face distinctive challenges which warrant specialist academic attention. We shall shortly return to consider some of these challenges facing practitioners. First, by way of setting the scene, we move on to record a few highlights of the rise of this specialist field of scholarship.

Changing times for practitioners and academics

The CVO originated in 1978 as a modest self-funding venture based at Brunel University (PORTVAC – Programme of Research and Training into Voluntary Action). It was still a time of political consensus in the UK that the state ought to be the funder and provider of essential welfare services. Health, personal social services, housing, education – all were regarded as natural inhabitants of the public sector domain. The organised voluntary 'sector' seemed content with its more limited role complementing and supplementing the mainstream work of the public sector.

It had not always been so. In his seminal book, *Social Policy*, Marshall (1967, p. 169) reminded us that in the inter-war years voluntary bodies and public services had 'met well-nigh on equal terms'. Indeed, Beveridge in his famous Report (1948, p. 8) had gone further and saw 'co-operation between public and voluntary agencies. . . . [as] one of the special features of British public life'. It was a 'special' relationship that was underpinned by what was regarded as the core characteristic of voluntary action – 'independence from public control'.

In those earlier days the equality of relationship with government was also seen to include professionalism in administration. Voluntary organisations were regarded as highly professional. In a phrase that may surprise today's readers, Marshall (p. 168) was able to draw attention to the 'up-to-date and efficient administration' of the national voluntary federations of the inter-war years. The same belief in the high administrative performance of voluntary organisations can be found in Beveridge's report where he quoted approvingly from Bourdillon's *Voluntary Social Services* (1945):

Nowadays many of the most active voluntary organizations are staffed entirely by highly trained and fairly-well paid professional workers (Beveridge, 1948, p. 8).

Attitudes to the voluntary sector had certainly changed by the late 1970s and the time of the foundation of the Centre. With the benefit of hindsight it seems a remarkably tranquil period. There was little interest in the administration of the myriad of organisations that made up this rather unassuming sector. Although there was a long and distinguished British tradition of academic writing about voluntary action, few were interested in the educational and training needs of those who worked in the sector. There were no other specialist university programmes. In our own particular area of interest – organisation and management – there were at that time few management consultants and scarcely any specialist management literature.

Today, the world of state welfare provision is in tatters. In some areas, such as residential care of the elderly, the private sector plays a prominent role. In other areas of social welfare we are in the midst of the contracting-out of services. We have seen, too, the establishment of new organisational forms which are said to have 'opted-out' of the state system or to have become 'self-governing'. Apparently, they have thrown off the shackles of governmental control and entered the voluntary sector. Even the organisational language, which describes many of these bodies as 'trusts' and 'associations' stresses their independence and affinity with the voluntary sector.

So the voluntary sector is back 'in business'. It is a business which not all in the sector find comfortable. The language of public policy statements may still be full of the old familiar comforting words of the special relationship with government – 'partnership' remains a favourite – but the really powerful concepts are those of policy implementation which are largely imported from the private sector. The new 'business' has brought with it increased demands for 'efficiency' and 'effectiveness', the search for 'market niche', performance indicators and the need for 'strategic planning'.

Readers who suspect that the editors are here betraying scepticism regarding the undiluted virtues of importing private sector management concepts into the voluntary sector are correct. This may appear a rather odd stance for those running a Centre devoted to better organisation and management. Nevertheless it is a stance which we defend on two grounds.

First, most organisational concepts and theories were designed for large-scale organisations, particularly in the commercial and industrial sector. Even there, as two of the world's most distinguished contributors (one a Nobel prize winner) to the field of organisation theory have recently emphasised, the utility of those concepts is far from certain: 'the literature contains many assertions, but little evidence to determine. . . . . whether these assertions really hold up in the world of fact' (March and Simon, 1993, p.24).

Second, there is a more personal reason for scepticism which emanates from the history of our Centre. The CVO was in fact established primarily as a result of the limitations of the then-existing management theory. The original agenda of problems presented to us by those working in the sector at that time (Billis, 1979; Harris and Billis, 1986) unequivocally pointed to the need for new and distinctive theories. Existing theories developed for other sectors went so far, but not far enough. We return to this general theme shortly, and in our concluding chapter.

The academic community, both in the UK and internationally, has travelled a long way since the days when our Centre was established. Then, one solitary scholarly journal (*Journal of Voluntary Action Research*) provided an outlet for the mainly North American research. Apart from our own fledgling effort, the only other university programme was that established at Yale University a year previously (Program on Non-Profit Organization). There were no specialist international conferences and no international network. However, the resurgence of the sector has been accompanied by a period of sustained academic initiatives. We are now much better placed to argue our own corner with the big battalions of the public and private sector theorists.

Within the last five years there have been dramatic changes in the scholarly field. Two additional journals (*Nonprofit Management and Leadership* and *Voluntas*) – both with international contributions and readership – have become well established and joined the revitalised pioneering journal, retitled *Nonprofit and Voluntary Sector Quarterly*. Others are poised to join them. There are scores of centres and programmes devoted to non-profit studies in the United States, several new initiatives in this country, and a fast growing number of centres in other countries. The establishment in 1992 of the International Society for Third Sector Research (ISTR) was yet another step towards the consolidation and development of this area of study.

Our field – voluntary, non-profit or third sector studies – has come a long way in the last fifteen years. A not-insignificant contribution to the success of this journey has been made by the participants in the 1994 CVO 15th Anniversary Conference.

Enduring challenges

Since we believe that keeping close to the organisational challenges
faced by practitioners is important for the development of our field,
it was natural for us to use those challenges as a starting point for
our conference, and for this book. In the final chapter we shall
draw on the essays of our contributors to look ahead and to attempt
some analysis of possible future challenges for academics and practitioners. Here our purpose is different. It is to reflect on the past
and present organisational challenges in order to provide a back-
cloth for the following conference papers.

How have the organisational problems changed in the past fifteen years? What challenges have endured?

There can be no unequivocal answers about a field as large and
complex as the voluntary sector. Indeed, the definition of the sector
itself is one of the enduring issues. Nevertheless, in attempting tentative answers to these questions, the editors can draw on a depth
and breadth of organisational experiences. In the past fifteen years,
more than 300 agencies have participated in our Centre's programme
of workshops. A similar number of agencies have participated in
off-site research and training activities ranging from lengthy action-
research projects, through to briefer workshops and seminars.

In February 1979, ten directors and senior managers from voluntary agencies took part in the first event organised by the CVO.
The workshop report (Billis, 1979) referred to the 'formidable list
of issues' that were raised. These were divided into three broad
groupings: aims and objectives, work organisation, and governance.
It is a salutary exercise to see what was occupying the attention of
sector leaders at that time. Under the heading 'aims and objectives',
one of the main anxieties surrounded the way in which objectives,
values and cultures were changing, seemingly in an uncontrollable
manner. For example, a traditional voluntary organisation originally
responding to problems of loneliness had become, for financial reasons,
a housing association. The director questioned whether the 'method
of housing associations comes to wag the dog of loneliness'. An
allied problem, even in those quieter days, was that of growth –
which was seen to bring a trail of further challenges in its wake:
for example, defining the boundaries with the statutory sector, changed
relationships with other voluntary organisations, and changes in ethics
and values.

A second category of challenges were those linked to the internal organisation of work. Amongst these, confusion over roles and internal structures loomed large as a major sub-set of challenges: poor and fragmented accountability; conflicts between aims and organisational structures; communications between the different parts of the agency; and coping with changing individual roles, made up the more detailed list. Another sub-set of issues revolved around recruitment, training and career development; for example the absence of career systems or training structures and the difficulties of attracting high calibre staff. There were other problems that were subsumed in this general category of work organisation. A few participants mentioned the need to develop leadership skills, and several emphasised the difficulties that appeared in the relationship between volunteers and paid staff.

The final category, and for today's observer the least surprising of all, was 'governance'. Under this heading we included also the relationships between national headquarters and local associations, as well as the doyen of voluntary agency management problems – the relationships between staff and management committees and between chief executives and chairpersons.

In 1993 – fourteen years and scores of workshops later – a similar group of senior people from the sector met to discuss their organisational problems. They too began by listing the major issues facing their voluntary organisations. A few of the words used may have altered, but many of the main themes remained constant.

The problems of what was now described as 'rapid' growth were highlighted. So, too, were the difficulties of changing aims and values, particularly those of adjusting to a new, more 'professional', culture which envisages a heightened role for paid staff. Several themes, such as difficulties in staff–volunteer relationships and confusion over accountability, still appeared on the list in our category 'work organisation'. Coping with structures of accountability continued to represent a challenge for the leadership, whilst issues of recruitment and training were less prominent.

But the category which remained the most problematic was 'governance'. All the earlier themes were restated. Agencies raised questions about governance structures that were seen to be too large to make effective decisions, about strained relationships between management committees and staff, and about tensions between headquarters and local groups.

We can reinforce this picture with several additional sources. A review of the 'Thatcher period' (Billis and Harris, 1992) and other recent empirical studies undertaken by the Centre (for example, Billis and MacKeith, 1993; Billis, Ashby, Ewart and Rochester, 1994; Hedley and Rochester 1991; Harris, 1993) provide more detail. Summarising these experiences leads to the conclusion that few themes have dropped completely from the organisational agenda, although certain of our original categories have intensified in severity and spread.

Amongst these are issues which we have put under the heading of *aims and objectives*. Clarification of mission was an issue for a few agencies fifteen years ago. We have pointed elsewhere (Billis and Harris, 1992; Billis, Ashby, Ewart and Rochester, 1994) to the widespread changes in core 'target' groups – from the less to the more severe cases of need – which many agencies have experienced in the past decade. The more turbulent public policy environment may well be a major contributory factor in the intensification of the challenges of growth and change which have been influential in raising questions of change in agency missions. Such is the widespread character of these challenges that the sector might well adapt the familiar chant of the football terraces ('here we go') and adopt 'where are we going?' as its theme song.

Policy turbulence is also a likely causal factor in the *governance* problems, another of the themes that have intensified and spread in severity. As Drucker (1990) put it: 'no subject provides more heated debate in the nonprofit world than that of governance'.

We have in this section attempted to provide a summary of key challenges currently facing voluntary sector leaders. It was against this background that our conference was planned. Our hope and objective was to make a contribution to this vast range of issues. We conclude this introduction by providing the reader with a brief tour of the book's contents.

Responses to the challenges

The essays in this book have passed through several stages. They began life as invited contributions to an anniversary conference. Each paper received a written response from a practitioner before the academic authors made verbal presentations to the conference, where each paper was the subject of substantial debate. The authors then revised their contributions for publication. All in all it was a lengthy period of gestation.

We open with a paper by Marilyn Taylor who picks up the theme of environmental turbulence which we have already highlighted as a potential contributing factor to problems of agency growth and change. Taylor emphasises the place of demographic change and government policy as important factors. She concludes that voluntary agencies will need to seek alliances within and beyond the sector in order to survive and develop.

Rob Paton, in a paper that gets to the heart of many current anxieties, explores another of the broader challenges facing agencies: the role of values. He argues that, although it is not possible to derive neat formulae for resolving value issues, the process for dealing with them may be as significant as the actual decision made.

From broad considerations of policy and values we then move to more specific challenges. Voluntary agencies do not operate in isolation, and our next five chapters focus explicitly on aspects of the relationship of agencies to their environment. We begin with a piece by Tony Marshall who describes some of the difficulties inherent in attempts to define the sector. He argues that the apparently heterogeneous parts of the sector are held together by their common role as mediator between the State and the individual. Next, Diana Leat demonstrates how the increased environmental complexity, noted in previous chapters, has led to further difficulties in understanding the chronic problem of accountability. Voluntary agencies are accountable to different people and groups at different times for different things. Leat sharpens our understanding of the complexity of managing accountability. David Wilson then addresses two central issues for agency managers and leaders. First are the dangers of importing practices from the private sector, and second the need for agencies to develop strategic alliances. Jane Lewis demonstrates how increased professionalism, greater formalisation of procedures and more complex lines of accountability have followed the introduction of contracts. Contracting, too, is the subject of Nicholas Deakin's chapter. However, his specific concern is with users. He traces the development of user involvement in all sectors and argues that the introduction of contracts has not led to increased user control, choice or involvement.

The following group of chapters deals with several of the most critical of the more 'internal' challenges (although all are closely linked in some way with the environment). We begin, appropriately, with the question of leadership. Richard Kay suggests that this can best be understood as a process of interaction between individuals and groups at all levels in the organisation. He suggests that they should adopt what he calls 'paradoxical thinking': to live with change and see situations from multiple perspectives, rather than trying to remove ambiguity.

We continue with what we earlier identified as 'top of the pops' of agency problems – governance – an issue which is inextricably linked to leadership. Margaret Harris reminds readers of concerns expressed within and outside the sector about the role of governing bodies. She not only suggests reasons why governing bodies may not perform as they should, but offers practical ways in which their effectiveness may be improved. Effectiveness is also the key theme of the following chapter by Martin Knapp. In an exhaustive review of the issues, he discusses the perspectives on voluntary sector effectiveness of the public sector, users, volunteers and the voluntary sector itself.

The impact of contracting appears again as a sub-theme in Justin Davis Smith's chapter, in relation to the management of volunteers. Smith examines the growth of 'managerialism' and the greater formalisation of the volunteer role. In questioning whether this is in keeping with the 'ethos' of voluntary action, the paper brings us back to the concerns of our opening chapters.

Our final two chapters return us more firmly to the opening themes of organisational change, policy turbulence and values. If voluntary agencies are to have a secure future in the new environment, they will certainly need to ensure that they have training programmes which respond to their distinctive values and needs. They will also require organisational models which help them make choices in that environment. Stephen Osborne discusses the first of these needs in his contribution to the continuing debate about training. After discussing ways in which training geared to specific needs might be provided, he cautions that, without a more integrated distinctive programme, the sector's contribution to society might be much reduced. The penultimate chapter by David Billis provides a model of agency change and survival which attempts to demonstrate the interaction between many of the themes of this book: value systems, governance, human and financial resources and accountability.

We close with a chapter which considers the broad themes which

cut across the individual contributions: organisational knowledge about
the voluntary sector; distinctive features of management and leadership; organisational environment; and the authentic core of the voluntary sector. Each of these themes encompasses numerous challenges
for the future.

References

Beveridge, Lord (1948) *Voluntary Action*, Allen & Unwin, London.
Billis D. (1979) *Voluntary Sector Management: Research and Practice*,
    Working Paper No. 1, PORTVAC, London.
Billis D. and M. Harris (1992) 'Taking the strain of change: UK local
    voluntary agencies enter the post-Thatcher period', *Nonprofit and Vol-
    untary Sector Quarterly*, 21 (4).
Billis D. and J. MacKeith (1993) *Organising NGOs: Challenges and Trends
    in the Management of Overseas Aid*, Centre for Voluntary Organisa-
    tion, London School of Economics.
Billis, D., J. Ashby, A. Ewart and C. Rochester (1994) *Taking Stock:
    Exploring the Shifting Foundations of Governance and Strategy in Housing
    Associations*, Centre for Voluntary Organisation, London School of
    Economics.
Bourdillon, A.F.C. (ed.) (1945) *Voluntary Social Services: Their Place in
    the Modern State*, Methuen, London.
Drucker, D. (1990) *Managing the Non-profit Organization*, Butterworth-
    Heinemann, Oxford.
Hall, P.D. (1993) 'Of books and the scholarly infrastructure', *Nonprofit
    and Voluntary Sector Quarterly*, 22 (1) Spring.
Harris, M. and D. Billis (1986) *Organising Voluntary Agencies*, Bedford
    Square Press, London.
Harris, M. (1993) *The Power and Authority of Governing Bodies: Three
    Models of Practice in Service Providing Agencies*, Working Paper No.
    13, Centre For Voluntary Organisation, London School of Economics,
    London.
Hedley, R. and C. Rochester (1991) *Contracts at the Crossroads*, Associ-
    ation of Crossroads Care Attendant Schemes, Rugby.
Independent Sector (1988) *Formal Education of Non-Profit Organization
    Leaders/Managers*, Report of the Academic Study Group, Washington,
    12 May.
March, J. and H. Simon (1993) *Organizations*, second edition, Blackwell,
    Cambridge, MA.
Marshall, T.H. (1967) *Social Policy*, Hutchinson, London.

2

What are the Key Influences on the Work of Voluntary Agencies?

Marilyn Taylor

> 'The time has come,' the Walrus said,
> 'To talk of many things:
> Of shoes – and ships – and sealing-wax
> Of cabbages and kings,
> And why the sea is boiling hot,
> And whether pigs have wings.'
> Lewis Carroll, *Alice Through the Looking Glass*

Introduction

To review the key influences on the work of voluntary agencies could be an immense task. Organisational theorists have produced a huge literature, analysing a vast array of influences on the objects of their study. The question of how far any organisation is a product of its environment, the resources on which it depends, internal dynamics or national cultures, to choose but a few, has provided ample debate over the years.

If the potential influences are legion, the term 'voluntary agencies' also masks an enormous variation. Will the influences that drive an environmental agency have anything in common with those that drive a training agency, a health project or an arts group? Within fields of activity there will be major differences: between large, medium and small; new and well-established; funded and unfunded; local

and national; rural, suburban and urban; self-help organisations and
those providing services for others; and so on. Even within a particular agency, the influences on someone who volunteers for a couple
of hours a month in a local project will be quite different from
those that drive the executive director in its national parent body.

Nonetheless, a newcomer to the field might be forgiven for assuming that, in recent years, voluntary agencies have been increasingly at the mercy of government in deciding what they do and how
they do it. In particular, fears have been expressed that the move to
a 'contract culture' will distort the values and goals of voluntary
agencies and change the nature of their contribution to welfare (Taylor,
1990; Gutch, 1992; Smith and Lipsky, 1992; Billis, 1993).

Government clearly has a significant influence, whether directly
as a major funder[1] or indirectly by shaping the environment within
which voluntary agencies work. But is government so dominant an
influence that it will outweigh all other external influences as well
as the motivations and values that drive these agencies from within? There are many others who contribute to the values and directions that voluntary agencies take. This chapter reviews both external
and internal influences and identifies some of the ways in which
voluntary agencies can balance the forces which would pull them
into a government agenda.

Why the sea is boiling hot

Demographic and technological change are placing ever greater
demands on voluntary agencies both as providers and campaigners
(for a more detailed discussion of these trends, see NCVO, 1990).
An ageing population in the UK is expected to make increasing
demands on welfare services. Technological change is demanding
new skills of the workforce, and the labour market offers few opportunities for the semi- or unskilled worker, creating a pool of
more or less permanently unemployed people and few prospects for
low achievers at school. Against a background of policies which
have emphasised wealth creation and choice, most commentators
would agree that the gap between rich and poor is getting wider.

This gap is not only financial. Migration patterns are cutting those
in need off from those with skills and resources. Rural and coastal
areas which attract elderly people on retirement are losing their

economically active population. People who can afford to move out of inner city areas and peripheral estates are doing so, leaving them bereft of skills, resources and alternatives. This physical separation means that many needs are not even visible to the majority of the population except as packaged by the media. Meanwhile, family ties are becoming more complex with the rising rate of divorce and remarriage. Households are getting smaller (Kiernan and Wicks, 1990). Women are being attracted back into the labour market: traditional patterns of informal caring are not being reproduced and past assumptions about volunteering are no longer valid.

This is a brief glance at an extremely complex set of changes. It does not begin to address the equally significant changes in other voluntary sector fields such as overseas aid and the environment. But it suggests that, while demand is increasing, resources are under more and more pressure, while the distance between those in need and those with resources is growing. This is a situation where the flexibility and resourcefulness that is claimed for voluntary agencies will be very much in demand.

Of kings and cabbage patches: government and the 'new institutional environment'

Within any public policy field, government defines the environment, not only for voluntary agencies, but for all organisations. In community care, as in other public services, it is creating a new institutional environment: a competitive market which is blurring the boundaries between public and private and encouraging new agencies into the field. In this new environment, voluntary agencies need to position themselves, not only in relation to the various arms of government but in relation to a diversity of other players, who may be allies or competitors.

As a significant funder, government provides the resources, directly or indirectly, for the work of many voluntary agencies in this field. As a regulator, it dictates the conditions under which aspects of this work are carried out, in terms of standards, qualifications required, financial accounting requirements and, through the Charity Commission, the conditions under which voluntary agencies may claim tax exemption. It makes a significant contribution to the climate of opinion that surrounds the work of voluntary agencies, including notions of what are deserving and undeserving causes. As a policy-maker, and still a significant provider, it is the target of many voluntary sector campaigns.

The influence of government on the voluntary sector as a funder is nothing new. In the eighteenth century it provided funds for the London-based Foundling Hospital on the condition that it provided its services on a country-wide basis. Owen (1964) documents how this condition swamped the Hospital and nearly brought it to a standstill. More recent examples of the power of government as funder can be found in its special employment programmes and its support for housing associations through the Housing Corporation, two major sources of government funding to the sector in the 1980s. Government's special employment programmes made a wide range of voluntary sector work possible, provided staff and premises for the first time to many community-based and minority ethnic groups, and encouraged a number of agencies to make a major investment in training work. But critics (see, for example, Addy and Scott, 1988) argued that those who took these funds were allowing themselves to be diverted from their own priorities and values and co-opted into the creation of low-paid temporary jobs. When the funding for these programmes was reduced and their direction changed to reflect more closely the needs of industry, many agencies found themselves left high and dry, no longer in the business for which they were set up, but no longer wanting to, as the critics saw it, massage the unemployment figures.

In the 1980s, Housing Corporation money was the vehicle used to transfer responsibility for building and managing social housing from the public sector. Again these funds opened up a lot of potential, but once more the rules have been changed. Housing Corporation funding rates have been significantly cut, with the result that Housing Associations are being forced to raise funds on the private market to survive and make economies of scale – something which makes it particularly hard for smaller associations to survive. They are also being forced to raise rents – a pressure which causes problems for those who still see their mission very much in terms of provision for people who are disadvantaged in the housing market.

There are fears that current moves to contracting may provide a third and even more potent example of the power of government funding to bend the sector to its own aims and incorporate its resources (see, for example, Gutch, 1992; Lewis, this volume). Special employment programmes were an extra pool of money which could, initially at least, be used for any purpose identified by the agency so long as it created employment or provided training. In community care, however, like housing, voluntary agencies are being invited to substitute for public sector provision, in a climate of financial restraint and with activities and outcomes clearly specified by government purchasers.

As an influence, however, government funding does not have to be restrictive. The Urban Programme, like the special employment programmes, spread the reach of government funds to an enormous range of activities and communities until it was first more expressly geared to economic regeneration purposes and then cut. There are also different sources of government funding. I have argued elsewhere (Taylor and Lansley, 1992) that the tensions between central and local government in the 1980s were beneficial to a sector which was courted by both sides. But the centralisation of government and the rationalisation of funding programmes in recent years is reducing the flexibility and pluralism of government funding. The principle of grant-aid for the general purposes of an agency, which allowed agencies more scope to define the purposes for which they wanted funding and offered flexibility in the use of the funds, is losing ground as the balance between grants and fees changes in favour of the latter (Taylor *et al.*, 1993). The advent of unitary instead of two-tier local authorities in many areas is likely to reduce further the potential for flexibility and, if the experience of the abolition of the metropolitan counties is repeated elsewhere in the country, may squeeze local authority support to voluntary agencies even further (Mocroft, 1992).

Nonetheless, voluntary agencies have always found windows of opportunity in government policy in the past. These continue to exist in advocacy, urban regeneration and crime prevention, for example, and as community-care purchasing policies develop across the country, there will probably be more room for manoeuvre than many fear (see Lewis, this volume). But there is likely to be less and less money available for the range of activities which voluntary agencies have developed as a complement to mainstream provision and in which this mainstream provision is embedded – development, self-help, social activities, preventative work are some examples. Furthermore, in a tight financial climate, it is unlikely that either funders or the agencies they support will be minded to take risks. Funders

will only fund what they feel is safe. Agencies will be less willing
to rock the boat. The interchange between campaigning and service
provision, which has been a strength of many voluntary agencies,
may well fade away.

If government funding is too restrictive, there are many smaller
voluntary agencies that survive without government money. And for
larger charities, government funding may be a small proportion of
their total income. But the influence of government extends beyond
what it funds directly. Within the voluntary sector, regulations, training
requirements, drives towards quality and more general forces to be
more business-like are shaping the 'cabbage patch' within which
voluntary organisations operate.

Despite the rhetoric of deregulation, research carried out by the
author[2] (see also Lewis, this volume) suggests that there is a reluctance in government to accept that the management processes appropriate to large public service bureaucracies or firms producing
private goods on the commercial market may not be appropriate to
the wide range of organisations operating in fields like community
care. Here, services are difficult to specify, choices are difficult
and the service user is often not the purchaser. Voluntary (and private) agencies in our research felt that their ability to get on with
the job was being threatened by inappropriate conditions and expectations about how to operate which come from all levels of government – local, national and European. In fact regulation is haphazard:
tight in some areas, lax in others and variable from inspector to
inspector, but voluntary (and private) agencies reported more time
taken up in administration (at the cost of face-to-face contact with
staff and service users) and a desire on the part of purchasers and
regulators to 'insure' against any kind of risk. The move into contracts is also forcing trustees of national charities to re-examine the
autonomy they can offer branches in the light of a sharper understanding of their liability.

There is a difficult balance to be maintained. Most voluntary
agencies in our research appreciated the need for good management,
but feared that inappropriate demands from funders and regulators
would be beyond the means of smaller agencies and would put the
commitment of volunteers and management committee members at
risk. One organisation's director asked how he was expected to tell
older people, who had been preparing food all their lives, that they
now had to be trained to do so. Others asked what would happen to

attempts to involve young mothers in play schemes, if they were expected to have qualifications. Where would they find the money this requires?

Similarly, many agencies welcome the language of quality that is flowing through the service world, but finding workable models and acceptable definitions of quality is another question altogether. The business models that are held up as leaders in the field are not necessarily suited to the provision of services to vulnerable people, especially by diverse small agencies.

As part of the 'move towards the market', central government is encouraging the adoption of 'business' values of efficiency, economy and competitiveness within government, central and local, and in the organisations it funds. A recent survey suggested that larger voluntary organisations now recruited one in three of their senior managers from the for-profit sector (Bruce and Raymer, 1992). Our own research found that people with business skills were being recruited to management committees and displacing members with different experience and contributions to offer. Some agencies felt this was appropriate, given the increasing complexity of the task; others that it made it far more difficult for them to involve service users and local people in running their activities.

Organisational theory has argued that, in any environment, organisations can be expected to adopt norms of behaviour which make it easier for them to survive (DiMaggio and Powell, 1983). This pressure may be *coercive*, as in the case of purchaser requirements and regulation. But it may equally be *mimetic* or *normative*. Organisations will adopt what they see to be accepted ways of doing things. They will learn a common language. They will imitate what they see as having succeeded elsewhere. They will thus tend to become more like each other.

The environment for many voluntary organisations is becoming increasingly turbulent. Many of the areas in which they operate are areas of high risk, unpredictable human services which require inventiveness, flexibility and diversity. Leading thinkers in the commercial world are also grappling with the need to find more flexible ways of responding to a high risk environment in a language which has some resonance for the voluntary sector. It would be a pity if, as Leat argues elsewhere (1993), voluntary agencies are forced into old bureaucratic moulds just as the leading thinkers of the commercial world are leaving these safe havens.

This assimilation into a common mould is not just a matter of style. Some fear that these forces are pulling voluntary agencies away from their roots altogether. The need to raise funds on the private market and raise rents, for example, has led housing associations to become more commercialised to the extent that a significant number of them no longer see themselves as part of the voluntary sector (Roof, 1992). In the US, research suggests that the move to 'the market' has meant that non-profit agencies are less likely to serve the poor (Clarke and Estes, 1992; Salamon, 1993). In the UK, voluntary agencies are learning to become more business-like in their fund-raising – a move that has prompted the invention of the term 'compassion fatigue': 'To emulate the world of show business and the sophistication of commercial merchandise campaigns was not perceived as the business of charity' (Fenton *et al.*, 1992).

Shoes and ships and sealing wax: founders, members, users and other influences

How then do voluntary agencies keep a part of them that is 'their own'? Diversifying funding, which many voluntary agencies are urged to do, will not be a solution in itself if it leads to the commercialisation suggested above. Potentially more powerful are the various constituencies that go to make up voluntary agencies themselves, some of whom have their feet in the external world as well. The multiple accountability of voluntary agencies has been identified by some commentators as a distinctive feature of the sector (see, for example, Leat, 1988, and this volume). Their management committees often bring together public authority representatives, members of the local community, people from other voluntary agencies, professionals from a variety of organisations and, now more frequently, service users. This multiple accountability could mean that no one voice is strong enough to resist co-option into a government or any other external agenda. It may even make it difficult to develop a clear identity and value base which can be maintained in the face of external pressure. On the other hand it could be a strong force against this pressure. Our research suggested that many people get involved in the voluntary sector because it is 'different', or set up a voluntary agency because they could not do what they wanted anywhere else. They will surely want to preserve these 'differences'.

It is relatively easy to list the players who may be a central influence on the work of voluntary agencies. It is far more difficult to generalise in any way about them. Different influences will come to the fore in different kinds of organisation. The influence of staff will vary according to numbers, occupation, personality, the power of other constituencies and a host of other factors. The power of members would be expected to be high in a user-based or ethnic minority organisation with a political commitment to empowerment, a professional association, or a campaign which relies on the size of its membership for political credibility. But in some other organisations, membership is a very hazy concept – anyone who has an interest – or even just a fundraising device. There are many organisations where the annual general meeting (as the ultimate decision-making body) struggles to find a quorum and membership is more a vote of confidence for the cause than a key influence.

There is not room to discuss every one of the voluntary sector's constituencies in this chapter. Several – volunteers, management committees, other agencies – are referred to elsewhere in this book. But, as suggested earlier, getting agreement amongst these constituencies as to the central aims and identity of the voluntary agency may itself be complicated. Voluntary organisations are sometimes defined as value-based organisations but, as Paton argues elsewhere in this volume, they may be as much defined by the inherent ambiguity and fluidity of their values. Maybe, in the light of Paton's argument, all a voluntary agency can aim to do is to be clear about its 'values debate', the ideas and needs that led to its existence and the need to engage constantly with a re-examination of those values in the light of changing needs and a changing environment. In doing so there are three further constituencies of importance: service users, founders and networks.

Service users are a constituency with growing power. The user movement cannot be stereotyped – there are many shades of opinion within it. But its organisations are concerned with empowering their members and giving them a political voice, and they will have some support from current policies in doing so (see Deakin, this volume). Despite the rhetoric of voluntary agencies as close to the consumer, the user movement rarely distinguishes between the sectors when it criticises services as disabling and disempowering: charity can and has been extremely patronising. User organisations have been highly critical of the imbalance of funding between organisations *for* disabled people and organisations *of* disabled people. They will be demanding considerable changes of existing organisations and equipping service users to make their voice heard within them. They will also, like minority ethnic communities, be demanding a greater share of the resources that are available. If they are not to be discredited or outmanoeuvred by purchasers who lay claim to a more direct relationship with user organisations, voluntary agencies will need to develop their own dialogue and alliances with user organisations and their own users.

But it is not only those currently involved in a voluntary agency who have an influence. Founders and other charismatic individuals in an organisation's history often live on and may be used as symbols to resist change – for good or ill. Organisations which have become quite bureaucratic in form may still hang on, either in rhetoric or in reality, to vestiges of earlier associational days. Those which have their roots in religion, working class or social movements often retain a strong value tradition which can help them to resist incorporation by other forces.

The influence of founders can fade. In our research, one national charity was 'moving away from the introspective belief that, because we have a lovely founder, all will be well . . . we will have to change in order to survive' (Taylor, Langan and Hoggett, 1995). Nonetheless, it could be argued that as symbols of the organisations' roots, they are part of the 'sealing wax' of the voluntary sector.

So too are the networks which the voluntary sector has developed over the years. The UK voluntary sector has a long tradition of network organisations, which now cover most areas in the country. The importance of these intermediary bodies was underlined by the 1978 Wolfenden Report. Alliances have also sprung up across fields of activity (for example, child care, youth provision) and more recently among groups who feel excluded from the more traditional networks. These networks have been an important source of influence through their provision of training and information, but also as a political channel through which the interests of the sector and those who use its services can be represented. In so far as they perform this role, they have the potential to act as a strong source of identity and carrier of values.

These networks are reinforced by the interdependence of many voluntary agencies in their working lives: sitting on each others' management committees, providing complementary services, developing new provision together, collaborating in consultation exercises. The interlocking nature of their work often makes it difficult to talk of voluntary agencies in isolation: a point of which purchasers need to be aware. For some smaller agencies, working in tandem with other similar agencies is the only way to maximise the few resources they have.

It is possible that a more competitive ethos and a climate in which each aspect of an agency's work needs to be costed will put at risk traditions of collaboration and co-operation. Wilson in this volume suggests that larger voluntary organisations may become increasingly isolated and insular. It is also possible that it will become increasingly difficult for umbrella bodies to get funding. Younghusband (1978) suggests that local councils for voluntary service grew significantly following the local government reorganisation of 1974. Larger umbrella bodies were needed to cover the new larger authorities created at this time and these larger authorities were able to provide financial support. If we are now reverting to smaller authorities, will the reverse be the case? In some areas, funding for training and information services is increasingly likely to be provided directly to the voluntary agencies who need it, rather than to umbrella bodies, in the expectation that individual agencies will go to the fast-growing private consultancy industry to have their needs met. If so, the political, networking and identity-reinforcing roles that intermediary bodies have played could well be lost. In these circumstances, it may be to the larger organisations that we need to look for the survival of the smaller. Melvyn Carlowe, in responding to this paper when it was originally presented, argued that such links between large and small organisations would also act as a reinforcement of values in the sector by prodding 'the existing charitable and voluntary organisations into remembering why they originally came into existence'.

Whether pigs have wings?

Figure 2.1 summarises the key influences identified in this chapter on voluntary agencies. I have described a situation where voluntary organisations are facing growing need against a background of restricted resources. The current policy environment, however, presents a prospect of increasing assimilation into a dominant government

Figure 2.1 *What are the key influences on the voluntary sector?*

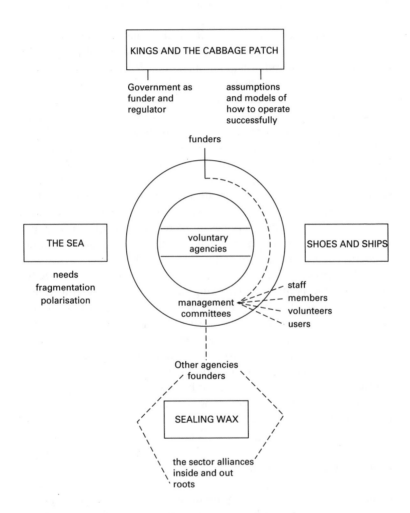

agenda, where the grey areas which have allowed voluntary agencies, at their best, to draw on a range of energies and resources and to provide flexible responses to need are being eroded.

It has, however, suggested that voluntary agencies will continue to find windows of opportunity, even as government and other funders tighten up on their conditions of funding. The language of consumerism, quality and community lends itself to the work of many in this sector and can be reclaimed to support their work, especially in alliance with user organisations – an alliance which could help other voluntary agencies to negotiate more effectively with purchasers and other funders and to resist pressures towards inappropriate regulation. The multiple constituencies on which voluntary organisations call, and the alliances which they create, can all be used to ensure that voluntary agencies address the needs outlined at the beginning of the chapter.

The ways in which voluntary agencies will respond to these different influences will vary. Some agencies will undoubtedly be assimilated into outside agendas, but others will not. They have long experience of managing uncertainty. The history of the sector suggests that whatever the environment in which they have to operate, people will continue to come together to find ways to address the issues that cause them concern. The diversity this represents is another force against co-option – voluntary agencies *per se* refuse to fit into boundaries determined by the outside world. But this diversity means also, of course, that some voluntary agencies will fundamentally disagree with what others are doing. Nothing in this chapter suggests that they have a uniform notion of the public good or even the good of those they were set up to serve.

A look into the crystal ball of the future offers two scenarios. The first supports the thesis that voluntary agencies will become more and more indistinguishable from others in their respective fields. Government or equally powerful large-scale institutions like multinational corporate firms will call the shots. A growing breed of 'professional' managers will populate a 'not-for-profit sector', competing with each other for public sector contracts and for a good image in the fund-raising market. Smaller agencies will continue to exist, sometimes on patronage from more powerful sponsors, sometimes out of a groundswell of dissatisfaction from below, but they will quickly burn out, overwhelmed by the pressure that caused them to form in the first place, and they will be isolated and fragmented

– easy to divide and rule. Those wishing to get public or private sponsorship will operate a strong degree of self-censorship, and will easily succumb to the pressures to formalise and grow in order to become viable. Or they will be subject to take-over and merger, as market principles spread across the organisational environment. User organisations will be co-opted. The divide between large service-providing and small campaigning organisations advocated in a recent report (Knight, 1993) could become an unwelcome reality as the identity of interests between larger and smaller organisations is eroded and those in the middle grow or die.

An alternative scenario recognises the immense variety that exists within the sector at present. Voluntary agencies, who already engage in a diversity of activities, may contract for certain elements of their work, but they will look for ways of supporting other work through alternative funding sources and, if they can get them, overheads on service agreements. They will find a way to exploit differences between the various arms of government – maybe government will recognise the value of pluralism in its own funding arrangements. Smaller organisations, unwilling to surrender values of participation and face-to-face working, will develop alternative ways of growing through franchises, consortia and other innovative organisational forms. People from voluntary agencies will seek allies from across the new institutional environment and take up opportunities for management education outside the MBA stable, which give them opportunities to engage and debate with leading edge practice in the commercial sector. User organisations will work increasingly with service users across all sectors to develop their ability to have a say in the organisations that serve them. As this becomes more common, regulation will depend more on the user voice and become more specific to the particular organisation concerned. Agencies across the sector will recognise that they need to network amongst themselves and with community and user-based organisations if their political role is to survive and if smaller organisations are to remain viable.

If the second scenario sounds rather idealistic, it is to be hoped that the first is far too pessimistic. But whatever happens in the new environment, it will be important to find allies wherever they present themselves. Small private agencies in the field of community care are facing many of the same pressures as small voluntary agencies and are equally resistant to pressures to formalise. There will be more and more people in local and health authorities who are looking for ways of recreating the 'grey areas' which are being squeezed out of the system. Our concern should not be with the notion of *sector*, but with the survival of the *work* that voluntary agencies want to do, ensuring that the scope remains within the new environment to develop diverse, flexible and co-operative services which can address the needs with which this paper started, and which can break down the increasing polarisation within society.

Notes

1. Kendall and Knapp have identified the proportion of voluntary sector funds coming from government as 40 per cent (Salamon and Anheier, 1994).
2. This research mapped voluntary and independent organisations in three localities, explored their different motivations and values, different approaches to management and the impact of changing policy. It was supported by the Joseph Rowntree Foundation and carried out at the School for Advanced Urban Studies by Marilyn Taylor, Joan Langan and Paul Hoggett (Taylor *et al.*, 1995).

References

Addy, T. and D. Scott (1988) *Fatal Impacts? The MSC and Voluntary Action*, William Temple Foundation, Manchester.

Billis, D. (1993) *Organising Public and Voluntary Agencies*, Routledge, London.

Bruce, I. and A. Raymer (1992) *Managing and Staffing Britain's Largest Charities*, VOLPROF, City University, London.

Clarke, L. and C.L. Estes (1992) 'Sociological and economic theories of markets and nonprofits: evidence from home health organizations', *American Journal of Sociology*, 97(4): 945–69.

Dimaggio, P. and W.W. Powell (1983) 'The iron cage revisited: institutional isomorphism and collective rationality in organisational fields', *American Sociological Review*, 48: 147–60.

Fenton, N., P. Golding and A. Radley (1992) 'Thinking about charity: report of a pilot study into public attitudes to charity and volunteering' in S. Saxon-Harrold and J. Kendall (eds) *Researching the Voluntary Sector*, Charities Aid Foundation, Tonbridge.

Gutch, R. (1992) *Contracting: Lessons from the USA*, National Council for Voluntary Organisations, London.

Kiernan, K. and M. Wicks (1990) *Family Change and Future Policy*, Joseph Rowntree Foundation and Family Policy Studies Centre, York and London.

Knight, B. (1993) *Voluntary Action*, Home Office, London.

Leat, D. (1988) *Voluntary Organisations and Accountability*, National Council for Voluntary Organisations, London.

Leat, D. (1993) *The Development of Community Care by the Independent Sector*, Policy Studies Institute, London.

Mocroft, I. (1992) 'The survey of local authority payments to voluntary and charitable organisations', *Charity Trends*, Charities Aid Foundation, Tonbridge.

NCVO (1990) *Directions for the Next Decade: Understanding Social and Institutional Trends*, National Council for Voluntary Organisations, London.

Owen, D. (1964) *English Philanthropy 1660–1960*, Harvard University Press, Cambridge, MA.

Roof (1992) 'No sign of movement', November – December: 21–5.

Salamon, L.M. (1993) 'The marketization of welfare: changing nonprofit and for-profit roles in the American welfare state', *Social Service Review*, 67 (1): 17–39.

Salamon, L.M. and H.K. Anheier (1994) *The Emerging Sector: An Overview*, Institute for Policy Studies, Johns Hopkins University, Baltimore.

Smith, S.R. and M. Lipsky (1992) *Nonprofits for Hire: The Welfare State in the Age of Contracting*, Harvard University Press, Cambridge, MA.

Taylor, M. (1990) *New Times, New Challenges*, National Council for Voluntary Organisations, London.

Taylor, M. and J. Lansley (1992) 'Ideology and welfare in the UK: the implications for the voluntary sector', *Voluntas*, 3 (2): 153–74.

Taylor, M., J. Kendall and A. Fenyo (1993) 'Survey of local authority payments to voluntary and charitable organisations', *Charity Trends*, Charities Aid Foundation, Tonbridge.

Taylor, M., J. Langan and P. Hoggett (1995) *Encouraging Diversity: Voluntary and Private Organisations in Community Care*, Arena, Aldershot.

Wolfenden Report (1978) *The Future of Voluntary Organisations*, Croom Helm, London.

Younghusband, E. (1978) *Social Work in Britain 1950–1975*, vol. 1, Allen & Unwin, London.

3

How are Values Handled in Voluntary Agencies?

Rob Paton

Introduction

The front page headline was '"Sacked because Catholic" claims agency worker'. The story, which ran onto an inside page, detailed a brief but bitter dispute between a volunteer co-ordinator and the management of the agency within which he was based. The dismissed worker claimed:

> I am a Catholic and although I am willing to work with gays and women who have had abortions, I could not actively promote those principles. . . . They wanted me to leave my religion at the door, which means they are discriminating against me because of my religious beliefs. They are putting the freedom to be homosexual and have abortions above the choice of being a Christian (*East Lothian Courier*, 1993).

The manager of the agency saw things differently:

'We have an equal opportunity policy . . . We are not judgmental towards anyone who comes to us . . . We asked – during his interview if there were any groups or organizations he could not work with and he replied "no".' But, she said, after several weeks in the post he had approached her stating that he did not feel comfortable promoting certain organisations. 'I was shocked and called for an emergency meeting of the full volunteer bureau committee. . . . He was basically refusing to do his job properly' (ibid.).

According to the dismissed worker, who was seeking legal advice, the notice of immediate dismissal pushed through his door gave no reason for his being sacked. He was replaced by his former assistant.

The dismissed worker took the case to an industrial tribunal and won compensation for unfair dismissal. It seems the tribunal was influenced by the fact that, a week after he joined, the organisation had adopted a new equal opportunities policy affirming that staff should not be subject to any form of discrimination.

What are we to make of this sorry tale? Is it a bizarre incident of no general significance – beyond the obvious point that if sensitive issues are ineptly handled then an unholy row will probably result? Is it explained simply by saying that 'equal opps' has often proved divisive? Or have we been here before? Is this incident redolent of other intense arguments and furious rows that we have been party to, heard about, or witnessed in voluntary agencies over the years? Indeed, is it not part of the folklore of the sector that disputes involving deeply felt personal and organisational principles can and do flare up, or in other cases lurk in the background haunting organisations for years? Consider the following instances:

- Staff and trustees of a religious charity are deeply divided over whether and in what sense staff of the organisation have to be 'practising Christians'.
- Staff of overseas development charities experience deep divisions over the representation of their beneficiaries in fundraising materials: marketing staff argue that to raise the funds the organisation needs they must communicate the reality of the suffering the organisation is responding to; the field staff complain that heart-rending pictures reinforce stereotypes and misconceptions that underpin the very social and economic disadvantages the charities aspire to eradicate (Lidchi, 1994).
- The Bishop of Oxford pursues the Church Commissioners to the highest court in the land in a dispute over the propriety of their investment policies.

This chapter argues that such incidents – which will be referred to as *values issues* – do indeed have features that distinguish them from other types of organisational conflict. Moreover, although values issues can (and do) arise in all sorts of organisations they are more likely to arise in voluntary agencies, social movement organisations, and religious bodies. The implications of this analysis for practising managers are explored. Since the significance of values *for the nature and incidence of conflict in organisations* seems not to have been considered before, this chapter can only be exploratory. It builds on relevant concepts as far as possible, and gives many instances of values issues, but is inductive and reflective in approach, aiming to elaborate the concept of values issues in a way that will be illuminating for practitioners. It does not report the findings of designed research, though the possibility of more rigorous empirical application and testing of the ideas is implicit.

Values issues as a type of organisational conflict

A values issue can be defined as *an organisational conflict which reflects emergent or unresolved tensions concerning the implications of a commitment central to the identity or mission of an organisation, or between two such commitments, where such tensions are perceived to have a clear ethical dimension.*

Thus, in the case of the dismissed volunteer co-ordinator, (*i*) two different implications of the equal opportunities policy seemed incompatible (giving priority to the full range of potential service users effectively excluded certain people – devout Catholics or Muslims for example – from employment; alternatively, respecting the concerns of such staff would undermine the commitment to the full range of service users); (*ii*) their interpretation of the equal opportunities policy was felt by the management to be so important to the organisation's mission that a dilution of its requirements was unacceptable; but, equally, the dismissed employee believed that his treatment was incompatible with the ideals of the organisation; (*iii*) each side to the dispute considered the other side's action not merely to be misconceived, but ethically questionable.

The characteristics of values issues

How then do values issues differ from other organisational conflicts? The following features are characteristic:

The appeal to higher values. At least one party, but usually both, will appeal to, and in some measure be motivated by, higher values, even if other (pragmatic, or ego-related) considerations are involved too. By contrast, in other organisational conflicts, arguments are generally couched in relation to the success of the organisation (profitability, market share, efficiency and so on), and motivations concern these factors as well as personal and departmental advantage, personal rivalries and so on. This distinction is apparent in the judgements that the opposing parties may make of each other: in a values issue the participants are likely to consider each other to some degree 'bad' (that is morally questionable), whereas in other conflicts the complaint is more likely to be that the other side is foolish, or perhaps endangering personal or organisational interests.

Organisational significance. The issues appear to be of far-reaching significance for the organisation – typically, they concern 'what we stand for', 'all we hold most dear' or 'the integrity of the organisation' ('practising what we preach'). Of course, other sorts of organisational conflict can also have far-reaching significance – for example disagreements over major restructuring, or over strategic investments or divestments. But many, probably most, concern tactical or 'frictional' matters (sectional struggles for degrees of autonomy, more advantageous resource allocation and so on). (Standard texts such as Handy, 1993, or Kakabadse *et al.*, 1988, discuss these issues in more detail.)

Personal significance. The issue is of considerable personal significance for some of those involved because it concerns their identity and sense of self. Identification with a cause or system of beliefs (which the organisation may also espouse) provides a basis for criticising policy or practice, and may generate a conflict of loyalties for members of the organisation who may act against what would normally be considered to be their interests (as in the case of the volunteer co-ordinator discussed above). By contrast, conflicts in business organisations derive overwhelmingly from interests, as perceived through the lenses of organisational roles and departmental identities and perspectives. As such, conflicts in business organisations are generally self-limiting and pursued with *relative* detachment (whether you win or lose, it is not in your interest to 'go too far' in pursuit of your aims). Of course, where those involved identify closely with their roles or departmental interests and fear that much is at stake, such conflicts will be very intense. So although values issues always have personal significance for some of those involved, intense personal significance does not in itself signify a values issue.

Limited scope for compromise. The issue will be one on which compromise is, or at least appears, difficult. Matters of principle cannot be negotiated in the same way as disagreements over next year's budget. To the extent that other organisational conflicts involve disagreements about amounts (for example of money, office space, staff time and so on) they are more obviously amenable to negotiation, compromise and 'splitting the difference'. But one cannot compromise or split the difference on, to take a stark and topical example, the ordination of women priests.

These aspects of values issues are a matter of degree, rather than categorical. Some organisational conflicts will be clear and relatively pure cases, but often conflicts in organisations mix up several different issues, one or more of which may have values dimensions. Nevertheless, taken together these four aspects allow us to distinguish between 'ordinary' organisational conflicts, those with a values dimension, and those that are *primarily* values issues.

Taken together, these aspects of values issues also explain two other common, but not essential, characteristics. First, values issues usually generate strong feelings, involving at best 'passionate argument' and at worst outrage and bitterness (Rothschild-Whitt, 1979, quotes one member of a value-based organisation as saying 'Plants die here from the heavy vibes'). Secondly, values issues are inherently prone to *escalation,* which may happen rapidly, leading to polarisation and even irreconcilable differences, expulsions or splits. The case of the dismissed volunteer co-ordinator, where the obvious compromise was letting the co-ordinator's assistant handle any cases he was uneasy about, illustrates both these points. Another instance was reported to the author by a former Director of Oxfam: some years ago, Oxfam staff, for whom the military were heavily implicated in many of the disasters Oxfam had to tackle, manoeuvred frantically to try to prevent the appointment of a high-ranking army officer to a senior position in the organisation – to the extent even of leaking stories to the press (thereby putting Oxfam's public reputation, fundraising potential and capacity to save lives, in jeopardy). This instance is interesting because 'anti-militarism' was not an explicit organisational commitment; informally, however, many staff evidently feared that such an appointment risked introducing values and assumptions that would compromise the character and commitments of the organisation.

Nevertheless, bitterness and polarisation are not *defining* characteristics of values issues. Whether a values issue develops in this way depends on how those involved express their concerns, how they react to each other, and how third parties contribute to the situation.

The contexts in which values issues arise

In what contexts are values issues likely to arise? Clearly, the legitimacy of appeals to 'higher values' is crucial. This suggests values issues will arise in public and voluntary agencies which exist to pursue humanitarian or religious goals. However, appeals to humanitarian values can arise in other organisations that do not explicitly espouse such goals. For example, new owners take over a paternalistic family firm in which the owner-managers have always looked after the employees. Long-serving members of staff are promptly made redundant to the outrage of everyone else – because the dismissal violates widely held assumptions about the way members of this particular community are treated. Until the new management has persuaded everyone of its view that 'really' such issues are purely economic, not moral, the resulting conflicts are likely to have many of the characteristics of values issues. Nevertheless, such issues would be considered exceptional in private sector companies, and it is reasonable to suppose that organisations with religious or humanitarian ideals are more likely to experience values issues.

Several other factors may contribute to the incidence of values issues. The first is the extent to which an organisation aims to bring about change in the wider society. Thus political and religious movements which are in some degree critical of the status quo are notoriously prone to intense dispute over fundamental tenets and principles. Indeed, they may contain within particular organisations many of the divisions and conflicts of the wider society which they are attempting to resolve. Batsleer (1992) provides a graphic illustration of this in his account of *Red Rope*, the socialist walking and climbing club, which aimed to allow socialists to enjoy outdoor leisure activities in the company of like-minded people and in ways compatible with their shared values:

'The manifest simplicity and common sense of the original principles and values were not sufficient to shield the organization from such great debates and schisms as the following:

- The usual doctrinal splits and rows over the ... meaning of 'socialism' – could 'progressive' people who did not see themselves as socialists belong to Red Rope?
- The development of more 'campaigning' work led to endless arguments about the ideals of Red Rope. Many people who were active in other campaigns and organizations joined Red Rope quite consciously to get away from the demands of the values and principles of the rest of their lives. ... Red Rope was 'time off' from politics. For other people, who were influenced by the notion that 'the personal is political', ... Red Rope's principles meant giving priority to the development of a particular life-style and culture within the club ...
- Red Rope's original commitment to enabling people to have equal access to the countryside meant that some support should be given to looking after the children of parents and guardians who would otherwise be unable to get away for a weekend's walking or climbing. ... The development of good practice in child-care was seen to be a core value of the organization – even though it resulted in such apparently bizarre situations as members who felt it was dishonest to give the child-care undertaking if they had no intention of fulfilling it, being prevented from attending a trip to Scotland for snow and ice-climbing at which no children would be present.
- In one form or another, issues of 'elitism' and 'individualism' led to rows and arguments. If the club was committed to income-sharing to ensure that unemployed people could attend Red Rope weekend trips, was it right to allow better-off members to use the club's publications to advertise for other people interested in going on costly, 'private', non-income sharing holidays to climb in the Alps or the Dolomites? ... Was it rampant individualism for the better rock-climbers to spend all their precious weekends in the mountains extending their own abilities and skills – and interests – rather than yet again losing a day taking novices up simple rock routes? ...
- Red Rope has had to contend with some of the wider cultural dilemmas and contradictions associated with outdoor pursuits. Were its values of co-operation, collective safety and equal access incompatible with some of the core, cultural values of mountaineering, which involves individual and often intensely private choices, commitments, risks and challenges? ... Was Red Rope endorsing behaviour and cultural stereotypes which

could be used to discriminate against disabled people?' (Batsleer, 1992, pp. 50–1).

This example suggests that the values and commitments of social movement organisations, especially small and medium-sized ones whose internal processes are more informal, are more likely to be ambiguous and hence open to conflicting interpretation. By contrast, in large and well-established organisations, especially those associated with the dominant values and beliefs in society, the meaning of values and commitments are to a greater extent governed by convention. Moreover, when those conventions are challenged, as in times of major organisational change, the values issues are more likely to be contained by being handled through formal organisational procedures (in the public sector, policy-making by elected members is quintessentially the arena in which values issues are debated and resolved).

Finally, to the extent that many voluntary organisations are participatively and consensually managed, they provide more opportunities for values issues to emerge and flare up. Equally, of course, they provide more opportunities for negotiating the meaning of organisational commitments (or the education/socialisation of staff or members), and hence for preventing and resolving values issues. But given the characteristics of values issues discussed above (especially the strength of feeling and tendency to escalate) it is virtually inevitable that conflicts will erupt from time to time. By contrast, a more authoritative (or indeed authoritarian) organisation will not provide the occasions where rival interpretations of organisational commitments can be expressed and promoted. Such rival views will therefore lack legitimacy within the organisation's decision processes, even if they are widely espoused among participants at a lower level, and indeed outside the organisation. In this way less participative value-based organisations (for example, in the public services) may avoid or suppress the conflict associated with latent values issues – though, as the phenomenon of 'whistle-blowing' in the National Health Service shows, such avoidance is not infallible.

Hence, although humanitarian values and associated organisational commitments permeate parts of the public sector and have been widely discussed in the academic and professional literature (see, for example, McKevitt and Lawton, 1994), they tend to be handled at higher levels in the organisation. Such policy level debates about values are also common in voluntary agencies. However, in addition, it seems that rows and disputes over values issues *in the course of day-to-day activities* arise more often in radical and campaigning voluntary organisations than in traditional service-delivery voluntary organisations or public sector organisations. It has been argued that this is because organisational values and commitments, being less governed by convention, are open to conflicting interpretations; and because the informal and participative processes within voluntary agencies allow concern about values issues to be expressed more readily.

The structure of values issues

While values issues can erupt in different ways in relation to a wide range of policies or practices, the underlying structure of the dispute in such conflicts will usually be quite familiar. Indeed, the opposing positions can usually be expressed as one or more of the following types of disagreement:

Arguments over the meaning *of commitments*

An example is the case of the meaning of 'practising Christian' for certain religious charities. This is the most fundamental difference which often underpins the other sorts of argument.

Arguments over the consistency *of action and commitment*

An example is the Bishop of Oxford's argument that the Church Commissioners' investment policies should be governed by ethical criteria. Such arguments have considerable rhetorical force, but on examination often prove to be somewhat problematic. Partly this is because they may be based on a particular interpretation of the relevant commitment, and hence mask an argument over its meaning (arguably, the Bishop of Oxford held a more restrictive view of the notion of Christian stewardship than the Church Commissioners). But more fundamentally, the problem is that organisations, like people, espouse many values and pursue multiple goals, which may be more or less ambiguous, and between which all sorts of tensions and inconsistencies inevitably arise. Thus if any single commitment is resolutely pursued, without considering the web of other related commitments in which it is embedded, the results will always be contentious and, indeed, morally questionable. In general, decision-making becomes ever more difficult the stricter and more diverse the criteria that must be satisfied. Hence the familiar strategies of functional separation of activities, the quasi-resolution of conflict, local rationality, and the sequential attention to goals (Cyert and March, 1963). Viewed this way, some inconsistency between values and action is inevitable – indeed it may even be desirable in maintaining the aspirations of an organisation. We know that organisational commitments (like personal standards of, say, honesty) can be important in influencing organisational behaviour even if they do not and cannot determine it in the short-term or in every case – this is the wisdom in everyday, conventional 'hypocrisy' (March, 1988). The argument that organisations cannot hope to be consistent, but only consistent *enough*, quickly generates the third form in which values issues are presented.

Arguments over the relative priority *of commitments*

An example would be an organisation racked by disagreements over whether it should spend a large sum of money paying for structural alterations to provide disabled access – at the expense of other ways of serving its clients. The case of the dismissed volunteer co-ordinator can likewise be seen as involving a clash between commitments to non-discrimination in client service and to other principles, such as the proper treatment of employees. These competing principles will often be incommensurate – most obviously when they involve a clash between the expressive and the instrumental purposes of the organisation (for example, between the Church 'bearing witness' or providing service). Hence the argument may not be reducible to 'managerial judgement' – in practice, a utilitarian calculus of costs and benefits, perhaps through an elaborate appraisal of different courses of action, aiming to justify a decision on grounds of maximum social benefit. To be sure, uncertainty over means-ends relationships and the outcomes associated with different courses of action will often contribute further layers to a dispute, but if some of those involved argue that a particular course of action is right more or less regardless of the cost or outcome, then such uncertainties are hardly the heart of the matter.

These different ways in which values issue arise or can be expressed are all illustrated in the case of Red Rope: what did its socialist commitments *mean* in the context of leisure activities in the mountains? To what extent did its own organisation have to be *consistent* with its socialist ideals? What *priority* should be given to the aim of being a socialist organisation (in the public domain and to some extent 'exemplary'), as opposed to the aim of being an organisation of and for socialists (a club for leisure pursuits and private enjoyment)?

One other general point about the structure of values issues follows from this and should be emphasised: they are conflicts of *right against right,* in the sense that they involve a clash of legitimate but contextually incompatible principles – be they rival interpretations of organisational identity, the familiar tension between idealism and pragmatism, or simply conflicting priorities. This obvious point is important precisely because it will often *not* be obvious to some, perhaps all, of those involved. Characteristically, whichever side they are on, those involved will, at least initially, tend to see the issue as a case of *right against wrong.* Arguably, this has crucial implications for the management of values issues.

Implications for practice

What are the implications for managers of the concept of a values issue and the perspective on voluntary agencies that it embodies? Clearly, earlier *caveats* about the preliminary status of the framework developed in this paper become more relevant than ever. That said, one test of the concept is whether it helps to make sense of the experience of staff and managers in voluntary agencies. To the extent that it clarifies significant features of some of the predicaments they experience from time to time, it may also enable more informed and discerning judgements to be made. But there can be no question of deriving formulae for the management of values issues – as if the judgements involved could be expressed in a 'how to do it' checklist. In other words, the sort of implications of the values issue concept that are relevant here concern the way practitioners might think about, respond to and approach values issues. Some of these are outlined in turn (they are discussed at greater length in the Open University Course 'Managing Voluntary and Non-Profit Enterprises'):

Recognising that values issues are inevitable

The core values of organisations are necessarily ambiguous in the
sense that reasonable people can disagree over their precise implications in many situations. This means that, as with legal principles,
everything depends on interpretation and precedent – the policies
the organisation has evolved and the practices through which it operates
– and on how the circumstances are construed. Hence any agreement on how best to pursue the organisation's commitments will be
provisional: new circumstances, new people and new ideas will all
have the potential to reveal tensions and inconsistencies among an
organisation's norms, strategies and assumptions. Moreover, voluntary agencies are affected by external influences. They are arenas
in which and through which currents of social concern and social
change are expressed. Thus in the 1970s when workplace democracy was high up the social agenda, 'non-hierarchical working' was
taken up by many as more consonant with their agencies' progressive aspirations and commitments. The ensuing debates and rows were
often typical values issues (Landry *et al.*, 1985; Stanton, 1989).
Currently, equal opportunities and user empowerment are powerful
currents of social concern that can reasonably be presented as cor-
ollaries of the progressive aspirations and commitments of many
agencies. Hence in many cases they provide a basis for challenging
policies, structures and practices – challenges which may themselves
flare up as values issues, and which provide scope for values issues
in the future as the (inevitable) uncertainty over the meaning and
scope of these new commitments emerges and has to be resolved
(Nadeau and Sanders, 1991).
    The inevitability of values issues arising means that they cannot
be seen as embarrassing aberrations or a sign of management failure. Rather, managing values issues has to be seen as a distinctive,
integral and decidedly challenging part of the job for those in responsible positions. Values issues may be more or less successfully
handled, but they cannot be avoided – except, perhaps, by having
less thoughtful and committed staff and volunteers.

Recognising the positive aspects and potential of values issues

The processes of institutionalisation are necessary evils for value-
expressive organisations. Goal displacement, through, for example,

the gradual dominance of the concerns of staff or funders, is a constant danger. Indeed, well-known occupational hazards for those in senior positions, especially in larger organisations, are seeing the continuance and success of the agency as an end in itself and considering the broad picture at the expense of the difficult and untidy details. The emergence of values issues, therefore, can be a welcome sign that an agency's values and commitments are still taken seriously. It is interesting to note that Batsleer concludes his description of Red Rope by pointing out that the bitter disputes:

> did not prevent Red Rope from growing successfully as a major outdoor organization. By the early 1990s, it had developed a complex national and regional structure; it published a monthly newsletter and a quarterly bulletin; it organized many trips each month, ranging from children's seaside outings to substantial mountain expeditions; it had become a recognised campaigning body in the areas of the natural environment and access to the countryside by running meetings, conferences and mass trespasses and generally acting as a pressure group within the Rambler's Association and the British Mountaineering Council (Batsleer, 1992, p. 51).

In general, advances are made precisely through confrontations between what is espoused and what is practised, and between different, somewhat inconsistent, commitments or practices. Arguably, the emergence of policies on 'positive images' in fund-raising also illustrates this point. This is not to romanticise values issues, nor to ignore the fact that they can easily become divisive, debilitating and a drain on managerial attention. The point is that they are also occasions for double-loop learning (Argyris and Schon, 1978), opportunities for inventing creative solutions that will allow an agency better to pursue its mission.

Recognising the political dimension

Conventional approaches to management have a rational, instrumental core involving the definition of objectives, the design of appropriate means of achieving them, the monitoring of progress and then error-correction as necessary. This instrumental core of management thinking and practice works well wherever goals can be reasonably well defined, a technology exists to achieve them (in the sense that means–ends relationships are more or less understood), and relatively unambiguous ways of measuring progress can be devised (Thomson, 1967). These conditions are often hard to meet in relation to higher values and goals concerned with social change.

Hence although there is still a place for an instrumentally rational approach in such situations, its contribution will be limited. We are in the realm of politics and value-expressive behaviour, rather than administration and instrumentally rational behaviour – and the discourse in these realms is conducted in quite different terms. The language of social concern and moral outrage (or indeed of theology) does not easily translate into the language of practical, pragmatic management. For society as a whole we give the job of straddling the divide between social ideals and practical possibilities to politicians. Although as a group they are not afforded much honour – being cursed for their duplicity or their incompetence (or both) – they may still have something to teach the managers of voluntary agencies whose roles likewise often involve reconciling high principles with messy practicalities. To be respected and effective, politicians have to demonstrate strong commitment both to practical results and to general principles and values; they have to work hard at translating principles and slogans into practical policies; and they require a talent for creative compromise, the workable agreement that achieves significant gains or opens up new possibilities, and that is widely acceptable. It seems likely therefore that such essentially political skills are an important part of effective leadership in voluntary agencies as well.

Attending to the process, as much as the decision

The fact that many values issues involve irresolvable conflicts between right and right, and the tendency for values issues to escalate and polarise, mean that *how* the issue is handled will often be more important than the particular decision that emerges – which may in any case be open to review. With this in mind, the following points may be relevant for those who are involved in values issues:

- Those involved have to be clear about their roles, distinguishing *personal values* and *organisational* commitments;
- Managers especially have to be clear when and whether they are *protagonists* in the argument or *facilitators* of negotiation and agreement among their staff;

- In either case it is helpful to highlight the conflicting rights, distinguishing as appropriate between *social* ideals, *organisational* values and standards of *personal* conduct;
- To prevent escalation, care will be necessary over the language employed, and it will be important to affirm as legitimate the underlying concerns of the different parties.

Conclusions

This chapter has argued that a particular type of organisational conflict – the values issue – is more likely to arise in voluntary agencies and other value-based organisations than in other contexts, and that so far this seems to have been neglected in the literature on non-profit management, even if, as seems to be the case, it is readily appreciated by the managers of voluntary agencies. The chapter has used a range of examples to illustrate both the variety and the common characteristics of values issues.

A key argument is that the inherent ambiguity and fluidity of organisational values, especially in changing circumstances, means that their meaning and practical significance will intermittently be contested. Thus, as well as binding organisations together in shared commitments, values will also on occasion threaten to divide them bitterly.

These arguments suggest that protecting, developing and negotiating the meaning of values, in order to preserve a more or less viable set of commitments, needs to be recognised as a crucial part of management in many voluntary agencies. Some practical implications of this perspective were sketched out, with the emphasis on the importance of process or political skills.

Note

The author is indebted to his colleagues, particularly Julian Batsleer and Dr Jill Mordaunt, and to students of the Voluntary Sector Management Programme, for their assistance in developing the ideas in this chapter. The usual disclaimer applies.

References

Argyris, C. and D. Schon (1978) *Organizational Learning*, Addison-Wesley, Reading, MA.

Batsleer, J. (1992) 'Change, Conflict and Culture' (Book 11 of the course 'Managing Voluntary and Nonprofit Enterprises') The Open University, Milton Keynes.

Cyert, R.M. and J.G. March (1963) *A Behavioural Theory of the Firm*, Prentice-Hall, Englewood Cliffs, New Jersey.

East Lothian Courier (1993), 21 May, East Lothian, Scotland.

Handy, C. (1993) *Understanding Organizations*, 3rd edn, Penguin, Harmondsworth.

Kakabadse, A., R. Ludlow and S. Vinnicombe (1988) *Working in Organizations*, Penguin, Harmondsworth.

Landry, C., D. Morley, R. Southwood and P. Wright (1985) *What a Way to Run a Railroad: An Analysis of Radical Failure*, Comedia, London.

Lidchi, H. (1994) 'Reality and representation: images of the developing world with particular reference to NGOs', unpublished PhD thesis, Open University, Milton Keynes.

March, J.G. (1988) *Decisions and Organizations*, Blackwell, Oxford.

McKevitt, D. and A. Lawton (eds) (1994) *Public Sector Management: Theory, Critique, Practice*, Sage, London.

Nadeau, J. and S. Sanders (1991) 'Equal opportunities policies: the cuckoo in the nest or the goose that laid the golden egg?' in J. Batsleer, C. Cornforth and R. Paton (eds), *Issues in Voluntary and Non-Profit Management*, Addison-Wesley, London.

Rothschild-Whitt, J. (1979) 'The collectivist organization: an alternative to rational-bureaucratic models', *American Sociological Review*, 44: 509–27.

Stanton, A. (1989) *Invitation to Self-management*, Dab Hand Press, London.

Thomson, J.D. (1967) *Organizations in Action*, McGraw-Hill, New York.

4

Can We Define the Voluntary Sector?

Tony F. Marshall

Introduction

This paper examines the lack of clarity associated with the concept of the 'voluntary sector' and the repercussions resulting from the sector's internal heterogeneity. It has been customary to view the voluntary sector as that which is not for profit (private) and not statutory (public). This residual view is, however, unsatisfactory, because it never says what the sector *is*, as against what it is *not*. In this chapter it is argued that the voluntary sector cannot be seen just in terms of service provision, but includes distinct (sub)sectors such as informal care, self-help and community activity, and action that has a religious motivation ('missionary') as well as organised voluntary service. Voluntary action can in fact move across sectors and much of the purpose of such action is to generate change in other sectors, although it also serves to preserve as well as change. The common element to all voluntary organisations is that they serve as mediators between the individual and the state, both holding society together and lubricating it for social change.

The current time is one of confusion about the nature of the voluntary sector and its role in society. Just as it has apparently become more central to public policy planning, so the barriers between the traditionally conceived sectors of private, statutory and voluntary have become increasingly unclear. Douglas (1983) points out that industry (private sector) is inextricably linked, for instance, with government contracts, universities and research institutes, employees' families, trade unions and political parties, while it is being pressed more and more by government to contribute to voluntary and community initiatives (for example Business in the Community).

The private and statutory sectors are usually more clearly defined, while the voluntary sector tends to be seen in negative or residual terms according to what it is not; that is, not for profit and not statutory. The tendency is for our society to be viewed primarily as a market economy and to assume that most transactions will occur individually via the marketplace. The concept of 'market failure' or 'contract failure' (Hansmann, 1980) explains the need for a complementary sector. The 'welfare state' concept gives the statutory sector dominance in this role of mopping up the market failures. The 'self-help' promoters, on the other hand, would give the voluntary sector dominance in this respect. Within the welfare state model the role of the voluntary sector is seen as dealing with what might be termed 'statutory failure', mopping up the needs of minority interest groups, extending provision beyond the basic, 'filling gaps', providing a more personalised approach – a safety-net below the safety-net, as it were. This whole way of viewing the sector is deficient. For one thing, it is historically inaccurate, in that the voluntary sector is primary and the growth of a market economy and of the state are later developments. For another thing, it fails to recognise that the voluntary sector stands for something positive, and cannot be adequately conceptualised as some kind of Polyfilla.

While we do not have an adequate conception of the voluntary sector in relation to other social sectors, the problem is compounded by the fact that the voluntary sector is internally fissile and lacking a corporate identity. (See the chapters by Osborne and Taylor in this volume for further discussion of the heterogeneity of the sector.) These divisions have become more important as organisations compete for contracts and diminishing pots of money.

In actual fact, this internal heterogeneity is just as much characteristic of the private sector (and increasingly the public sector too) as it is of the voluntary sector. The unifying feature of the private sector is normally taken to be the profit motive, but this cannot be assumed without question. While some businesses do exist to maximise profits, others exist because of their directors' interests or skills in specific economic activities, which are employed in such a way as to 'make a living', but not necessarily to extract every possible cent from customers. Thus self-employed manual workers may charge according to customers' abilities to pay, including some work below cost or even free for, say, poor elderly people. Research institutes and consultancies have usually been set up to enable their staff to take forward their own interests, while being able to support themselves by selling their products. Many craftspersons and artists choose to spend substantial time creating what is rewarding for them, with only a secondary consideration of what will sell or what is in demand (often supporting themselves by routine products which can be made quickly and fill a ready market niche, and maximising time spent on activity that may not be profitable). The distinction between private sector organisations that are simply profit-orientated (which are often conglomerates and derive investment from shares) and those that are orientated towards some other end, while affording employees a decent living, is seldom made, but crucial to analysis of the role of the private sector. Creation of this second sub-category of organisations that are *not* seeking to maximise profits enables one to place universities, research institutes, certain kinds of consultancy (for example environmental, or management of voluntary organisations), private schools, some organisations involved with cultural products (art galleries, museums, leisure activities), charities' trading outlets and some service providers (such as some homes for the elderly or prisons run by NACRO (the National Association for the Care and Resettlement of Offenders). Bodies such as these are often seen as akin to, sometimes as part of, the voluntary sector, even though they operate at market rates. Opted-out schools and hospitals might also be seen as inhabiting a similar category.

The voluntary sector is similarly associated with a variety of motives. In *Voluntary Action*, Barry Knight (1993) makes a common and simple distinction between service-providers and campaigners, which is superficially meaningful in theory (although not adequate to cover the full variety) and impossible to maintain in practice. Billis (1989) employs an organisational dimension of informality/bureaucracy. More complex taxonomies usually employ a sectoral concept akin to the way government departments are divided according to subject-matter – health, education, unemployment and so on. But the list is almost endless and, while it may be useful for some purposes to group voluntary organisations in this way, it is entirely artificial if one is concerned to capture variations in the roles of organisations, and their relationship to society.

I have approached the issue of classification elsewhere (Marshall,

1994) and will not be further concerned with it here in its own right. Suffice it to say that the classification developed in that publication makes fundamental distinctions among voluntary organisations between: religious congregations; religious charities; church-based voluntary service to the community; charitable trusts; secular voluntary service; reform groups; co-operatives and credit unions; self-help, community and sports/leisure associations; political parties and pressure groups; and universalist movements (green, peace, human rights, consumerism and so on). This classification can be further developed – for example, by differentiating voluntary groups that are essentially appurtenances of statutory agencies – parent teacher associations, neighbourhood watch, victim support, school governors, friends of hospitals, for example. One may also choose to extend the 'religious' categories to include activities predicated on secular beliefs like humanism. The only purpose it serves in this paper, however, is to indicate the variety of activities and organisations that can be lumped under the general heading of 'voluntary'. The distinctions I shall want to make here are rather broader ones, each of which subsumes several of these categories.

The ambiguities of voluntarism

Before more systematic analysis it may be instructive to look at some common conceptions of the voluntary sector and make brief reference to some of the evidence that suggests a more complex picture.

1. Voluntary organisations are about volunteering

They sound and look much alike, but the two terms have distinct connotations which are far from co-terminous. There are many voluntary organisations that do not 'employ' volunteers at all, apart from their trustees. There are vast numbers of volunteers working on behalf of, or organised by, statutory agencies (Darvill and Munday (eds), 1984; Lynn and Davis Smith, 1991, and see Davis Smith, this volume).

2. The voluntary sector is more personalised, closer to the community: the statutory sector is bureaucratic

This is largely mythology. Bureaucracy *may* be well-managed complexity; the alternative *may* be chaos. Bureaucratic systems at least offer clear rights to assistance and guidelines for equal access (even if these are not always well implemented); voluntary services *can* be provided haphazardly and idiosyncratically. The degree of personal contact is more a matter of resources than sector. When my house was burgled recently, a policeman spent some time ensuring we were able to cope and exploring security issues; a victim support volunteer pushed a small scrap of paper with a phone number on it through the letter-box and then fled before I could get to the door. One can get short-changed in quality of service by organisations in any sector. Similarly, client/customer representation is not necessarily more prevalent in the voluntary sector than in the statutory sector. Indeed, the ideology of philanthropy may militate against it, while many statutory agencies are now taking quality of service and client participation much more seriously. (See Deakin, this volume, for further discussion of these issues.)

3. The statutory sector serves consensus values: the voluntary sector is able to respond to minority values

This is not entirely true. The state does take steps to protect minority rights, and all statutory agencies now have equal opportunities policies. This cannot be said of all voluntary groups – some actively resist the extension of their services to minority groups. The voluntary sector, moreover, is not aimed primarily at minority values – most major organisations serve universal values in the same way as statutory ones. (This is not to deny the role of certain organisations in the voluntary sector in successfully promoting the interests of minorities or of disadvantaged sections of the community – see Knapp, this volume, for example.)

4. The private sector serves private good: the statutory and voluntary sectors serve the collective good

This almost sounds truistic, but it actually contains little truth at all. Most services in all sectors are provided on an individualistic basis. In so far as collectivities need services, they are just as able (in general) to purchase them in the market as to rely on alternative provision. The private sector provides jobs and incomes which may be essential to the maintenance of local communities. A great deal of community activity takes place on the premises of public houses, which are profit-making businesses. The only glimmer of truth is that the *impetus behind provision* in the private sector is *private interest*, and in the other sectors *collective interest* (Blau and Scott, 1963).

5. The voluntary sector is primarily concerned with the disadvantaged

Although far from being entirely the case, there is some justification for this view, especially in the case of philanthropic organisations. In the case of self-help and community groups, there is no necessary connection with disadvantage, of course; indeed, there may be a reverse tendency in some respects, as the more advantaged have the greater skills and resources for organising themselves (Bulmer, 1986). However, both the statutory and the voluntary sectors are to some extent redistributive in a way that the private sector cannot be (as will be seen below).

6. Control in the voluntary sector lies with the community, not with investors (private sector) or the government (statutory)

What is 'community'? Control in the voluntary sector in actual fact rests most often with an existing organisation, for example a church or with a small self-selected clique of like-minded (even if well-meaning) individuals. Research into membership of voluntary agencies' management committees suggests little competition for places and selective recruitment procedures (Kramer, 1965; Middleton, 1987). If one is talking about democracy, then the statutory sector may be closer to popular control than many voluntary organisations.

7. The voluntary sector has a strong relationship with moral values

There is no evidence to suggest that activity in self-help groups and community organisations is any less self-interested than action in the private sector (Richardson and Goodman, 1983; Hatch and Hinton, 1986). The fact that the statutory sector is framed in terms of legal rights does not mean that those legal rights are not ultimately based on moral decisions, rather than ones of calculation.

8. The voluntary sector is creative, innovative, flexible and quick to respond

These are not universal features of voluntary organisations, nor are they necessarily absent from other sectors. As Knapp points out elsewhere in this volume, several writers have suggested that the voluntary sector is no more innovative than the public (Brenton, 1985; Kramer, 1981).

Extensive privatisation has recently led many to ask whether there is a limit to the transfer of statutory functions to charity. An example is provided by Harwood (1993), who discusses the attempts to persuade voluntary organisations to tender for the provision of secure accommodation for young offenders. They have been reluctant to do so, he says, because 'Firstly, the proposals to introduce the private [and voluntary] sector will result in poor child care practice. Secondly, the decision to lock up a child is such a major one it should only be carried [out?] by the state.' The second argument is the crucial one. But what is the difference between paying statutory sector staff to execute government policy and paying staff through some other kind of organisation, assuming that appropriate objectives and oversight are in place? This question applies to 'contracting out' in general. The only *necessary* difference, in fact, is in who pockets any profits (or savings). In all other respects a voluntary agency merely becomes an agent of the state, losing all independence and flexibility in favour of the detailed terms of a contract and legal rights or duties. In the case of custody this is quite appropriate, but why might one ever think that *avoiding* obligations and uniform service is a good way of going about matters? The answer to this question is crucial to our conception of the sector.

The answer is crucial because one cannot, in fact, justify the provision of valued services on other than either an eqalitarian or an ability-to-pay basis. The point is that the voluntary sector is not simply about service provision. If one views it in that way, one inevitably has to conclude that it is an inefficient and haphazard way of organising provision that has little credibility. One is left with the argument that voluntary organisations can be cheaper, because they may use volunteers. But statutory agencies can use volunteers, too, and often do. To the volunteers, it is the perceived value of the service they are helping provide which is often crucial, not the nature of the organisation managing their contribution. One may work just as willingly for one's local school as for Age Concern.

If one persists in viewing the voluntary sector as just another means of service provision one will never understand its real nature. To judge it in this way is to impose an inappropriate agenda set by the private and public sectors. It leads to the dominance of objectives like cost-effectiveness (see Knapp in this volume) and accountability (see Leat, also in this volume), and the language of business plans and contracts. These considerations are not irrelevant to the sector, but its essence cannot be so tightly constrained.

To make any progress, however, we shall have to stop talking about *the* voluntary sector and begin a discussion of the multiplicity of voluntary sectors.

Four (or more) voluntary sectors

The accompanying table differentiates 'sectors' (which might be defined as 'distinct spheres of organised action') according to the criteria for allocating action and the associated loci of control. (By 'control' is meant 'the ability to direct decisions on the form, quality, organisation and distribution of action'.) The final column of the table represents the different implications for social change associated with each sector, which will be discussed below in detail. It is this, in fact, which will provide the clue to what the voluntary sector is all about, as well as the reason for its apparent incoherence and lack of clarity.

Two sectors are essentially individualised: one is that of informal action on behalf of kin, neighbours, friends and so on, where aid is predicated on common group membership and is a matter of personal choice, albeit within the constraints of cultural norms of duty, helpfulness, sociability and reciprocity. The other is that of commercial relations, the so-called private sector, where aid has its price, and the extent and social distribution of action is determined largely by market forces and hence broadly by the distribution of wealth.

Table 4.1 *Sectors of organised action*

Sector	Criterion for allocation of action	Source of control	Contribution to social change
Private	Economic: who can pay?	Market	Does not alter inequality
Statutory	Legal: who is entitled?	Government	Systemic redistribution
Religious	Moral: who is seen as deserving?	Religious group	Local redistribution
Philanthropic	Moral: who is seen as deserving?	Providers	Local redistribution
Community	Political: who can mobilise?	Beneficiaries	Empowerment
Informal	Social: who belongs?	Culture	Reproduces community

The statutory sector corresponds to that action which governments have determined as their own responsibility. Provision does not therefore depend on the social position or economic power of recipients, but on legislation and national policy, although entitlement may be defined in terms of social or economic disadvantage. Although Parliament is the immediate source of control, legislation provides some continuity beyond particular governments, and the ultimate control in a democracy is visualised as one of public consensus, or at least of majority values.

The major division among the remaining three sectors is whether control rests with those who benefit from the action or with others (the providers). In the first instance individuals group together for mutual advantage in furthering their self-interest, whether this is purely for association, as in much community activity, or for the achievement of greater economic or social power. In societies where communities are not defined in ascriptive terms, such as kinship groups or clans, this sector is important as the source of social solidarity and the creation of 'community' itself. Such communities need not be geographically defined – they may be associations representing shared interests spanning the whole country (or the world).

Although many community groups are formed as a response to members' common feeling of social disadvantage, such groups are not restricted to the lower echelons of society. They might include, for instance, the residents of a block of expensive flats who organise a self-help system of security to defend themselves against burglary and attack from outside. They would also include elite clubs like the Carlton, as well as professional associations and working-men's clubs.

The remaining two sectors are both characterised by action by a relatively favoured group of people on behalf of others. The distinction between the two rests on whether the organisational context for action is that of existing religious institutions or purpose-built organisations of a secular kind. This distinction is important because of the size and historical importance of the religious sector in most countries of the world, even in those which are seen to be the most secularised. It is also important because the pre-existing organisational base of religious action is an important resource physically, in terms of social acceptance, and for the mobilisation of volunteers. In other respects it is similar to the secular philanthropic sector in that action is determined by providers, not beneficiaries, and that the criterion is what those providers see as a deserving or priority cause, according to religious or other views.

The difficulty of defining boundaries between sectors, noted in the first part of this paper, can now be seen as one which is inherent to the subject-matter. When one adopts the position of the policy-maker rationally allocating services across commercial, state and voluntary organisations, the lack of clarity is problematic, but, if one adopts a neutral historical perspective, one can see that activities move, *and are intended to move*, across boundaries over time. These sectors are not a matter of rational planning, but are evolutionary social phenomena that develop (and change their nature) in interaction with each other. The end-point of a great deal of action in the community sector is precisely to achieve influence on the other sectors – to gain economic power through combination in order that members will be better placed to operate in the private sector (through co-operatives, for example), to generate credibility for their cause and stake a claim as a group deserving of public help (which may recruit philanthropic support), or to influence government to change or create legislation in their favour. That sub-category of philanthropic action that consists of reform movements, empowerment and social advocacy is also concerned with the same movement of groups across boundaries – whether it is advancing their economic position, advocating appropriate legislation, or helping the intended beneficiaries to mobilise and organise themselves. The nature of most of these sectors is therefore closely tied to the workings of the political system.

Both the private and informal sectors tend to conserve the current state of affairs, the one economically and the other socially. The informal sector reinforces mutual help among the closely related, which may match the preference of beneficiaries to be assisted by those they know rather than by strangers, even though the latter may be more knowledgeable or skilled (Billis, 1989). The informal sector relieves society as a whole of a substantial economic burden of care for its members, especially at the extensive low-skilled end of the range, such as caring for the sick at home or providing the immobilised with transport (Hadley and Hatch, 1981). Even more importantly, this sector is the very foundation of community, not only in terms of mutual help, but also in terms of association, cultural attachment and a sense of belonging and status. Although the informal sector includes 'service', it is primarily about the construction of relationships without which life would be anomic, unrewarding and threatening. Mutual help in this sector, like informal social gatherings and celebrations, is part of the fabric from which society is built, not the sector's main rationale.

While the informal sector constructs community on the basis of ascriptive and personal ties, the community sector proper achieves a wider basis for association on the basis of weaker, or merely potential, ties, such as residence in the same neighbourhood or the sharing of common interests. It is a sector which has grown with the social fragmentation of neighbourhoods and the breakdown of extensive kinship networks and clan groupings. While the stuff of politics in a kinship-based society is the manoeuvring of different clans for dominance and relative advantage, the informal sector in Western society tends to be relatively weak in this respect, and the main force for change now comes from aggregations of people who are less intimately associated, through community groups of various kinds. Again, like the informal sector, much of the activity is concerned with association and cultural celebration, and, in so far as material interests are concerned, there is the building of a network of mutual help and the chance for people to work together to pursue common ends, as in tenants' associations and local protest groups, co-operatives and trade unions (Brenton, 1985). The community sector differs from the informal in that it works through purpose-built organisations (which may, however, be transient) rather than personal ties. Although the sector is not directly redistributive, because members pool their current resources to help themselves, it may empower disadvantaged groups to achieve change in other sectors.

The philanthropic and religious sectors are redistributive to a degree, usually on a local basis and only to the extent that providers can afford, and choose, to share their resources of money, time, equipment, and so on, with those they wish to serve. The redistribution is therefore limited, often local and patchy (see, for example, Wolpert, 1993). The power to define who are to be considered 'deserving' recipients, moreover, remains in the hands of providers, and is a reflection of the existing distribution of social power. However, some philanthropic activity (both secular and religious) does contribute to the empowerment of groups in the community sector, and thus may lead to more substantial social change. While some philanthropic activity is dedicated to promoting association and building community, it is much more concentrated in service-provision (including financial help) than the informal and community sectors.

The statutory sector, finally, is the main means by which systematic redistribution can be achieved. While it may favour community-building, it is mainly concerned, in its direct action, with service-provision.

Volunteering, the state and mediating institutions

The term 'volunteering' is often used to refer to services provided free by individuals working through voluntary organisations, generally of a philanthropic (secular or religious) kind. One could interpret 'volunteering' in a much wider way, however, and see it as covering any action that individuals *choose* to contribute for the greater social good (as they see it), through whatever means or sector they prefer. (See Davis Smith, this volume, for further discussion of this issue.)

The voluntary sector, similarly, is not discrete; it permeates and underlies all social activity. Those organisations that lie outside the

statutory or private sectors, moreover, depend on resources to survive, which may come from those two sectors (including public giving)
or by transfer between voluntary organisations, as in funding by
charitable trusts. Those based in major religious institutions may be
resourced by them, and self-help groups may be able to survive on
members' fees or voluntary effort, but philanthropic groups will
eventually have to attract government support if they are to survive, unless they are among the few with a sufficiently high public
profile to attract large sums by individual giving or massive en-
dowments.

If one defines the voluntary sector, however, as any of those
sectors which is neither for-profit nor state action, there is a sense
in which these sectors have something in common which is distinct. Berger and Neuhaus (1977) argue that the two major political
ideologies in the modern world – individualism and statism – both
fail to create a meaningful relationship between the individual and
the state. Either ideology may lead to anomie and alienation, the
one because society has no place, the other because it becomes
overbearing and all-pervasive ('Big Brother'). Both may therefore
lead to feelings of individual impotence and to lack of social commitment. Berger and Neuhaus therefore assert the importance of
'mediating institutions': groups or communities not so large that
individuals cannot identify with them, nor have some meaningful
and effective involvement in them, and which themselves link the
individual to the nation-state. State services and governmental func-
tioning, in their view, operate through such mediating institutions,
maintaining a baseline of economic and social well-being, and ensuring fundamental human rights, while encouraging the vitality of
institutions by allowing maximum freedom for grassroots activity,
and bottom-up rather than top-down definitions of need and decision-making. Gladstone (1979) uses these ideas as the basis of his
theory of 'welfare pluralism'.

Such mediating institutions can take a multitude of forms – for
example, residential communities, workplaces, schools, churches, ethnic
or cultural communities, charities, political groups, kinship networks
– indeed any form of collectivity in which individual members can
directly participate. This is the same constellation of activity that
makes up the informal, community, philanthropic and religious sectors defined in this paper. While the private sector allows play for
individualism, and the statutory sector for those basic services that

should be available to all members of society, the voluntary sector comprises those mediating institutions through which individuals can share in, and contribute to, meaningful association, the cultural stock of the nation, the material and psychological commonweal, and political action.

So what is the voluntary sector?

The reason for many of the ambiguities explored earlier in this chapter now becomes clear. The boundary problems follow from the assumption that sectors of organised action should be distinct, when they are in fact overlapping (Billis, 1989). Traditional philanthropic voluntary service organisations can actually operate in virtually any sector. They may act in the private sector, by providing services for fees; they may act in the statutory sector on contract, or by close relationships of interdependence; they may work through the support of informal carers; they may collaborate with church groups; they may stimulate self-help community action.

The internal heterogeneity of the 'voluntary sector' can be encompassed by seeing it as an amalgam of several sub-sectors, each with a different impetus and character. Some of these are more concerned with the creation of community, some with helping the disadvantaged, others with mutual self-help or grassroots innovation. All these strands help to make up the sector, but none of them characterise it as a whole. The only common feature is their mediating character – the fact that they give individuals a role and a place in social life and, potentially, social change. They represent action that is both collective and yet personal. If the private sector constitutes the marketplace for material negotiation, the voluntary sector provides the marketplace for negotiating social values and social relationships. (The contributions by Billis, Paton and Taylor in this volume show how much of the life of a voluntary organisation is about value negotiation.) The public sector can, correspondingly, be seen as the marketplace for negotiating legal rights.

This is not to deny that certain organisations, whose origins are certainly within the voluntary sector, may evolve away from these characteristics, such that they become more like private enterprise or statutory provision. If the sector is about social change, it is therefore about malleability and movement over time. De Tocqueville

(1956) came close to defining the essence of voluntarism when he identified it as the mainstay of democracy – communal decision-making, grassroots organisation, campaigning – a role more evident to him in nineteenth-century America when the state was still in a relatively early stage of development than it is to us today. But 'democracy' itself is a concept imposed from outside (like the service-delivery agenda), representing the ideology of a particular type of political order. The voluntary sector is just as important a market-place for social values and relationships in other kinds of state – in Communist China and South American dictatorships for example – as in Western 'democracies'. In all of these states the voluntary sector provides both the adhesive which holds them together and the solvent which allows them to change. It is both used by, and helps to shape, governments. Thus we end, as we started, with the peculiar ambiguity of the voluntary sector.

Acknowledgements

I am grateful for the comments of those who contributed to the Symposium giving rise to this book, and other voluntary sector researchers and practitioners with whom I have discussed such ideas from time to time. I am sure I have not satisfied them all, but I have tried to incorporate their valuable ideas and insights. I regard the ideas in this paper as in a state of permanent evolution (rather like the voluntary sector itself) rather than a definitive statement, and I look forward to continuing discussion of these themes. Two papers by Stephen Osborne came to my attention too late to incorporate into this discussion, but greatly overlap with my own chapter and provide more substantial underpinning for some of the ideas, as well as developing lines I have not been able to broach here (Osborne, 1993a, 1993b).

References

Berger, P. and R. Neuhaus (1977) *To Empower People: The Role of Mediating Structures in Public Policy*, American Enterprise Institute for Public Policy Research, Washington DC.
Billis, D. (1989) *A Theory of the Voluntary Sector: Implications for Policy and Practice*, Working Paper no. 5, Centre for Voluntary Organisation, London School of Economics, London.

Blau, P.M. and W.R. Scott (1963) *Formal Organizations*, Routledge & Kegan Paul, London.

Brenton, M. (1985) *The Voluntary Sector in British Social Services*, Longman, London and New York.

Bulmer, M. (1986) *Neighbours: The Work of Philip Abrams*, Cambridge University Press, Cambridge.

Darvill, G. and B. Munday (eds) (1984) *Volunteers in the Personal Social Services*, Tavistock.

De Tocqueville, A. (1956) *Democracy in America*, Mentor, New York.

Douglas, J. (1983) *Why Charity? The Case for a Third Sector*, Sage, London.

Gladstone, F. (1979) *Voluntary Action in a Changing World*, Bedford Square Press, London.

Hadley, R. and S. Hatch (1981) *Social Welfare and the Failure of the State*, Allen & Unwin, London.

Hansmann, H.B. (1980) 'The role of nonprofit enterprise', *Yale Law Journal*, 89: 835–98.

Harwood, S. (1993) 'Where the work of charity stops', *Third Sector*, 9 September.

Hatch, S. and T. Hinton (1986) *Self-Help in Practice: A Study of Contact a Family, Community Work and Family Support*, Joint Unit for Social Services Research, Sheffield University.

Knight, B. (1993) *Voluntary Action*, Home Office, London.

Kramer, R. (1965) 'Ideology, status and power in board-executive relationships', *Social Work*, 10, October.

Kramer, R. (1981) *Voluntary Agencies in the Welfare State*, University of California Press, Berkeley and Los Angeles, California.

Lynn, P. and J. Davis Smith *The 1991 National Survey of Voluntary Activity in the UK*, Volunteer Centre UK, Berkhamsted.

Marshall, T. (1994) *The Assessment of Local Voluntary Activity: Developing the Method*, Home Office, London.

Middleton, M. (1987) 'Nonprofit boards of directors: beyond the governance function' in *The Nonprofit Sector: A Research Handbook*, ed. W.W. Powell, Yale University Press, New Haven and London.

Osborne, S. (1993a) *Understanding Voluntary Organizations in Contemporary Western Society*, Aston Business School, Birmingham.

Osborne, S. (1993b) *Toward a Theory of the Voluntary Sector? A Review of Theories of Voluntary Action*, Aston Business School, Birmingham.

Richardson, A. and M. Goodman (1983) *Self-Help and Social Care: Mutual Aid Organisations in Practice*, Policy Studies Institute, London.

Wolpert, J. (1993) 'Decentralization and equity in public and nonprofit sectors', *Nonprofit and Voluntary Sector Quarterly*, 22(4): 281–96.

5

Are Voluntary Organisations Accountable?

Diana Leat

Introduction

This paper does not purport to provide any straightforward answer to the question posed. Instead I shall raise a series of further questions and draw a number of distinctions which underpin discussion of the accountability of voluntary organisations. I shall then consider some of the potential difficulties faced by voluntary organisations in responding to demands for greater accountability.

Before embarking on this task it is worth making some preliminary remarks on voluntary organisations' public accountability. First, voluntary organisations are in a somewhat odd position in relation to accountability, reflecting their position between the public and private sectors. In theory, organisations in the commercial sector are accountable, in a sense, to their funders and customers/beneficiaries via market mechanisms. Public organisations are publicly accountable, both to their funders and their users via the democratic political process. In theory, voluntary organisations are accountable neither via market mechanisms nor the electoral process. Indeed some argue that accountability is a peculiarly public sector concept (see, for example, Vinten, 1992).

Thus it might be argued that voluntary organisations exist in a (semi) private domain, between market and state, in which issues of accountability do not arise. Interestingly, in discussion of this paper during the CVO 15th Anniversary Conference it was suggested that precisely because voluntary organisations exist between market and state it is necessary to build in means of accountability. Secondly, voluntary organisations have been criticised as 'private governments' subject to the 'iron law of oligarchy' (Kramer, 1987). Thirdly, in Britain, charities' record on public accountability has been at best patchy. A House of Commons Committee on Public Accounts in 1989 expressed astonishment at the lack of public accountability displayed by charities, and subsequent reports expressed similar disquiet. The philosophy behind the Charities Act 1990 was said to be that 'charities should be accountable to the public who have put their money in the public domain' (Hansard, HLPBC, col. 93, quoted in Warburton, 1992). Fourthly, and paradoxically, alongside worries regarding the accountability of voluntary organisations there is a vague notion that voluntary organisations are somehow more accountable to, or at least closer to 'the people'. This broad notion is often linked to that of voluntary organisations as mediating structures and vehicles for 'empowerment'(see Marshall, this volume). The empirical evidence to support these claims is, however, lacking (see, for example, Kramer, 1987).

The final introductory point is that there is little data on how voluntary organisations define accountability, what priority they attach to it and what systems and procedures they have in place. Studies raising the issue of accountability tend to be concerned primarily with accountability to statutory funders (for reasons suggested above this may be significant in itself). If accountability is a useful concept, and if it is important or relevant in relation to voluntary organisations, further empirical research is needed. What follows is, of necessity, based on speculation, related data, personal accounts of charity managers and sparse research evidence.

Demands for accountability

The question 'are voluntary organisations accountable?' may be read as implying that voluntary organisations *should* be accountable. But should they? And if so, to whom and for what?

In Britain questions regarding the accountability of voluntary organisations (as distinct from charities) appear to be of relatively recent origin and have a somewhat unclear rationale. Questions regarding the regulation, control and accountability of charities have a much longer history, as events leading up to the creation of the Charity Commission in the nineteenth century demonstrate

(Chesterman, 1979). In part, issues of public accountability are built into the concept of charity via the notion of public benefit which is central to legal definition. Furthermore, the existence of the Charity Commission creates an expectation of public accountability, both in the sense that that is part of its function and in so far as its registration functions are seen to provide organisations with a 'seal of public approval', encouraging people to give to those organisations. Thus the 'halo effect' of charitable status may be seen to generate its own demands for public protection and maintenance of public trust via accountability.

Issues of public accountability also arise from the fiscal and legal privileges conferred by charitable status. As the scope and scale of taxation has grown, the value of the tax advantages enjoyed by charities has also grown. This may have had two effects. Firstly, as charitable status became more financially valuable there may have been greater concern to bestow this status more carefully and to police it more effectively. Secondly, as the sums of 'lost' public revenue grew, there may have been greater concern regarding the use of such monies.

But aside from these fiscal trends (relevant only to charities) there have been other wider social changes which may have (rightly or wrongly) increased interest in the accountability of voluntary organisations more generally (Leat, 1988; Leat, 1990).

The mixed economy of welfare

With the development of a mixed economy of welfare provision, voluntary organisations assume a new significance, in policy if not in practice. The voluntary sector may not be important in terms of expenditure or contribution to total provision, but it is no longer marginal within the ideology of provision. Greater attention is paid to the accountability of voluntary organisations, not merely because such organisations may be in receipt of larger sums of state funding, but also, and more significantly, because instead of providing the 'extras' voluntary organisations are now regarded as central players in the provision of services for which the state accepts some responsibility. Two other factors have contributed to further attention being paid to the accountability of voluntary organisations: first, increasing emphasis in both local and central government on ensuring efficiency and effectiveness in the spending of government money, including that on voluntary organisations (Home Office, 1990); second, involvement of voluntary organisations in more closely monitored 'experimental' central and local government initiatives.

Professionalism

For various reasons, beyond the scope of this paper, voluntary organisations have increasingly employed paid professional technical and general managerial staff (Kramer, 1990; Bruce and Leat, 1993). But in charities, responsibility for policy-making and the overall conduct of the organisation must remain with unpaid volunteer trustees. With the separation of policy-making and implementation, issues of accountability for 'appropriate' or 'adequate' implementation arise. Furthermore, if workers are paid/employed to implement policy, then the issue of employee-employer accountability is introduced. If, in addition, those employed to manage the organisation and to implement policy claim some professional competence, then accountability takes on a new and potentially troublesome dimension; the role of the management committee must be reconciled in theory and in practice with the claims of managers and employees to professional authority and autonomy. These problems are not peculiar to voluntary organisations, but may be of special significance in so far as governance by independent volunteer trustees has been considered a defining characteristic (on the issue of definition see, for example, Salamon and Anheier, 1992).

Consumerism

Finally, the voluntary sector, along with the for-profit and public sectors, has been influenced by the ideology of consumerism – that the demands of the ordinary person, the consumer, should be taken into account. The growth of consumerism has led to changes in the internal structure and culture of some voluntary organisations, as well as a change in the overall shape and character of the sector as a whole, as new organisations started by consumers for consumers have joined the ranks of the philanthropic paternalists. There is nothing new in organisations started by consumers for consumers, but the growth of such organisations in the 1970s and 1980s appeared to go against the trend of greater professionalism discussed above. In addition, the growth of consumerism indirectly led to voluntary organisations being used by local authorities, and other statutory bodies, as representatives of 'the community' or of a particular client group. Accepting, or claiming, a representative role may have had two further effects. By stepping into the local political arena and onto the toes of local authority members, voluntary organisations made increased questioning of their accountability inevitable. And secondly, for various reasons, some voluntary organisations appeared to identify legitimacy with some notion of democratic accountability.

The discussion above indirectly raises a number of questions and distinctions. First, it may be important to distinguish between:

1. Charities which by definition enjoy state 'approval', indirect financial 'subsidy' and may also receive direct state funding;
2. Voluntary organisations in receipt of state funding;
3. Voluntary organisations not in receipt of state funding, either directly or indirectly.

Receipt of public funding, directly or indirectly from the state, or as a result of a 'legal halo', provides one important rationale for demands for voluntary organisations, of whatever type, to be publicly accountable. Secondly, in discussing issues of voluntary organisations' accountability, it is important to distinguish between 'external' and 'internal' accountabilities. Not only are the issues, and tensions, different, but it is arguable that the one does not imply the other; furthermore, demands for greater external accountability may in practice create problems and tensions in internal accountability. Thirdly, accountability to members, users and beneficiaries may be an important source of legitimacy for some voluntary organisations, but it is not the only source of legitimacy (Rein, 1975); it is therefore important to distinguish between accountability and legitimacy (Leat, 1988).

It is also important to distinguish between accountability and democracy. Voluntary organisations may (or may not) be accountable to specified groups, but this does not imply that they are internally democratic. A detailed discussion of voluntary organisations and democracy is beyond the scope of this paper. But it is worth noting that the 'celebration of voluntary organizations as an important democratizing force has ... been called into question by the composition and the decision-making processes of their governing bodies and the prevalence of minority rule' (Kramer, 1987, p. 245). Others have argued that voluntary organisations' contribution to democracy lies not in their internal structures but in their contribution to pluralism through advocacy (see, for example, Perrow, 1970). Yet another view is that the virtue of voluntary organisations lies not in its representativeness but in its particularism (see, for example, Douglas, 1983).

Types of accountability

As Kramer has remarked, popularity of the concept of accountability is exceeded only by the lack of agreement about its meaning (Kramer, 1982).

Elsewhere I have distinguished different forms of accountability. *Explanatory accountability* means being required to give an account, to describe and explain. Those owed accountability claim the right to require an account, to express disapproval or criticism, but do not have the power to impose sanctions (other than public criticism, which may in some circumstances constitute some form of sanction). *Accountability with sanctions*, on the other hand, involves not only the right to require an account but also the right to impose sanctions if the account or the actions accounted for are unacceptable. The sanctions involved are likely to be relatively tangible and immediate – loss of office or loss of funding, for example. The third type of accountability is *responsive accountability*. This is the weakest, and probably the most widespread, type of accountability, requiring only that those who are accountable take into account or respond to the views or demands of those to whom they are accountable. 'There are no formal sanctions involved although failure to be accountable in this sense, or to be responsive, may lead to loss of support from those who expect to have their views taken into account' (Leat, 1988, p. 20).

Accountability for what?

Organisations may be required to account for the proper use of money – fiscal accountability. They may be required to account for their use of proper procedures – process accountability. They may be required to account for the quality of their work – programme accountability. They may be required to account for their choice of priorities, the relevance and appropriateness of their work – accountability for priorities.

These distinctions are important in clarifying the nature and scope of accountability. They are also important in discussing what voluntary organisations may be regarded as accountable for and to whom. Voluntary organisations may be accountable to different groups for different things, to the same group for different things and to different groups for the same things (Leat, 1988). 'Inappropriate' accountability may arise in part from lack of clarity regarding the accountability requirements of each particular group. For example, difficulties sometimes arise between voluntary organisations and funders because the funder regards the organisation as owing fiscal, process and programme accountability, whereas the funded organisation sees itself as accountable only for the proper use of money. Conversely, other voluntary organisations complain that some funders are only interested in a decent set of accounts (fiscal accountability) and take no interest in the quality of their work (programme accountability).

Accountability to whom?

One of the often-stated differences between for-profit and voluntary non-profit organisations lies in the range of constituents to whom they may be regarded as in some sense accountable. For example, Drucker, discussing public service institutions which have no results out of which they are paid, has argued that such organisations have to satisfy everyone (Drucker, 1985). Discussing non-profit organisations, Drucker has suggested that one of the most basic differences between non-profit organisations and businesses is that the typical non-profit organisation has a multitude of constituencies and has to work out a different relationship with each of them (Drucker, 1990). Of course, not all relationships imply accountability, but it might reasonably be argued that if the term 'constituencies' is to mean anything then it must include some notion of accountability, even if only responsive accountability.

What does this 'multitude of constituencies' include? Hinton, discussing the accountability of the Save the Children Fund, provides one list:

But aside from the trustees, a seemingly endless number of other stake-holders would consider SCF to be accountable to them to a greater or lesser extent: children, families, eight or nine different national governments, the United Nations and its family of 40-plus agencies, the European Community, sponsors, corporate donors, the purchasers of goods in Save the Children shops, individual donors, or the executors of legacies, or indeed anyone who happens to read about Save the Children in the press or hears about the organisation on the television – all would appear to feel from time to time that the organisation is wholly or in part accountable to them (Hinton, 1993, p. 9).

The groups to whom in theory voluntary organisations may be regarded, or may regard themselves, as accountable include the following: the general public/community; the Charity Commission; the Inland Revenue; central government; local government; users; other voluntary organisations; professional bodies; the Registrar of Companies; various regulatory bodies; various watchdog bodies on particular issues; various funders, including central and local government departments; quangos; trusts; the general public; corporate and commercial givers (Leat, 1988). This is merely the 'outer wheel' of potential constituencies. Within this wheel there is a further set of relationships involving various types of accountability between volunteers, paid staff, chief executive, board/management committee, sub-committees, membership (individuals and/or organisations), special programme/project committees, parent body (if any). Users may or may not be included within this 'inner wheel', either as a special category or in their capacity as members.

Lists of constituencies to whom an organisation is regarded, or regards itself, as accountable will differ between organisations, and for the same organisation over time. Some types of voluntary organisation are, of course, likely to share a common core of constituents – for example, all charities are accountable to the Charity Commission and to the Inland Revenue – but it is worth making the point that not all organisations are accountable to funders (endowed foundations, for example).

What factors are likely to affect the nature and number of an organisation's constituencies *and* the type (explanatory, with sanctions, responsive) and scope (fiscal, process, programme, priorities) of accountability in relation to each group? The following section suggests some variables for further research.

Accountability variables

Legal status (charitable status), legal form and individual constitutional structure are obviously important variables. For example, charities are accountable to the Charity Commission and the sub-set of charities registered as companies are also accountable under company as well as charity law. Not all charities have members and those that do may have different accountability arrangements built into their constitutions. It is worth re-emphasising here that not all charities and voluntary organisations are constituted as internally democratic bodies, though they may nevertheless be regarded or regard themselves as owing responsive accountability to a wide range of groups.

Level and type of resource dependence and sources of income are two other important variables in considering both the nature and number of groups to which organisations are regarded, or regard themselves, as accountable. These variables are also important in analysing the types and scope of accountability owed to different groups. As Young and Finch have suggested, voluntary organisations have varying degrees of organisational 'slack' (Young and Finch, 1977). Different degrees of organisational slack give organisations different key constituencies and different degrees of freedom to ignore what would be constraining constituencies for another organisation.

Perhaps the most extreme example in this context is the endowed foundation which is accountable to the Charity Commission but has no dependency upon any external source of finance or legitimacy and may, if it chooses, carry on its work in complete secrecy and without reference to the expectations or demands of others. Indeed some endowed trusts robustly defend their right not to be accountable to any external body (accountability to the Charity Commission may be only grudgingly granted as a legal requirement). The endowed foundation may be contrasted with a heavily resource-dependent operating charity receiving grants and contracts from a wide range of funders, each able to demand accountability with all too real sanctions, and each (potentially) requiring fiscal, process and programme accountability.

It may be important to distinguish not only between degree of resource dependence and sources of funding but also type or terms of funding. The type and scope of accountability required of the organisation is likely to depend upon the nature of that funding, whether it is given as grant-aid or within a contract; and if the latter the precise terms of the contract. Kramer, and others, have highlighted the fact that in practice accountability for grant-aid may amount to little more than responsive accountability, and may be primarily restricted to fiscal accountability (see, for example, Brager and Holloway, 1978; Hartogs and Weber, 1978; Leat, Tester and Unell, 1986; Leat, 1988; Knapp, Robertson and Thomason, 1990; Kramer, 1981 and 1990). We have yet to see whether the effects of contracts on accountability of voluntary organisations will be the same in Britain as those reported in the US (Gutch, 1992; Bernstein, 1991). The possibly dramatic effects of contracting on accountability relationships within voluntary organisations (for example, in a federated structure) and between voluntary organisations and their dual 'customers' (users and funders) is one of many areas requiring further research (see below).

Internal organisational structure is another very important variable in considering constituencies and accountability. As Billis has highlighted, many voluntary organisations combine in one structure elements of a service bureaucracy, a voluntary membership association and a pattern of informal social relations (Billis, 1989; 1993). These three elements may imply different, and possibly incompatible, types of accountability. In practice, of course, voluntary organisations differ radically in their formal and informal internal structures. They differ in terms of whether or not they employ paid staff, at what level, with what responsibility; in use of volunteers; in committee structures and responsibilities; in user and member involvement, and so on.

Of particular interest and practical importance here may be federated organisations, in which accountability between the national and local organisations (and/or any regional layer) may be especially complicated and fraught. For example,

> the majority of our Trustees come from Age Concern local organisations. Many of these trustees are professional Chief Executive Officers whose organisations and roles were created by us. A conflict of interest can arise between national aims and local priorities. People are usually very loyal but complications can arise, for example, when we raise money across the country but give our grants for specific projects and work, according to certain criteria. . . . . if we were not to behave in this way, our redistributive role – getting programmes off the ground where

most needed – would not exist and all the money would go back to the few areas from where it is usually raised. We have to spend time demonstrating to new Trustees particularly precisely what it means to be Trustees of the national body, where their primary allegiance must lie (Greengross, 1993, p. 77).

Kramer further underlines the difficulties of accountabilities in federated agencies, referring to the 'persistence of power struggles in agencies where representatives of the local affiliates have a veto power over the actions of the governing board. The relationship between the bureaucratic national organisation and their local affiliates are "loosely coupled" and reflect their top-down origin and authority structure' (Kramer, 1990, p. 42).

I suggested above that accountabilities change over time. One reason for those changes may be related to changing sources and types of income; these may change accountabilities in themselves, but also spark off further change via their effects on organisational structures. For example, if a charity seeks to derive significant income from trading, it is usually well-advised to set up a separate trading company. The directors of the trading company may be staff and trustees of the charity. Again Sally Greengross describes the new complex internal accountabilities and tensions this may create:

for instance, I have become Director of a company with Age Concern colleagues, one of whom is managing director, to undertake direct everyday management of the company. As a board of directors we determine the policy of the company. Now, I think that I know what I am paid to do as a charity director, but some of the members of the board are accountable to me as director of the charity. And the shareholders are our trustees, or at least they are part of the team of shareholders if it is a joint initiative. So you can see the complications when directors are not equal as one of them is accountable to those shareholders who are trustees of the parent organisation (Greengross, 1993, pp. 80–1).

In considering accountability in relation to internal organisational structure, it is especially important to distinguish theory from practice. All organisations which employ paid staff necessarily create accountabilities between employers and employees. In charities, employers are typically the board of trustees who are responsible

for the policy and overall conduct of the organisation; paid staff are
employed to implement the policy of the board and are typically
accountable to the board. That is the theory. In practice, in some
but not all organisations, accountability of paid staff to the board
may mean little more than responsive accountability – although of
course the board always has available the option of accountability
with sanctions (ultimately to fire the employee). Kramer's conclusion from a study of twenty British voluntary organisations was
that generally there is a balance of power between board and executive with the executive tending to predominate (Kramer, 1990).
(On board/staff relations and who manages the organisation see for
example: Kramer, 1965; Senor, 1965; Harris, 1992).

Other important variables will affect the number and range of
groups to which an organisation regards itself, or is regarded, as
being accountable. These variables will also affect the nature and
scope of those accountabilities and include: the history and stage of
development of the organisation; its need for, and possible sources
of, legitimacy; environmental factors (including the degree of resource or policy 'turbulence' and the presence of competitors for
funds or for reputation as leader in the field); the mission, ethos
and culture of the organisation and the visibility and vocality of its
potential constituents including key beneficiaries/users.

It is worth stressing here that 'assigning' accountability is an
interactive process: some accountabilities are thrust upon us by others
and may be difficult openly to reject, other accountabilities are ones
which we choose or at least accept as necessary/legitimate. Thus
characteristics of those who are, or who claim a place, within the
organisation's broad domain, may make an important difference to
the demands for accountability made on, and accepted by,
organisations.

Managing accountability in practice

What accountability means in practice will vary between organisations and constituencies. But it is reasonable to suppose that organisations will share certain common problems in practising
accountability. These problems range from nitty-gritty 'how' problems to ones which have to do with resources, structures and cultures.

Accountability entails costs. Depending on the size of the constituency and the particular form and level of accountability required, being accountable is likely to consume time and other resources. Reports to funders take time and cost money; so do annual reports, news-sheets and thank-you letters to donors. Some may argue that such feedback is important as a requirement, as a courtesy, as good public relations or as a fundamental principle. But for some voluntary organisations, the financial and staff resources required to practise accountability, on any scale, may be prohibitive, and for all organisations the costs are likely to raise difficult ideological and public relations problems. Questions may be raised about who the organisation exists to serve – donors, funders or beneficiaries – and whose needs come first in spending priorities. Anxiety may also be expressed that the costs of accountability come under the heading of administration, upon which donors (and others) do not look kindly. Donors themselves may actually be put off giving to a charity which is seen to have money to spend on regular mailings of reports and accounts.

There are various conflicting factors at work here. In part, the difficulties may stem from the fact that voluntary organisations typically (but not always or in all of their work) look two ways to funders and users. In part the difficulties stem also from confused expectations of voluntary organisations and, perhaps in particular, charities. On the one hand they are expected to show that they are accountable and grateful; on the other to spend money only on direct services to beneficiaries and as little as possible on administration. The tensions may stem also from the import of principles and practices derived from marketing and public relations in the for-profit sector without, in the voluntary sector, the money or the ideology which makes the necessary expenditure acceptable.

In addition to costs, accountability may also provide benefits. Structures and systems for accountability may be seen as a way of spreading risk, responsibility and blame; as ways of 'managing' constituencies, criticism and conflict and as a way of 'listening to customers' (see, for example, Hinton, 1993; Wardrop White, 1993).

Although the typical structure of some voluntary organisations may have benefits in terms of spreading risk and responsibility, it may also create special problems in making accountability meaningful. Accountability of staff to unpaid, part-time volunteer board members is riddled with difficulties. There are difficulties inherent in the tension between employing (often highly paid) professional specialists and managers for their expert knowledge and the principle that part-time board members (often selected for reasons other than their expert knowledge) govern the organisation. Where, in practice, is the dividing line between governance and management? There are practical difficulties arising from the fact that board members usually have limited time to give to the organisation and board meetings may be infrequent; meanwhile work must go on, managers must make decisions and offer an account later.

In membership organisations, there are practical problems in bringing together often large numbers of geographically dispersed members, and in achieving their real involvement and understanding of the issues under consideration, given that they are likely to have different purposes and interests in belonging to the organisation, different skills and knowledge.

In federated organisations, there are difficulties in identifying who is accountable to whom, wearing what hat (see above) as well as practical problems in bringing together geographically dispersed and busy representatives. In both for-profit and voluntary non-profit organisations, a federated structure may pose particular problems in reconciling corporate standards and local autonomy. In the voluntary sector, these problems may be heightened in so far as local independence is seen not merely as good management, but as a fundamental and jealously guarded principle.

In those voluntary organisations which involve volunteers, there are theoretical and practical problems concerning the accountability of volunteers within the organisation (see Davis Smith, this volume). For example, in what sense and for what may volunteers be held to account? And at a practical level the sheer number and turnover of volunteers may create difficulties in designing systems of accountability. Furthermore, the presence of volunteers within an organisation may create tensions in relation to the accountability of paid staff. Two standards and systems of accountability may be required, but may cause confusion and resentment (Young, 1987).

The predominance of technical professionals in many voluntary organisations may create problems of accountability, not only in relation to the board, but also in relation to senior general managers, who may face special problems in requiring accountability from their technical professional staff (DiMaggio, 1988).

As a general rule, it seems reasonable to suppose that volunteer–staff and staff–staff, as well as board–staff, accountability problems will increase the larger the size of the organisation, the greater the number and diversity of professional staff, and the more diverse the

range and scope of activities. It is also worth making the point here
that organisations which produce services, rather than goods, in whatever sector, face special problems of supervision and quality control (see, for example: Normann, 1991). These difficulties, combined
with the very nature of the many services which must be provided
on-line in dispersed sites, are likely to give added significance to
arrangements for *post facto* accountability.

Cultural and ideological factors within voluntary organisations
may create other problems or underline those referred to above. So,
for example, many voluntary organisations are heavily dependent
upon externally provided resources, especially those from the state.
But at the same time it is part of the ideology of many voluntary
organisations that they are 'independent', especially from the state.
Many voluntary organisations subscribe to ideologies stressing equality
and participation; at one level this may encourage internal accountability; at another level it may create difficulties in identifying the
limits of accountability and the difference between accountability
and control and hierarchical management. At worst, the emphasis
on equality and participation may mean that everyone is accountable for everything and nothing (Landry *et al.*, 1985). It is also part
of the ideology of some organisations that the organisation is in
some sense accountable to users. Again there are theoretical and
legal difficulties in this notion. Furthermore, it is not clear how
users' views are heard and how any conflicts of interest are reconciled. In practice, is there any difference between accountability
to users and good management techniques which emphasise keeping close to the customer? (see, for example, Peters and Austin,
1985). In producing services users want, is accountability any more
or less effective than the sort of market research described by Bruce
at the RNIB and widely practised in for-profit organisations (Bruce,
1993)? This raises a wider question about the nature of accountability – is accountability an end in itself or is it a means to an
end? If it is a means to an end, what end[s]? And are there other
equally or more effective and efficient ways of attaining those ends?

Contracting and accountability

In his response to this paper at the CVO 15th Anniversary Conference, Stuart Etherington raised a number of important issues for
voluntary organisations in future. Many of these arise from contracting,

and include questions concerning an organisation's relative accountability to purchasers and donors. Does contracting require or encourage closer accountability to purchasers, and less accountability
to donors? Contracting also raises questions concerning the changing role of trustees *vis-à-vis* purchasers; changes in relationships
with users as specialist voluntary organisations act as 'poacher and
gamekeeper', setting standards and pitching to provide services. Other
issues raised by contracting include the development of customer
satisfaction indices and the ways in which these may challenge the
views of other stakeholders; as well as issues to do with greater
attention to employees as stakeholders. Etherington sees some hope
in the development of measures of benefits to beneficiaries as a
means of assessing the effectiveness of charities: 'if we cannot do
this, then it is likely that the sector as a whole could degenerate
into a series of conflictual relationships between stakeholders rather
than grow on the basis of agreement between stakeholders as to the
measures they will adopt in order to exercise effective accountability'.

Conclusion

Are voluntary organisations accountable? The answer in this paper
has been: it depends on what you mean by accountability, by and
to whom, for what. Should voluntary organisations be accountable
and why does it matter? Here the relevant question may be: 'compared with other organisations spending public money, are voluntary organisations more or less accountable?'

Compared with organisations in the public sector, voluntary organisations spending public money appear in some respects to be
less accountable. In the public sector, there are various ombudsmen
to take up consumer complaints, and in recent years the courts have
made judgments which suggest, in certain areas and circumstances,
that consumers have a contract with the supplier and the rights which
go with that. In the case of charities, there is no ombudsman, but
there is the Charity Commission which responds to complaints on
behalf of the public. Under what circumstances donors or users might
be deemed to have a contract with a charity is (to me at least)
unclear. Given that there are also ombudsmen in certain for-profit
industries, and that the consumer typically has recourse to contract
law, it could also be argued that in many respects voluntary organ-

isations are rather less accountable than for-profit organisations.

Increasingly, however, the standards of public accountability applied to statutory bodies may be the exception rather than the rule in spending public money. The dramatic growth in quangos in health, education and policing has led some to warn that Britain is facing a 'crisis of accountability' and a growing 'democratic deficit' (The *Guardian*, 'The quango explosion' 19 November 1993). In so far as voluntary organisations have certain characteristics in common with quangos, they too may be seen as contributing to this crisis of accountability. It is worth noting here that Sir Patrick Nairne, ex-Permanent Secretary at the Department of Health and Social Security (DHSS), discussing the growth in the use of charities as a conduit for public money, remarked: 'the advantage for government is that people can't ask questions in the House' (quoted in Lattimer, 1990).

One very simple practical test of accountability to users is the procedure for dealing with complaints. Research is needed on voluntary organisations' complaints procedures and how these compare with those in the for-profit and public sectors. Increasingly, both public and for-profit organisations are 'rediscovering' users and placing them centre stage; complaints procedures are now required in social services departments. How many voluntary organisations even have a clearly specified complaints procedure?

This paper started with one question and has raised many more. Despite the rhetoric of user-empowerment and the role of voluntary organisations in democracy, we are a long way from understanding the principles, the aspirations and the practice of voluntary organisations in making themselves accountable.

References

Bernstein, S. (1991) *Managing Contracted Services in the Nonprofit Agency*, Temple University Press, Philadelphia.

Billis, D. (1989) *A Theory of the Voluntary Sector: Implications for Policy and Practice*, Working Paper no. 5, Centre for Voluntary Organisation, London School of Economics, London.

Billis, D. (1993) *Organising Public and Voluntary Agencies*, Routledge, London.

Brager, G. and S. Holloway (1978) *Changing Human Service Organizations: Politics and Practice*, Free Press, New York.

Bruce, I. (1993) 'Social Marketing' in I. Bruce (ed.) *Charity Talks on Successful Development*, VOLPROF, City University Business School, London.

Bruce, I. and D. Leat (1993) *Management for Tomorrow*, VOLPROF, City University Business School, London.

Chesterman, M. (1979) *Charities, Trusts and Social Welfare*, Weidenfeld & Nicolson, London.

DiMaggio, P. (1988) 'Nonprofit Managers in Different Fields of Service: Management Tasks and Management Training', in M. O'Neill and D.R. Young (eds) *Educating Managers of Nonprofit Organizations*, Praeger, New York.

Douglas, J. (1983) *Why Charity?*, Sage, Beverly Hills, CA.

Drucker, P. (1985) *Innovation and Entrepreneurship*, William Heinemann, London.

Drucker, P. (1990) *Managing the Nonprofit Organization*, Butterworth Heinemann, London.

Greengross, S. (1993) 'Accountability', in I. Bruce (ed.) *Charity Talks on Successful Development*, VOLPROF, City University Business School, London.

Guardian newspaper (1993) 'The quango explosion', 19 November, London.

Gutch, R. (1992) *Contracting: Lessons from the US*, NCVO/Bedford Square Press, London.

Harris, M. (1992) 'The role of voluntary management committees', in J. Batsleer, C. Cornforth and R. Paton (eds) *Issues in Voluntary and Non-profit Management*, Open University/Addison Wesley, London.

Hartogs, N. and J. Weber (1978) *The Impact of Government Funding on the Management of Voluntary Agencies*, Greater New York Fund and United Way, New York.

Hinton, N. (1993) 'Planning for growth', in I. Bruce (ed.) *Charity Talks on Successful Development*, VOLPROF, City University Business School, London.

Home Office (1990) *Efficiency Scrutiny of Government Funding of Voluntary Organisations*, HMSO, London.

Knapp, M., E. Robertson and C. Thomason (1990) 'Public funding, voluntary action: whose welfare'? in H. Anheier and W. Seibel (eds) *The Third Sector: Comparative Studies of Nonprofit Organizations,* de Gruyter, Berlin and New York.

Kramer, R. (1965) 'Ideology, status and power in board executive relationships', *Social Work*, 10: 107–14.

Kramer, R. (1981) *Voluntary Agencies in the Welfare State*, University of California Press, Berkeley.

Kramer, R. (1982) 'From voluntarism to vendorism: an organisational perspective on contracting', PONPO Working Paper no. 54, Yale University, Prentice Hall.

Kramer, R. (1987) 'Voluntary agencies and the personal social services', in W.W. Powell (ed.) *The Nonprofit Sector: A Research Handbook*, Yale University Press, New Haven and London.

Kramer, R. (1990) 'Change and continuity in British voluntary organisations, 1976 to 1988', *Voluntas*, 1(2): 33–60.

Landry, C., D. Morley, R. Southwood and P. Wright (1985) *What a Way to Run a Railroad: An Analysis of Radical Failure*, Comedia, London.

Lattimer, M. (1990) 'Whitehall wisdom', *Trust Monitor*, February.

Leat, D. (1988) *Voluntary Organisations and Accountability*, NCVO, London.

Leat, D. (1990) 'Voluntary organizations and accountability: theory and practice', in H.K. Anheier and W. Seibel (eds), *The Third Sector: Comparative Studies of Nonprofit Organizations*, De Gruyter, Berlin and New York.

Leat, D., S. Tester and J. Unell (1986) *A Price Worth Paying? A Study of the Effects of Government Grant-Aid to Voluntary Organisations*, Policy Studies Institute, London.

Normann, R. (1991) *Service Management, Strategy and Leadership Service Business*, 2nd edn, John Wiley, London.

Perrow, C. (1970) *Complex Organizations: A Critical Essay*, Scott, Foresman, Glencoe, IL.

Peters, T. and N. Austin (1985) *A Passion for Excellence*, William Collins, London.

Rein, M. (1975) 'Social planning: the search for legitimacy', in R. Kramer and H. Specht (eds) *Readings in Community Organisation Practice*, Prentice Hall.

Salamon, L. and H. Anheier (1992) 'In search of the non-profit sector. I: The question of definitions', *Voluntas*, 3(2): 125–52.

Senor, J.M. (1965) 'Another look at the executive board relationship', in M.N. Zald (ed.) *Social Welfare Institutions, A Sociological Reader*, Free Press, Glencoe IL.

Vinten, G. (1992) 'Reviewing the current managerial ethos', in L. Willcocks and J. Harrow (eds) *Rediscovering Public Services Management*, McGraw-Hill, London.

Warburton, J. (1992) *Charities Act 1992 Current Law Statutes Annotated (chapter 41)* Sweet & Maxwell, London.

Wardrop White, D. (1993) 'Response to N. Hinton', in I. Bruce (ed.) *Charity Talks on Successful Development*, VOLPROF, City University Business School, London.

Young, D. and S. Finch (1977) *Foster Care and Nonprofit Agencies*, Lexington Books.

Young, D. (1987) 'Executive leadership in non-profit agencies', in W.W. Powell (ed.) *The Nonprofit Sector: A Research Handbook*, Yale University Press, New Haven and London.

6

How do Voluntary Agencies Manage Organisational Change?

David C. Wilson

Introduction

This paper argues that a common response in voluntary organisations to managing organisational change has been the adoption of managerial practices and recipes from the commercial business sector. The disadvantages of this approach are discussed, and a potential alternative way forward suggested, focusing on the use of collaboration and alliances. A framework is introduced to indicate the utility of adopting specific strategies in particular operating contexts, the most important elements of which are public image and popularity and the level of competition. The paper concentrates on how factors external to the organisation impact upon internal practices, and concludes by speculating that organisational learning needs to take place in order to manage strategic change successfully and to facilitate organisational growth and survival.

Change is a constant feature of organisations in the voluntary sector. The speed and direction of these changes have also been increasing significantly over the last decade. For example, the picture portrayed in the Wolfenden Committee's Report (1978) of voluntary organisations as partners, gap-fillers and providers working alongside Government agencies is virtually unrecognisable today in the enterprising, professionalised and contracting 1990s (Shirley, 1993).

The details of contextual changes in the voluntary sector will be discussed later, but their overall impact has been consistently to focus attention on strategic decision-making in voluntary organisations not only to ensure survival but also to facilitate future planning and sustain the momentum of change. This paper concentrates largely on relations with the external environment. This is not to deny the importance of the internal organisational context, which is dealt with in some detail by David Billis elsewhere in this book. Empirical research indicates that in order to capture a full picture of organisational change, both internal and external contexts should be examined together (Leavy and Wilson, 1994) and the reader interested in change could benefit from reading both this and the chapter by David Billis. This chapter concentrates on organisational strategies developed in anticipation of, or more usually in response to, changes in the organisation's external environment. Both researchers and practitioners in the voluntary sector have become increasingly concerned about organisational strategy and its application to charitable organisations. Strategy here is defined as a concerted effort to produce fundamental decisions and actions to shape the nature and direction of organisational activities within legal bounds. It is the long-term goals of the organisation and the shorter-term decisions required to achieve these goals.

Organisational strategy and the voluntary sector have not always been so closely related. Ware (1989) documents the strategic changes in charitable organisations over the last twenty years, concluding that there has been a substantial shift from their being perceived as appendages to the welfare state to their playing an important and unique role in the British economy (and beyond) in the 1990s. Medley (1988), for example, recalls that strategic planning was introduced to the World Wildlife Fund (UK) in 1978 to help achieve planned organisational actions, cohesive team work and set clear objectives. He also recalls that the implementation of strategic planning in the 1970s was fairly novel in the voluntary sector, requiring individuals in the organisation to 'take a wholly professional and sound business approach to their work' (Medley, 1988, p. 46). It is telling that as Medley (1992) writes of the strategic reformulation of the Worldwide Fund for Nature (UK), as it is now called, in the 1990s, virtually every major voluntary organisation will have embarked upon some form of strategic plan (see Edwards, 1992, for examples).

Building upon earlier research (for example Butler and Wilson, 1990, and Wilson, 1992), this paper outlines the changing face of strategy in the voluntary sector and identifies some of the key challenges for organisational change and continuity into the next decade. To do this effectively, it is first necessary to give a brief analysis of strategies adopted by voluntary organisations (either intentionally or by default) in order to show the context in which future voluntary activities will have to take place.

Strategic change in voluntary agencies

Strategic change can be planned, or can emerge from a series of steps taken, almost becoming a strategy by default. Emergent strategies only become strategies once they are recognised after the event as patterns in a number of actions taken. Bryson (1988) notes that few voluntary organisations have engaged extensively in formal strategic planning. Strategies, therefore, tend to be emergent. Empirical evidence bears this out. A primary reason appears to be organisational survival; since funds are limited and services are required immediately, the 'strategy' of many voluntary organisations is to focus on the needs of immediate circumstances rather than on longer-term projects. The short-term versus long-term dilemma is obviously an enduring characteristic, especially for smaller agencies which do not have the luxury of some financial slack. However, the planned versus emergent continuum is too broad to reveal the subtle but marked changes of strategies undertaken by voluntary agencies as they have responded to changing economic and political contexts.

The Wolfenden Committee (1978) characterised flexibility as the primary advantage of voluntary organisations. Any disadvantages (that is a reduction in flexibility) were largely due to financial dependence, particularly on government agencies. The effects of this dependence over eroding autonomy and constraining innovation in voluntary agencies have been detailed by many researchers (for example Leat, Smolka and Unell, 1981; Saxon-Harrold, 1985). These studies showed that strategies emphasised maintaining autonomy as a primary objective. The socio-political context was characterised by Gladstone (1982) as 'gradualist welfare pluralism'. For Gladstone, pluralism describes the state and the voluntary sectors as partners. Whilst the state often funded specific voluntary organisations for the provision of specific services which it was itself unable or unwilling to provide, the idea that state and voluntary organisations should work hand in hand was dominant under the banner of welfare pluralism. The strategy of voluntary organisations in this context appears clear, with the benefit of hindsight.

First, achieving *independence* from state funding became important. Where total independence could not be achieved, then state monies which had explicit 'strings attached' concerning how they should be spent, were to be avoided if possible. Voluntary organisations should try to achieve autonomy over the scale and nature of state funding they received. In this way, they could retain *autonomy* from a set of political stakeholders (state agencies) which would ensure that, in theory at least, they remained as independent as possible.

By the early 1980s, many researchers had begun to doubt the ability of the pluralist frame of reference to explain fully the strategic developments of both voluntary (and commercial) organisations (see, for example, Streeck and Schmitter, 1984; Shearman and Burrell, 1987). The seeds were sown for a wider perspective, which concentrated on sectoral groupings of organisations. Strategies could then be mediated by associations such as the National Council for Voluntary Organisations (NCVO). The emphasis became one of representation, getting one's organisational voice heard and trying to achieve lobbying strength in numbers.

The Conservative Government began the steps to eradicate what it termed the 'dependence culture'. For the managers of voluntary organisations this meant that another major set of strategic changes were about to be forced upon them. A shorthand term for the context of these changes is known as the 'enterprise culture' (see Wilson, 1992). The major change facing managers of voluntary agencies was to survive through increased levels of competition, both within the voluntary sector and between voluntary agencies and commercial and public organisations. This kind of strategic 'survival of the fittest' was evident across all sectors. The public sector was busy being privatised and deregulated and the commercial, for-profit, sector was subjected to extreme competitive conditions. Internal markets were seen as the best way of reducing costs and the processes of contracting became commonplace. The voluntary sector, however, highlights some of the massive shifts in emphasis that took place in the late 1980s (see Taylor and Lansley, 1992). They include:

1. Creating a culture of enterprise (NCVO, 1990) in which voluntary organisations competed along commercial lines (for example, achieving leading brands and securing competitive

advantage). Voluntary organisations were encouraged to become like commercial organisations and to see successful for-profit operations as role models for change.

2. The professionalisation of management often characterised by hiring senior management from outside the voluntary sector to bring in commercial practice.

3. Reorganisations of organisation culture and structure to achieve increased decentralisation, facilitate project management and secure distinctive competence as a service provider.

The transitions experienced by Housing Associations are good examples of the above succession of strategic changes. As Ashby[1] notes, they have moved through stages of being gap fillers, through welfare pluralism, the mixed economy of welfare (Webb and Wistow, 1982) to provider dominance. They have largely escaped the full rigours of contracting, but must now competitively bid against each other for grant funding and must raise the balance of their total expenditure (around £2.2 billion in 1992–3) from private funders. They therefore have to cope with an internal market regulated by the Housing Corporation as well as the private sector. Housing Associations have also been under pressure to become more 'professional' through becoming more 'businesslike'. They have embraced a range of private sector techniques as part of this process. In some cases, these techniques have been imposed. For example, Scottish Homes requires all Scottish Associations seeking regular development programmes to submit annual business plans. The Housing Corporation has required financial ration analyses and, in the wake of a recent fraud, has required associations to establish internal audit arrangements.

The context of economic recession has also had a major impact on the strategies of most voluntary organisations. This is having the effect of forcing the pace of strategic focusing outlined above (but not its general direction). For example, in Britain some voluntary agencies are being forced to consider redundancies. They are having to 'downsize'. Large organisations such as Oxfam are also directly affected by economic recession. Trading throughout Oxfam's 850 shops has been hit by the slow-moving housing market, since the majority of second-hand goods donated to shops are given when people move house.

Between 1980 and 1990 the level of volunteering did not significantly increase (Charities Aid Foundation, 1992), but the demand for services from voluntary organisations increased significantly. More has to be achieved with less in the way of human resources. Recession has hit aid budgets at all levels (government and individual) and the overall aid income to charities has been reduced. Alison Davies, Divisional Director of Scotland Save the Children, noted that the knock-on effect of increasing pressure to cut aid budgets in richer countries would result in competition amongst developing countries, forcing more countries into crisis and meaning less money for everyone (Davies, 1993). Voluntary organisations in the international aid sector, however, are competing increasingly strongly for scarce resources. The level of competitive strategy has merely been heightened.

Some of the results of competition in the voluntary sector can already be seen. Wilson (1989) predicted that fragmentation could easily occur, with smaller charities unable to survive in harsh funding climates and large charities becoming increasingly dependent upon their funders. Smaller charities would be forced out of business by larger charities, especially those with larger and more flexible budgets. Empirical evidence suggests that some of this prediction is coming to fruition. Figures from the Charities Aid Foundation (CAF, 1992) reveal that although overall income to the sector is reduced, the voluntary income of the top 400 charities has increased, with many showing substantial growth. The larger charities are growing. They have higher levels of managerial professionalism, are less dependent on government grants and spend more on advertising, direct mail and legacies than smaller and medium-sized charities. Many of the latter are having difficulty in surviving. Even in sectors which are growing overall (international aid, for example) smaller charities with the least flexible budgets are declining. These include organisations which are dependent on Overseas Development Administration funding and are without block grants (ODA, 1992). Looking further ahead, competition will increase if (as predicted) there is a reduction in the government's overseas aid budget (this was maintained in 1992) and if the ODA's budget remains static with an increasing number of voluntary organisations seeking funding. Organisational failures will increase and those that survive will face increasing dependencies on their funders.

Other contextual changes have also reinforced the adoption of competitive strategies in the voluntary sector. A detailed exposition of these socio-political changes is beyond the scope of this short paper, but key factors would include demographic shifts; macro-political restructuring; moves toward information and service-based economies; changing values and volatile world economies. To cope with these changes, voluntary organisations will need not only to develop detailed strategic plans, they will also need to ensure that they have the necessary infrastructure to implement them. It is also becoming increasingly evident that the adoption of competitive strategies will benefit only the few. Many more organisations will simply fail in their bids to compete, contract or manage change.

Dark clouds also lurk in the areas of fiscal and legal regulation. The cherished status of being a registered charity (with all its attendant benefits) has recently been called into question as archaic and inappropriate in stand-alone Britain. The report 'Voluntary Action' (Knight, 1993), a sizeable sample drawn from over 1,200 national voluntary organisations, is critical of charitable status and argues for the eventual abolition of the Charity Commission. It concludes that many of the larger voluntary organisations are already like their commercial counterparts, with senior staff more interested in pay, status and perks than in the clients the organisation is meant to serve. More Darwinistic is the suggestion that many organisations are:

> cumbersome, moribund, outdated and so riddled with error that nothing could touch them. . . . no one seems to have devised a method of removing voluntary organisations that have outlived their useful life (quoted in the *Guardian*, 6 October 1993)

Those organisations that survive can be divided into two categories, the report concludes: one category being large organisations providing services on contract with the loss of tax concessions (by removal of charitable status) recoupable subject to meeting government performance targets (such as user satisfaction surveys). The other category will be non-service providers – smaller organisations with a mission to be ideological, achieve change and reform.

Whether or not the report is able to influence governmental policy, it is noticeable that a great deal of time and effort was spent by all types of organisations in the late 1980s trying to become the 'best' provider of specific goods and services in the context described earlier. The academic literature of organisation theory and related disciplines became saturated with the concept of 'excellence' and 'best practice' (Peters and Waterman, 1982; Peters and Austin, 1985; Kanter, 1983, 1989). Voluntary organisations also were recipients of this elixir of performance but, like many for-profit organisations, were to find that adopting such normative concepts was not so easy in practice. The concept of excellence was firmly rooted in the pursuit of competitive strategies which were clustered around the core product or service. This placed enormous constraints on organisations. First, it required them to rank strategies in order of importance. Peripheral concerns were to be underplayed and central concerns were to be pursued vigorously. Butler and Wilson (1990) showed how such demands had led to conflict and disagreement in a number of charities in the late 1980s. Second, good practice was defined as the best commercial practice, leaving little scope for managing the vast range of contextual contingencies faced by most voluntary organisations. Third, achieving excellence required close monitoring and centralised control. As Young (1990) pointed out, this was in many respects perceived to be counter-cultural for many organisations in the voluntary sector.

The impact of strategic changes in the voluntary sector

The relatively small amount of empirical evidence available suggests that excessive competition and commercialisation are likely to stifle rather than facilitate flexibility and innovation. On the positive side, the changes demanded by the political context and economic recession have prompted some concerted action within the voluntary sector. NCVO has been active in this regard, and practitioner journals such as *Professional Fundraising* have emerged. Some thoughtful work looking at good practice within and outside the sector has emerged. Areas such as the management of volunteers (Hedley, 1992); good practice in evaluation (Ball, 1988); effective and efficient fundraising (Burnett, 1992) and principles of good general management (Holloway and Otto, 1989; Adirondack, 1989) have all been disseminated widely. These authors are also careful to tailor their recommendations to the specific context of voluntary organisations and eschew blanket recipes from the for-profit sector. This kind of work may provide a way forward. At present it is still highly normative and empirically weak. Stronger, more reflective, empirical research is beginning to emerge from universities such as the Centre for Voluntary Organisation at the London School of Economics, from the Open University and from Aston University.

On the more negative side, evidence is emerging which suggests that the way forward for most voluntary organisations is not the direct application or the tailoring of management ideas developed in for-profit organisations. Paton and Cornforth (1992), for example, highlight the resource-dependence perspective whereby voluntary organisations will be subject to the influences of different stakeholders. These can, for example, be clients, government agencies, funding bodies and other organisations. Each stakeholder will present a variety of contingencies which must be managed, but which are unlikely to be homogeneous across a range of organisations. Therefore the heterogeneity of stakeholders and their demands in the voluntary sector precludes the adoption of blanket managerial recipes just taken from commercial practice. Taking stock of the influences of just one stakeholder (government funders), Knapp, Robertson and Thomason (1987) reveal that the effects on voluntary organisations include financial dependency and the erosion of autonomy; over-regulation; a propensity to adopt bureaucratic structures and to modify organisational goals in line with those of the funders. These contingencies alone would preclude adopting an entrepreneurial, competitive strategy.

Dartington (1992) is more pessimistic. He argues that the prevalence of management ideas from the for-profit sector (fuelled by the enterprise culture) is both inappropriate and paradoxical: inappropriate, because such managerial prescriptions do not fit with the reality of voluntary operations; paradoxical, because many voluntary organisations are explicitly designed around their role to work with and for the un-enterprising. Bielefeld (1992) notes that neither the resource-dependence perspective (organisations are driven by contingencies) nor the institutional perspective (organisations are moulded by the demands of the socio-political environment) adequately explain the strategies of the sample of non-profit organisations he studied (approximately 200 non-religious organisations). He noted that voluntary organisations 'were not uniformly adopting the strategies either that resource dependence or institutional theory specified' (Bielefeld, 1992, p. 67). Therefore, strategy was more likely to be prompted by a combination of factors rather than a single cause and variation between organisations was likely to be greater than the homogeneity that the two theoretical perspectives suggested.

Wilson (1992) suggested that one way out of the seemingly deterministic logic of resource dependencies, or enterprise-driven competition, was for voluntary organisations to adopt co-operative strategies. A number of for-profit organisations have adopted co-operative strategies (termed variously, joint ventures or strategic alliances), despite the myth that they are all competing at cut-throat intensity. Both Japanese and North American for-profit organisations (perhaps the most stereotypically entrepreneurial) have been working co-operatively with suppliers, customers and peer organisations for many years. In some cases the voluntary sector and the for-profit sectors may actually change places, with the former becoming more competitive and the latter more collaborative.

The need for co-operative strategies was given emphasis by Wilson (1992) and Billis *et al.* (1994). Motivation to co-operate is achieved through needing to accomplish some or all of the following:

- growth and development of a greater scale of operations,
- adoption and utilisation of information technology;
- organisational integration;
- support for changes in the operating environment;
- establishment of cartel advantages in specific areas of competition;
- formalised links with complementary service providers;
- the securing of economies of procurement.

The logic of the co-operative argument is that it can increase the scale of strategic planning by the more efficient use of resources. At the same time, flexibility is not impaired since co-operation is not for life. Organisations can choose the duration and the degree of any alliances or joint ventures. Co-operation also allows organisations to share in the benefits of technological developments, since innovations in information technology can easily outstrip the ability of any single organisation to use them. Finally, co-operation facilitates integration between technology, planning, innovation and information, as well as organisational learning.

Co-operation and organisational learning

Collaboration between voluntary agencies has its supporters and detractors. Dartington (1986) pointed out that collaboration in the care of the elderly and mentally infirm was unworkable. Ashby[1] argues that Housing Associations are characterised by, and have benefited from, the adoption of collaborative strategies. The trade association (the National Federation of Housing Associations) is widely supported to lobby on behalf of all associations. Special groupings fight particular corners including special needs housing, the interests of small associations, black associations and so on. Collaboration is strong between small and large associations. Four separate intermediary organisations have been established to raise funds in bulk for distribution to their members. In the highly competitive development field, large and small associations have collaborated by forming consortia to develop large sites, and have formed partnerships to bid for funding. Collaborative arrangements occur between associations and specialist caring organisations. Within the mental health field, this has resulted in consortium companies mainly set up by housing associations which have agreements with health authorities and social services departments.

Huxham (1991) argued that collaborative relationships, whilst difficult to sustain, brought considerable strategic benefits and reduced overall costs. She argued that the adoption of flexible multi-organisational teams was a key factor in sustaining collaboration. Mordaunt (1992) highlighted the advantages of collaborative strategies since they create informal networks and alliances. Information and its dissemination between organisations thus becomes a key factor in collaborating successfully. If Deacon and Golding's (1991) research is typical, then voluntary organisations have been following individual strategies for too long. A continued lack of collaboration meant that they were effectively isolating one another from information vital to strategic planning. They note:

> It is particularly interesting to note the high priority assigned to information about other voluntary and community groups. The insularity of many voluntary and community groups and ineffective networking within the voluntary sector are often mentioned, as is the duplication of activity rather than co-operation that results (Deacon and Golding, 1991, pp. 76–7).

The highest priority for information was for knowledge of funding sources, followed by details about other voluntary and community groups.

Although co-operative strategies seem a logical alternative to competition, it is likely that variation will occur in the extent to which collaboration is both necessary and desirable. International comparisons are beyond the scope of this paper, but it is likely, for example, that any increase in the availability of European Commission monies to various sectors (international aid, for example) will allow many organisations successfully to pursue competitive strategies in isolation from their sister organisations. At least in the short term, the pressure for collaboration will not be felt.

Organisations (or rather their managers) need to learn to be self-reflexive and consciously adopt strategies which not only make the best use of human resources, but which are also tailored to the specific needs of the organisation's operating context. The key question, of course, is what are the critical factors in the context? Harris (1987) provided a first clue in her review of governance models of voluntary organisations (and see Harris, this volume, for further discussion of this subject). Within the sector there is wide variation between the 'traditional' model, the 'membership' model and the 'entrepreneur' model. Each sets the *internal context* of the organisation to a model of governance which in turn sets 'the rules of the game' for all operations. This internal context will mostly have a strong history behind it. It will have been developed and sustained over quite substantial time periods. Managing change in this internal context means unravelling a great deal of organisational history. It is unlikely, for example, that entrepreneurial models of governance will readily embrace the logic of strategic collaboration. There is a degree of mutual exclusivity between the two approaches amounting to a conflict of organisational philosophy. Certainly, more empirical research is needed here to help individuals in organisations to unlearn some of the taken-for-granted behaviours and relearn in a future context. One of the rather depressing findings (from the public and for profit sectors) is that organisations resist such changes until they are forced to confront their own *idée fixe* by the onset of a crisis (Pettigrew, 1985). In the voluntary sector, the onset of crisis (financial or managerial for example) may leave little room for organisational change or learning and may signal the ultimate demise of the organisation.

Adapting to the *external context* (the organisation's operating environment) represents another stream of tailoring strategies to context. Bielefeld (1992) argued that competitive and co-operative strategies were too crude a distinction to make them an either/or choice for managers. It appeared that organisations could be successful without being forced too far one way or the other. Empirical studies from Canadian non-profit sports organisations also support this view. Slack and Hinings (1992), Thibault, Slack and Hinings (1993) and Thibault (1993) argue that successful non-profit sports organisations balance their strategies according to key factors in the operating environment. Some of these (such as cost of equipment and the number of trainers available) are obviously sector-specific, but their findings mirror earlier works on strategy such as Butler and Wilson (1990), Kramer (1990), Drucker (1990) and Nutt (1984). Taking evidence from these sources reveals two key elements which are important in the external context:

1. The level of organisational appeal to funders (for example image or type of service provision);
2. The level of competition from other voluntary and statutory organisations.

The appeal or image of an organisation will have an immediate impact on the extent to which it will attract funds. Some concerns (such as the environment or green issues) tend to be fashionable, attracting funds at the peak of their popularity. Other services (such as international aid and sea rescue) are more enduring and perhaps are considered the 'traditional' area of service provision. Others (such as mental welfare or AIDS agencies) tend to be less well off in terms of public appeal (and hence donations). The level of appeal to funders (image and/or type of service) is one dimension. A second dimension is competition (how many other organisations provide a similar service?).

Putting level of appeal and level of competition together allows the creation of a contingency framework in which potentially successful strategies may be identified. For example, organisations which have a less immediately high profile public image would be advised either to become a *specialist provider* (when competition is high) or to try *innovating* (when competition is low). In the latter case, the strategy would be to increase public image and awareness to accrue more funds. The low level of competition gives space for such a strategy. Organisational size is likely to be a mediating factor in the pursuit of this strategy since some small organisations may not have the time or the resources to experiment and innovate.

Organisations which have a relatively high public image and attractiveness appear to have two options. When competition is fierce, they can seek *distinctive competence* by becoming perceived as the best, most efficient, provider of services, but at the same time sticking to a central core of services. Oxfam would be a case in point – it is likely that in the future they will have to expand beyond shops to aid income. Core services will, however, remain the same. In a context of less competition, organisations can choose to increase the distance between them and competitors by *adding new services*. In summary:

- Organisations with less appeal to funders should establish a specialist niche when competition is high and innovate when it is low;
- Organisations with more appeal to their funders can seek distinctive competence when competition is high, or add new services when competition is low.

Collaborative strategies could apply to cases where level of appeal is relatively high. Organisations could become more efficient by collaborating with others for information or new technology, for example. Equally, they could add new services by engaging in temporary alliances with other providers. Co-operation is likely to be less attractive when appeal is low. In this context, voluntary agencies need either to become more specialised, and thus offer a distinctive service, or to innovate (perhaps to stay in continued operation). Nevertheless, to achieve this, managers will need information about their sister organisations and about new developments in general (Deacon and Golding, 1991). They will need to collaborate with others in order to achieve this level of intelligence.

Collaboration is, therefore, a plausible strategy to pursue under various combinations of factors in the external context (levels of appeal and competition). It is equally unlikely that many voluntary agencies will find themselves in absolute situations where, for example, their level of appeal is low and competition is high. It is more likely that voluntary agencies will be operating in many combinations of external factors. For example, Ashby[1] notes that housing associations, along with many other voluntary agencies, operate in a complex environment and may find themselves facing different contingencies at the same time. The utility of the above strategy-context model is that it allows managers to assess the relative strength of key contingencies, and thus adopt a particular configuration of strategies (innovation with efficiency, for example).

Advocates of collaborative strategies should not, however, overlook the influence of different interest groups (or stakeholders) in strategy formulation. Contingency models can seem over-rational without also carrying out an analysis of stakeholder influence. For example, there can be multiple funders with different influences and expectations as well as stakeholders who are not funders. Thus, the level of competition will vary in relation to different stakeholders, as will the level of acceptance in relation to different funders. The objectives of the main stakeholders are often quite different and, sometimes, the objectives of the same stakeholder will be contradictory. Ashby[1] gives, as an example of this, the Housing Corporation pressing for more expert and commercially minded committees while simultaneously exhorting them to be more accountable to tenants and local communities. There can also be stakeholders *internal* to the organisation. Billis (this volume) refers to this as the 'explanatory system' whereby different values underlie the strategy-making process. What is certain, however, is that organisations need to manage change internally and externally if they are to thrive and survive.

Voluntary agencies may also present a political face whereby an external observer might be misled into thinking that the organisation was pursuing a wholly competitive strategy. They may actually be presenting themselves to funders in the way they judge that funders want to see them. Thus, appearing to embrace practices from the commercial sector might in fact be largely part of playing (or being seen to play) the funding game.

Recognition of the changing external context will, however, facilitate choosing a mix of strategies which are more appropriate than others. In this way, organisations can become adaptive systems which create and sustain learning. They can thrive and survive despite operating in a range of different contexts. They discard the notion of a one best way of organising. Strategic choices informed by contextual factors should also ensure that voluntary agencies thrive by adopting a particular mix of innovative, niche, efficiency or competitive strategies. They will also help preserve central values of most voluntary agencies, such as equal opportunities, good gender and ethnic balance, representation channels and a high degree of accountability (although as Billis notes, this in itself is never easy, given the range of different internal stakeholders). However, a strategy of competition alone will fail to achieve this complex and delicate balance both externally and internally.

Note

1. I am grateful to Julian Ashby of the Housing Association Consultancy & Advisory Service (HACAS) and the Centre for Voluntary Organisation for his comments on an earlier version of this paper. The examples given from Housing Associations were provided by him in a written commentary delivered at the 15th Anniversary Conference of the Centre for Voluntary Organisation, London School of Economics, London, 23 and 24 March 1994.

References

Adirondack, S. (1989) *Just About Managing*, London Voluntary Service Council, London.

Ball, C. (1988) *Evaluation in the Voluntary Sector*, The Forbes Trust, London.

Bielefeld, W. (1992) 'Non-profit-funding environment relations: theory and application', *Voluntas*, 3 (1): 48–70.

Billis, D., J. Ashby, A. Ewart and C. Rochester (1994) *Taking Stock: Exploring the Shifting Foundations of Governance and Strategy in Housing Associations*, Working Paper no. 16, Centre for Voluntary Organisation, London School of Economics, London.

Bryson, J.M. (1988) *Strategic Planning for Public and Non-Profit Organizations: A Guide to Strengthening and Sustaining Organizational Achievement*, Jossey-Bass, California.

Burnett, K. (1992) *Relationship Fundraising*, White Lion Press, London.

R.J. Butler and D.C. Wilson (1990) *Managing Voluntary and Non-Profit Organizations: Strategy and Structure*, Routledge, London.

Charities Aid Foundation (CAF) (1992) *Charity Trends*, 15th edn, Charities Aid Foundation, Tonbridge.

Dartington, T. (1986) *The Limits of Altruism: Elderly Mentally Infirm People as a Test Case for Collaboration*, King Edwards Hospital Fund for London, London.

Dartington, T. (1992) 'Professional management in voluntary organisation: some cautionary notes', in J. Batsleer, C. Cornforth and R. Paton (eds) *Issues in Voluntary and Non-Profit Management*, Addison-Wesley, London.

Davies, A. (1993) *The Changing Face of Charity*, Keynote Address to the SCVO Jubilee Forum, Edinburgh.

Deacon, D. and P. Golding (1991) 'The voluntary sector in the information society', *Voluntas*, 2 (2): 69–88.

Drucker, P. (1990) *Managing the Non Profit Organization: Practices and Principles*, Harper Collins, New York.

Edwards, K. (1992) *Contracts in Practice: A Practical Guide for Voluntary Organizations*, Directory of Social Change, London.

Gladstone, F. (1982) *Charity Law and Social Justice*, Bedford Square Press, London.

Guardian (1993), 6 October, London.

Harris, M. (1987) *Management Committees: Roles and Tasks*, Working Paper no. 4, Centre for Voluntary Organisation, London School of Economics, London.

Hedley, R. (1992) 'Organising and managing volunteers', in R. Hedley and J. Davis Smith (eds) *Volunteering and Society: Principles and Practice*, Bedford Square Press, London.

Holloway, C. and S. Otto (1989) *Getting Organised: A Handbook for Non-Statutory Organisations*, Bedford Square Press, London.

Huxham, C. (1991) 'Facilitating collaboration: issues in multiorganizational groups', *Journal of the Operational Research Society*, 42 (12) 1037–46.

Kanter, R.M. (1983) *The Change Masters: Corporate Entrepreneurs at Work*, Allen & Unwin, London.

Kanter, R.M. (1989) *When Giants Learn To Dance: Mastering the Challenges of Strategic Management and Careers in the 1990s*, Simon & Schuster, New York.

Knapp, M., E. Robertson and C. Thomason (1987) *Public Money, Voluntary Action, Whose Welfare?* PSSRU Discussion Paper 514, University of Kent, Canterbury.

Knight, B. (1993) *Voluntary Action*, Home Office, London.

Kramer, R.M. (1990) 'Change and continuity in British voluntary organisations,' *Voluntas*, 1 (2): 33–60.

Leat, D., G. Smolka and J. Unell (1981) *Voluntary and Statutory Collaboration: Rhetoric or Reality?* Bedford Square Press, London.

Leavy, B. and D.C. Wilson (1994) *Strategy and Leadership*, Routledge, London.

Medley, G.J. (1988) 'Strategic planning for the World Wildlife Fund,' *Long Range Planning*, 21 (1): 46–54.

Medley, G.J. (1992) 'WWF UK creates a new mission,' *Long Range Planning*, 25 (2): 63–68.

Mordaunt, J. (1992) *The Funding Game: A Case Study of Voluntary-Statutory Relationships*, unpublished PhD thesis, University of Edinburgh.

NCVO (1990) *Effectiveness and the Voluntary Sector*, Report of a Working Party chaired by Lord Nathan, NCVO, London.

Nutt, P.C. (1984) 'A strategic planning network for non-profit organizations', *Strategic Management Journal*, 7: 251–65.

ODA (1992) *Report of the Working Party on ODA/NGO Collaboration*, ODA, London.

Paton, R. and C. Cornforth (1992) 'What's different about managing in voluntary and non-profit organisations?' in J. Batsleer, C. Cornforth and R. Paton (eds) *Issues in Voluntary and Non-Profit Management*, Addison-Wesley, London.

Peters, T. and N. Austin (1985) *A Passion for Excellence: The Leadership Difference*, Guild, London.

Peters, T. and R. Waterman (1982) *In Search of Excellence: Lessons from America's Best Run Companies*, Harper & Row, New York.

Pettigrew, A.M. (1985) *The Awakening Giant: Continuity and Change in ICI*, Blackwell, Oxford.

Saxon-Harrold, S.K.E. (1985) *Strategy in the Voluntary Sector*, unpublished PhD thesis, University of Bradford.

Shearman, C. and G. Burrell (1987) 'The structures of industrial development,' *Journal of Management Studies*, 24 (4): pp. 325–45.

Shirley, H. (1993) 'Pick up of job market awaits charities that can measure up', *Charity Magazine*, 10 (4): 30.

Slack, T. and C.R. Hinings (1992) 'Understanding change in national sport organizations: an integration of theoretical perspectives', *Journal of Sport Management*, 6: 114–32.

Streeck, W. and P.C. Schmitter (eds) (1984) *Private Interest Government: Beyond Market and State*, Sage, London.

Taylor, M. and J. Lansley (1992) 'Ideology and welfare in the UK: implications for the voluntary sector', *Voluntas*, 3 (2): 153–74.

Thibault, L. (1993) *Strategy in Nonprofit Sport Organizations*, unpublished PhD thesis, University of Alberta, Canada.

Thibault, L., T. Slack and C.R. Hinings (1993) 'A framework for the analysis of strategy in nonprofit sport organizations', *Journal of Sport Management*, 7: 25–43.

Ware, A. (ed.) (1989) *Charities and Government*, Manchester University Press, Manchester.

Webb, A. and G. Wistow (1982) *Whither State Welfare?* RIPA, London.

Wilson, D.C. (1989) 'New trends in the funding of charities: the tripartite system of funding', in A. Ware (ed.) *Charities and Government*, Manchester University Press, Manchester.

Wilson, D.C. (1992) 'The strategic challenges of co-operation and competition in British voluntary organizations: toward the next century', *Non-Profit Management and Leadership*, 3 (2): 239–54.

Wolfenden (1978) *The Future of Voluntary Organisations: Report of the Wolfenden Committee*, Croom-Helm, London.

Young, D. (1990) 'Organizing principles for international advocacy associations', *Proceedings of the 1990 Conference of the Association of Voluntary Action Scholars*, Centre for Voluntary Organisation, London School of Economics, London.

7

What does Contracting do to Voluntary Agencies?

Jane Lewis

The significance of contracts

Since the passing of the 1990 National Health Service and Community Care Act and the copious guidance that has followed it, 'enabling authorities', the 'mixed economy of care' and, with them, contracts, have become the subjects of discussion and much speculation as to their possible effects.

The empirical evidence for this country is as yet slim. There is a massive literature on contracting in the USA (Gutch, 1992, draws on this), but considerable caution has to be used in applying it, given the very different context in the United States. Statutory services were never providers on the same scale in the US; the pattern of funding of American voluntary organisations has been rather different, with agencies relying on funds from a multiplicity of government organisations and on non-governmental sources for core activities, development and advocacy; and the shift to contracts has been very different. Whereas the US 'drifted' into a contracts culture, in Britain the change has been dictated by government policy. And whereas contracts were introduced in the United States during the 1960s as a means of expanding welfare provision, in Britain they have been accompanied by a commitment on the part of government to reduce statutory provision.

In a study of contracts within one voluntary organisation – Crossroads – Hedley and Rochester (1991) found only 15 per cent of the local organisations to be operating under contract. While there was evidence that negotiations preceding the contract had usually been protracted, Hedley and Rochester concluded that the problems of growth and formalisation that they observed would 'have arisen independently of the development of contracting arrangements' (para 13.6). They conceded that the organisations might be in something of a 'honeymoon' transitional period regarding contracts; most services under contract were still complementary, but they were on the whole optimistic that voluntary organisations would remain favoured providers.

The Volunteer Centre UK (Davis Smith and Hedley, 1993) contacted 500 organisations in May 1993. They received 190 replies, out of which 37 per cent were running contracts. Of these, 40 per cent said that contracts were an improvement and only 10 per cent said that they considered their organisations to be worse off. In their more detailed study of twelve contracts, Common and Flynn (1992) emphasised the degree of trust characterising contracts with the voluntary sector. While relationships between voluntary agencies and statutory authorities became more formal during the period of negotiation, they tended to relax afterwards, although there was variation in the degree of formality with which the contract was managed.

Two points may be made from this evidence: first, the surveys are valuable for reminding us that contracts have not swept the board overnight. They are still a minority form, although the NCVO's local authority funding survey has shown that voluntary organisations lost £12 million in grants during 1992–3, while contract fees increased by £78.4 million (134 per cent) (*NCVO News*, 1993). Indeed, as I shall demonstrate, the policy environment is changing rapidly, such that the 'grant aid culture' is dying and a more 'formalised' financial relationship with government funders is replacing it. Of course, as Billis (1993) suggests, voluntary agencies do not have to accept government money. Indeed, the response of many has been to seek funds from elsewhere. However, there is the world of difference between the effects of contracting on agencies who have no objection to contracting on the one hand, and on those who do object, but have little choice in the matter, on the other. Money is tight and the new 'contracts culture' is bound to have an impact on organisations that are predominantly government-funded. Organisations that are heavily reliant on government money have not found that they are able to refuse new proposals regarding their funding put forward by statutory authorities (Hoyes and Means, 1991; Davis Smith and Hedley, 1993). Second, where contracts have been introduced, the effects both on the relationship between (usually) the local authority and the voluntary agency, and also on the voluntary agency itself, are necessarily as yet unclear. Common and Flynn's (1992) study focused on the former, and found considerable variation in contract management styles. Given the variation in the speed and nature of the changes taking place in local authorities, this is not surprising. Most commentaries on contracts have been snapshot pictures of the situation at a particular point in time, rather than providing an idea of the changes that may take place over a longer period.

In what follows I shall look at the rapidly changing policy context, in which commissioning is coming to the fore of the agenda in local authorities, and then make some observations about the impact of contracts on voluntary organisations, drawing on a research project which has traced the effects of moves towards contracts on voluntary organisations belonging to the same national organisation in four London boroughs over a two-and-a-half-year period. Only two of the organisations are running contracts. One moved to contract for the borough's day care service, part of which was previously delivered under grant aid, very early on, in April 1990. For the other, there was no discussion of contracts until early in 1992, after the local authority imposed swingeing budget cuts and the Social Services Committee began to talk about the desirability of the 'voluntarisation of services'. In a third organisation, it was also the need to achieve cuts in expenditure that prompted a review of grant aid and a substantial 'tightening' of the conditions for, and monitoring of, grants; this is part of what I term the process of formalising financial relationships. The fourth organisation has also been asked to collect information regarding a number of performance indicators, but without any suggestion that the basis of the current arrangements will be changed. Finally, I shall offer some comments regarding the changing nature of the relationship between the statutory and voluntary sectors and whether it is still appropriate to refer to this as a 'partnership'.

The policy context

The 1989 White Paper on community care set out six key objectives, the fourth of which stressed the need to promote the 'independent sector'. Making social services departments into enablers, who purchase more than they provide, and so promote a mixed economy of care, was portrayed in the official guidance as central to achieving user choice and services that are both high quality and cost effective. Both private and voluntary organisations were included in the designation 'independent', but the pressure behind this particular aim of the White Paper may be identified as coming primarily from the private nursing and residential homes lobby, as well as from the Government's own opposition to local government. The idea was to break the local authority's monopoly provider status, but its success depended on a set of market conditions that often do not exist. Achieving greater choice depends in large measure on the kind of social care market that exists or can be created. One large private or voluntary sector organisation contracting with the local authority does not increase user choice.

The Draft Guidance issued in 1990 suggested a firm functional split between purchaser and provider functions for social services departments, along the lines of the changes taking place in health authorities, and thus also implied a quasi-market relationship between the statutory authority and any possible voluntary organisation provider. Both local authorities and the voluntary sector reacted strongly against this idea. The Association of Metropolitan Authorities (1990) and the NCVO (National Council for Voluntary Organisations) (1990) both deplored any move towards contracting on the basis of price-based competition and talked of the need to preserve a redefined notion of 'partnership'.

The revised 1991 Guidance, and in particular the Price Waterhouse document (DH and PW, 1991) on purchaser/provider roles within social services departments, substantially modified the earlier conception of a profound shift in statutory/voluntary relationships. The document acknowledged that one of the chief strengths of the current position was the closeness of contact with in-house and community providers, and concluded that the new relationship was best conceived of as 'being a contract culture involving close ongoing relationships with providers, rather than being based upon anonymous short term price competition' (p. 11).

The 1990 Act laid a duty on local authorities to consult widely (including the voluntary sector) in the production of a community care plan, and to assess those appearing to be in need of service. Local authorities were instructed to concentrate first on the production of a community care plan, which they did by the middle of 1992.

Full implementation of the Act was delayed until April 1993, but the Department of Health set out eight key tasks to be accomplished by that date. These highlighted the need to make sure that the following were in place: assessment systems for individuals; agreements with health authorities regarding new arrangements for hospital discharge and for clients in nursing homes; purchasing arrangements for nursing and residential home beds; and information for the public about the arrangements for assessment and care provision in the form of the community care plan. Thus prior to 1993 most authorities concentrated their attention on assessment procedures and, given the scarcity of resources, ways of prioritising assessed needs and of developing eligibility criteria for service. Few made stimulation of the independent sector a priority and most voluntary agencies would have experienced contact with the new changes only in the form of consultation over the community care plan, which in many places was rather a hit and miss affair.

However, the six key tasks set out by the NHS Management Executive and the Social Services Inspectorate for 1993–4 refer both to the need to begin to shift the balance of resources towards non-residential care and the development of joint commissioning with health authorities (DH (93) 18/CI (93) 12). In fact, while in 1992 Wistow and colleagues reported that only three of the twenty-four local authorities they looked at were enthusiastic about enabling, since the beginning of 1993 social services departments have shown considerably more interest in commissioning strategies. Furthermore, the purchasing structures within authorities are beginning to look complicated.

There is a tendency for authorities to move to implement a high and firm purchaser/provider split, operating from the second management tier right down through the department. Authorities are also grappling with the balance to be achieved between micro- and macro-purchasing; how far, in other words, to devolve budgets. Very few plan to devolve to the frontline, care manager level. In London, there seems to be a model emerging whereby decisions regarding purchasing are taken centrally within the social services department (including contract specifications, and negotiations in respect of prices), which result in a menu of services from which care managers will be able to draw. The idea of joint commissioning adds another possible layer to purchasing, although authorities are unclear as to whether to interpret this more as population needs planning, or as agreements on what to purchase and on contract specifications. Joint commissioning in terms of pooling budgets is far off.

All this has significant implications for voluntary agencies. First, the machinery for funding voluntary organisations has changed significantly. In the case of one London borough, grants were decentralised to the social services department in 1986 with a named person in charge of their administration. At the end of 1991, the department began what promised to be a long review of funding in consultation with the voluntary sector. But in the middle of 1992 the department reorganised, implementing a purchaser/provider split. At that time a commissioning unit came into being and grants management was relocated there. The contact person for voluntary agencies was, however, located in another division, strategic planning. Thus in this authority the funding of the voluntary sector became part of the Social Services department's wider commissioning strategy virtually overnight and voluntary agencies were no longer sure whom to approach within the department. In another London borough, the allocation of grants has passed to the joint commissioning teams that were set up at the end of 1992, while services under contract are managed by the contracts unit.

The climate is changing rapidly and voluntary organisations are very much subject to the shifts within the social services departments. It seems increasingly clear that voluntary agencies are regarded as providers, and as purchaser/provider splits become firmer this has important implications. In some authorities voluntary sector representatives played a part in the production of the first and second community care plans, as opposed to just being consulted. They did so usually by virtue of being invited onto the joint planning machinery. However, as joint planning becomes joint commissioning, so statutory authorities are raising questions about the membership of the joint commissioning groups/teams. The 1993 Guidance on Joint Commissioning suggested that if voluntary agencies were to continue to participate, then they might need to separate their advocacy and provider roles, just as the social services department has separated its purchaser and provider functions (DH, SSI, NHSME, 1993).

Perhaps most significant and most clear (albeit least quantifiable) is the rapid disappearance of a grant-aid culture and with it the 'special relationship' with the voluntary sector. Voluntary agencies may still be preferred as providers, not least because of the considerable quantities of volunteer labour they can deliver, but local authorities are increasingly talking about the importance of 'level playing fields' for independent providers of all kinds and for their own in-house providers.

The research evidence: the effects of contracting on voluntary agencies

The approach to contracting has tended to be informal (Common and Flynn, 1992; Hedley and Rochester, 1991). My research into the effects of contracts on voluntary agencies found that, in the case of the voluntary agency experiencing a rapid move to introduce contracts in 1992–3, negotiations were conducted by telephone and the local authority was reported as having little idea of what it wanted to see in the contract other than the budget total. This may indicate a high level of trust/discretion, but it is hard to generalise. Even within a single contract, some elements may be strictly specified and others not. And the way in which a contract is managed over time may change dramatically. In the case of the agency operating the day care contract, the contract was initially managed through the active involvement of staff from the local authority (analogous to Common and Flynn's 'partnership' management model). The local authority then implemented a purchaser/provider split and brought in a contracts manager from industry, whereupon the model for managing the contract shifted to Common and Flynn's 'contract manager' model. The new contracts manager was not familiar with social care, and active officer involvement was replaced by more detailed specification and monitoring. On the face of it, the management of the contract was less intrusive and hands-on and its review was less testing, but it was also less supportive and developmental. Thus, the relationship between the signatories to the contract is hard to predict over time and may not follow the simple line from more to less formal that has been outlined in studies to date.

With regard to the effects on the internal dynamics of voluntary agencies three major areas may be highlighted:

(i) Professionalisation and formalisation

There is some evidence to support the Government's claim regarding the greater clarity that contracting brings; in the words of one staff member involved in drawing up the respite care contract, the process of drawing up specifications 'stopped us doing it all'. The staff were forced closely to define the scope of the service they were prepared to offer and the model of care. Above all, it was felt that working out a contract stopped particular areas of work being taken for granted and not being subjected to evaluation. However, as the Association of Metropolitan Authorities (1990) has suggested, running a contract requires both new and more skills than managing a grant. It may be suggested that these have particular implications for the job descriptions of senior members of paid staff, and for the relationships between volunteers and paid workers.

In the case of the organisation running the day care contract, the Director undertook regular visits to each day care centre, instigated six weekly staff meetings in each centre, chaired six weekly day care group meetings attended by centre managers and local chairmen, carried out one-to-one professional supervision for day care managers, took responsibility for collecting quarterly the statistical information necessary for monitoring, offered training to paid staff and volunteers, and sought to improve liaison both with local voluntary groups, the local authority and the health authority. Little work could be delegated because the office was staffed by largely volunteer, untrained administrators and secretaries. Indeed, the Director continued to undertake the day-to-day office administration as well. When the local authority moved to joint commissioning, she became a member of the joint commissioning team for the elderly. The Director estimated that as much as 75 per cent of her time was absorbed by running the contract. She found herself working at a wide range of levels and the heavy degree of responsibility tended to open up the divide between her and the other paid and volunteer staff.

When the contract began, half the managers of the centres were volunteers, who found the formalisation of procedures demanded by the contract oppressive and resented in particular the time required to fill in the performance indicator returns, which they felt diminished the time they could spend with clients. One of these volunteers resigned and was replaced by a paid manager. The paid managers tended to welcome the new openness about practices and the clarity of a strict monitoring regime which 'kept them on their toes'. The management of volunteers also became more challenging as more attention was paid to developing uniform practices. For example, managers had to face the issue of how to 'retire' a volunteer who could no longer be trusted to carry out tasks satisfactorily. The contract imposed 'professional' standards of assessment, management and evaluation, which met with some resistance from some, but not all, voluntary staff; inevitably volunteers have very different agendas when volunteering, some welcome the chance to train and absorb new ideas, some do not (see Davis Smith and Knapp, this volume, for further discussion of these issues). Volunteers on the executive committees of all the organisations examined in the research expressed opposition to the demand from local authorities for more details about expenditure and more information about activities.

(ii) Governance and accountability

The role of executive members raises particularly difficult issues. Their advice on policy direction is increasingly needed, but they may be insufficiently aware of the context in which the agency is working. Commenting on American non-profit organisations, Powell and Friedkin (1987) have noted that as technical complexity increases, broad-based governance declines. In the contracts culture, accountability is increasingly to the purchaser in the first instance, which leaves the position of the trustees ambiguous. Margaret Harris (1987, 1989, 1991) and Hedley and Rochester (1992) have provided commentaries on the problems of executive committees in the new climate.

It was noteworthy that the executive committee for the organisation providing day care had no clear grasp of the community care changes and seemingly little appreciation of the changed ways of working of the organisation's staff. Lines of accountability also became confused. Day care managers found themselves responding to the Director of the organisation, but also to the chairmen of their local groups. Common and Flynn (1992) emphasised the problem of divided accountability between voluntary agencies and local authorities for contracted-out services, but the lines of accountability within the voluntary organisation may be additionally blurred (see also Leat, 1990).

(iii) Goals

As has been more generally reported, the period of negotiation of the day care contract was protracted. The most strongly contested issue was the client group to be served. While the voluntary organ-

isation had a commitment to taking clients who were socially isolated, the Local Authority wished to ensure access for the more
dependent elderly. The contract specified that all clients would be
assessed by the Social Services department, with 60 per cent being
required to meet Social Services' criteria for admission. This example
illustrates how contract specifications may change voluntary organisations' established aims and objectives with regard to a service.
Given that local authorities are having to target services more
efficiently, then it is likely that voluntary agencies contracting to
provide mainstream services will find themselves dealing with a
more dependent population (which also has implications for the work
of volunteers). As another organisation commented, if the local authority sends only five people to the day care centre but they are
doubly incontinent, the other users of the centre may then feel that
they do not want to attend.

More broadly, voluntary organisations have expressed the fear
that in being invited to contract for services their advocacy, campaigning and information services will suffer (Flynn and Common,
1990). This fear may become more real as the overview of voluntary organisations' grant aid moves into commissioning units within local authorities. As voluntary agencies become more firmly
identified as providers, so it is more likely that local authorities
will become more specific about the services they will purchase.
Both the Griffiths Report (DHSS, 1988) and the Home Office
Efficiency Scrutiny (1990) stressed the importance of preserving core
grants, but it is likely that in this, as in all else, local authority
practice will vary.

The Volunteer Centre UK's 1993 survey of volunteering and the
contract culture suggested that the positive effects of contracting
were greater funding security, the fact that voluntary organisations
tended to play a large role in the drafting of contracts, and that
contracts forced a reassessment of the way in which the organisation was governed and managed (Davis Smith and Hedley, 1993).
In fact, it is hard to generalise about any of these. For example, the
organisation running the day care contract welcomed the idea of a
three-year contract and the security it provided. But negotiations
for renewal were started by the local authority two years into the
contract and, furthermore, the authority decided to put the contract
out to tender. This organisation also found that after the first year
the local authority decided that it wanted an evaluation of user

satisfaction, which had not been included in the original budget, but which the organisation had to pay for.

One other organisation experienced arbitrary reductions in the agreed payment for services and found that there was little it could do about it. Voluntary organisations are not accustomed to drafting contracts (any more than local authorities have advanced purchasing skills) and while they have had a major say in many of the specifications, there has been a tendency to undercost crucial items, especially costs associated with using volunteers and in negotiating and running the contract (see also Meadows, 1992). Voluntary organisations must rapidly develop expertise in costings, particularly in respect of volunteers, who all too often are assumed to be 'free'. As professionalisation takes place, so the training costs for volunteers may be expected to rise. Formalising funding arrangements may also serve to expose the 'hidden' subsidies to the voluntary agency and open them to review.

In addition, what are considered to be advantages in one set of circumstances may turn out to be disadvantages in another. In one voluntary organisation, for example, the tightening up of conditions for grant aid, coupled with its reduction, forced a major review of staffing and structure and seems to have resulted in a promising three-year development plan. Another voluntary agency, however, was faced with the new contracts culture only a year after it had undergone a major review and taken the decision not to become a service provider, but rather to concentrate on campaigning.

The future of the 'new partnership'

Many argue that contracts are not new to the voluntary sector and that little will change as a result of contracting. The first point is undoubtedly true, but the conditions under which contracting is now taking place are significantly different. Voluntary organisations are in many instances being asked to become alternative rather than supplementary or complementary providers. As for the second point, this is likely to be true only for large, niche service providers. For them the argument in the American literature that stresses the extent to which contracts offer voluntary agencies the opportunity to become partners rather than supplicants may hold good. However, in the case of agencies that are funded largely by government, even large ones, it is difficult to see how the balance of power can ever rest with the voluntary agency. Within the new contracts culture (inside social services departments as well as between voluntary and statutory authorities), purchasers 'call the shots'. If a voluntary organisation becomes a large, monopoly provider of a hitherto mainstream local authority service, it may have considerable bargaining power, but it should be remembered that the *aim* of the reforms is to avoid replacing monopoly local authority providers with single independent providers.

Furthermore, if social services provision does become increasingly competitive, then voluntary agencies will face competition from private agencies. So far this has been limited for anything beyond residential and nursing homes, but the Government would certainly like to see independent homes diversify into other forms of provision. Voluntary organisations may feel confident that they retain their trump card of volunteer labour, but volunteers are not entirely 'free', for example in terms of training; voluntary organisations that have costed them as such are already bearing a heavy burden in relation to contracts.

Contracts tend to assume that the contractor is the same form of organisation as the purchaser and do not make allowance for different forms of management. Taylor and Hoggett (1993) have considered the potential for remaking contractors in the image of the purchaser. If indeed the historical role of the voluntary sector is to undergo profound change, such that it ceases to be either complementary or supplementary to the statutory sector (Kramer, 1981) and becomes an alternative provider, possibly of first resort, then the implications for mission, management and governance are huge. Salamon (1987) has suggested that at present the voluntary and statutory sectors are complementary in terms of their strengths and weaknesses, making collaboration sensible, but quasi-market relationships are not inherently sympathetic to a collaborative form of partnership. Indeed, there is a profound tension between the injunction to develop competition on the one hand, and the trust necessary for joint working on the other (Hunter, 1992). The precise form the new partnership will take in the new contracts culture is hard to predict.

Billis (1993) has warned of the dangers of an instrumental use of the voluntary sector which emphasises only those attributes that are of direct use to government. The process of contracting, which carries with it the idea of formalising arrangements between the parties and/or producing uniform, high quality services, highlights both the tensions inherent in the relationship between the statutory and voluntary sectors and the ambiguities inherent in the nature of voluntary organisations. Billis (1989) has argued that while voluntary organisations are primarily associational, they overlap both the personal and bureaucratic worlds. The management of ambiguity requires an understanding of the ground rules of both the associational and bureaucratic worlds, an appreciation of both membership, mission, informality and democracy on the one hand and managerial authority and accountability, levels of decision-making, career progression, staff development, conditions of service and explicit policy-making on the other. Voluntary organisations balance the demands of bureaucracy and association. It may be suggested that contracting will tend to shift the balance towards the former. Certainly, Barry Knight's (1993) report on voluntary action, in which he pushed 'enabling' to its logical conclusion and advocated dividing voluntary organisations into autonomous campaigners on the one hand and a 'third sector' of contracting service providers on the other, rode roughshod over the participatory and associational nature of voluntary agencies. The term 'partnership' has served to gloss over the problems inherent in a relationship between a formal bureaucratic statutory organisation and one that is more ambiguous. The new basis for partnership may be firmer in so far as voluntary organisations may come to adopt more bureaucratic features, but this also implies a significant change in the nature of voluntary organisations which may not be cost free.

References

Association of Metropolitan Authorities (1990) *Contracts for Social Care: The Local Authority View*, AMA, London.

Billis, D. (1989) *A Theory of the Voluntary Sector: Implications for Policy and Practice*, Working Paper no. 5, Centre for Voluntary Organisation, London School of Economics, London.

Billis, D. (1993) *Organising Public and Voluntary Agencies*, Routledge, London.

Common, R. and N. Flynn (1992) *Contracting for Care*, Joseph Rowntree Foundation, York.

J. Davis Smith and R. Hedley (1993) *Volunteering and the Contract Culture*, Volunteer Centre UK, Berkhamsted.

DH and Price Waterhouse (1991) *Implementing Community Care, Purchaser, Commissioner and Provider Roles*, HMSO, London.

DH, Social Services Inspectorate, National Health Service Management Executive (1993) *Joint Commissioning for Community Care: 'A Slice through Time'*, DH, London.

DH (93) 18/CI (93) 12 Department of Health letter 'Implementing caring for people', 15 March 1993.

DHSS (Department of Health and Social Security) (1988) *Community Care: An Agenda for Action*, HMSO, London.

Flynn, N. and R. Common (1990) *Contracts for Community Care*, Community Care Implementation Documents, CCI 14. HMSO, London.

Gutch, R. (1992) *Contracting Lessons from the US*, NCVO, London.

Harris, M. (1987) *Management Committees: Roles and Tasks*, Working Paper no. 4, Centre for Voluntary Organisation, London School of Economics, London.

Harris, M. (1989) *Management Committees in Practice: A Study in Local Voluntary Leadership*, Working Paper no. 7, Centre for Voluntary Organisation, London School of Economics, London.

Harris, M. (1991) *Exploring the Role of Voluntary Management Committees: A New Approach* Working Paper no. 10, Centre for Voluntary Organisation, London School of Economics, London.

Hedley, R. and C. Rochester (1991) *Contracts at the Crossroads*, Association of Crossroads Care Attendant Schemes.

Hedley, R. and C. Rochester (1992) *Understanding Management Committees: A Look at Volunteer Management Committee Members*, The Volunteer Centre UK, Berkhamsted.

Home Office (1990) *Profiting from Partnership: Efficiency Scrutiny of Government Funding of the Voluntary Sector*, Home Office, London.

Hoyes, L. and R. Means (1991) *Implementing the White Paper on Community Care*, School for Advanced Urban Studies, Bristol.

Hunter, D.J. (1992) 'To market! To market! A new dawn for community care?' *Health and Social Care*, 1: 3–10.

Knight, B. (1993) *Voluntary Action*, Home Office, London.

Kramer, R.M. (1981) *Voluntary Agencies in the Welfare State*, University of California Press, Berkeley.

Leat, D. (1990) 'Voluntary organisations and accountability' in H.K. Anheier and W. Siebel (eds) *The Third Sector: Comparative Studies of Nonprofit Organizations*, De Gruyter, New York.

Meadows, A. (1992) *Reaching Agreement*, NCVO, London.

NCVO (1990) *Working Party Report on Effectiveness and the Voluntary Sector*, NCVO, London.

NCVO News (1993) 'The ups and downs of local funding', no. 47, 4–7 September, NCVO, London.

Powell, W.W. and R. Friedkin (1987) 'Organisational change in non-profit organisations', in W.W. Powell (ed.) *The Non-Profit Sector: A Research Handbook,* Yale University Press, New Haven.

Salamon, L.B. (1987) 'Partners in public service: the scope and theory of government and non-profit relations', in W.W. Powell (ed.) *The Non-Profit Sector, A Research Handbook*, Yale University Press, New Haven.

Taylor, M. and P. Hoggett (1993) 'Quasi-markets and the transformation of the independent sector', paper presented at the conference: *Quasi-Markets in Public Sector Service Delivery: the Emerging Findings*, School for Advanced Urban Studies, University of Bristol, 22–24 March.

Wistow, G., M. Knapp, B. Hardy and C. Allen (1992) 'From providing to enabling: local authorities and the mixed economy of social care', *Public Administration*, 70: 25–45.

8

What does Contracting do to Users?

Nicholas Deakin

Existing policy and provision

An open conspiracy has developed on both left and right to stigma-
tise the way in which welfare has been delivered in this country. In
his commentary on a recent critical publication about the Citizen's
Charter, William Waldegrave congratulates his critics on getting one
thing right, at least: correctly identifying the 'problems caused by
the way in which the welfare state has been structured throughout
most – if not all of its life' and 'the remoteness and insensitivity of
public service bureaucracies . . . and the principle of uniformity which
has been evident throughout the welfare state' (Waldegrave, 1993a).

This is rewriting of history on a truly epic scale – and about as
crass, in its way, as the idle chatter on the left about the postwar
dominance of 'Fordist' modes of welfare production. Issues about
the way in which welfare should be delivered and the impact on its
users go back to the beginnings of the welfare state in its modern
form; and concern about the situation of citizens has been part of
the debate from very early on (see Cole in *Planning for Britain*
(1943); Beveridge in the original *Voluntary Action* (1948)). Leviathan's mode of operation was a matter of urgent public debate long
before a younger Waldegrave set down ways in which he believed
the beast could be bound (1978: in which, oddly enough, there is not
the faintest prefiguration of any of his current policy preoccupations).

In particular, the shortfall in responsiveness to service users and
means of redressing it was a central preoccupation of that much
maligned decade, the sixties (when the welfare state was still only

two decades old). Planners, faced with extensive critiques of their practice towards communities (Skeffington, 1969), were inching their way painfully up Sherry Arnstein's (1971) ladder of participation; and the Seebohm Report (1968) portrayed reorganisation as the means by which users of the new social services could be enabled to participate in their delivery. Even in the innermost citadel of welfare values, the National Health Service, there was dawning recognition of a need to secure patient satisfaction (Cartwright, 1969) and a push towards greater accountability to users which eventually led to the establishment of Community Health Councils (CHCs): institutions still unique within the welfare system.

More than this, the campaigns undertaken by what the French sometimes call the '*soixantehuitards*' were directed not merely to fighting the existing system but to constructing alternative structures outside it for those whose needs were not recognised there. Community action campaigns, for example, led to an efflorescence of self-help activities (for example, campaigning for the homeless, promoting tenant co-operatives, even self-build schemes). The same process was also seen at work in the impact made by 'second wave' feminism and the mutual support organisations that emerged from the experience of common problems. More important, when these organisations grew (as many of them did) and crossed the line into service provision, most tried as they did so to take values of involvement (or active participation) of the users of their services with them. All this was reflected in the revitalisation of voluntary activity which added a whole sequence of new campaigning-cum-delivery organisations to the roster (Gladstone, 1979). Later, the crossover went one stage further when graduates from the new voluntary sector began to colonise local government, both as officers and as members – sometimes both at once – and some of them took the same sets of values with them.

So challenges to existing structures were already familiar, and criticisms of its shortcomings in general and lack of responsiveness in particular well understood (both inside and outside the system) by the time a new Government brought a new approach to bear after 1979 to the issue of user involvement. This approach (following Wistow and Barnes (1993), but simplifying grossly) was fuelled at least in part by a belated discovery on the part of the private sector of the need to pay greater attention to customer preferences and demands. This development was given (some) intellectual respectability by the management gurus with their obsessional talk about promoting passion for responsiveness. Later, it was imported into government by the supermarket barons, Lords Rayner and Griffiths, the embodiment of one of the few authentic British economic success stories. The solutions they proceeded to offer were accordingly based on proven success in forms of delivery that bore some superficial resemblance to the task of providing welfare. Customer choice therefore became, and has continued to be, the centrepiece of what was being attempted. The defining characteristic of the programme derives from a concept of users that stresses consumption at the point of delivery (often as a single act) at the expense of any other definitions based on what the users of public services actually experience – usually longer-term relationships, often mediated through other institutions or individuals.

The long march of 'supermarket values' (Gilmour, 1992) through the public service took the best part of the decade; at times, it sat uncomfortably with an alternative agenda – the Treasury's preoccupation with attempts to achieve reductions in public expenditure. Their declared concern was with aggregates; the exercise of individual choice was therefore threatening if it had long-term public expenditure implications (compare the Treasury reaction to Norman Fowler's 1985 attempt at pensions reform: Lawson, 1992). For the Treasury, whose main weapons were cash-limits and targeting of spending, the promotion of greater efficiency was not a user-enabling but a cost-cutting device. So although the two objectives of Government policy – enhancing choice and rationing expenditure – ran in double harness, they increasingly came to pull in different directions. And the stakes rose as the pressure generated by the widely perceived decline in quality of public services (especially those managed by local authorities) mounted during the decade of the eighties.

However, user dissatisfaction generated in this way could be used as part of the rationale for further reform. Furthermore, local authorities had independently attempted to address the problem, in a variety of ways. First, there was an effort to promote value change by stressing the importance of a public service orientation and an approach through 'enabling' (Stewart and Clarke, 1988); and, second, structural changes designed to improve access and strengthen accountability were introduced – in particular, decentralisation of services (Gaster, 1993). These changes were pushed along by pressure both from above, through the Audit Commission, as well as by direct government intervention, and from below, as already-active users' movements gained greater confidence (Hatch, 1980). This emerged through the rapid growth of self-help organisations and the appearance of another wave of voluntary sector activity based on past exclusions – for example, the normalisation movement and the new black voluntary sector, both of which promoted the insistent claims of service users in opposition to both old (medical) and new (social work) provider professions.

All this effervescent new wine was being poured into the old bottles of the existing welfare state structures, left virtually unchanged in the first two terms of Conservative Government (Deakin, 1987; Hills, 1990). However, all that altered after 1987. The subsequent changes have been marked by a new emphasis on the importance of changing values, with the introduction of market-based models providing the means and empowerment of customers through enhanced choice as the end. As we now know, Margaret Thatcher never believed that the public sector could provide services of the same quality as the private sector (Ridley, 1992). Hence, she thought, self-interest should always lead the alert customer to choose the latter, provided they could afford it; failure to do so was seen as an unmistakable signal of willingness to accept passive-dependent client status. But in the interim the public sector could make progress by devising passable imitations of private provision. This was to be achieved by the creation of quasi-markets, which have spread across the range of main welfare services during the period of intense legislative activity from 1987 to 1990.

Quasi-markets take different forms in different service areas; but all of them have in common the creation of new structural relationships between the purchasers and providers of services, and the steady withdrawal of state agencies from the latter role in favour of private and 'independent sector' (sic) providers (Le Grand and Bartlett, 1993). This reflects the principle that diversity of provision is a good in itself; and also the view that competition will benefit the customer by enhancing their range of choices. With this goes the importation of new devices for managing the relationship between purchasers and providers, among which contracts for delivery of service have been especially prominent. All services have experienced changes of operating style and the attempt to implant new management values, centred on meeting customer demands, and with rewards geared to the effectiveness of the response to them. They have also been kitted out with all the paraphernalia of mission statements, a new vocabulary and various presentational devices, like livery and logo, often (mis)taken as having some value in their own right.

In all these reforms the centrality of users' interests has repeatedly been stressed. The Citizen's Charter, perched like a rather wobbly glacé cherry on top of the vast cake that the Government has been baking, enshrines that principle in its stated objective of 'raising the standard of public services by making them more responsive to the wishes and needs of users' (HM Government, 1993, p. 5). William Waldegrave, as Minister for a specially created new Department, the Office for Public Services and Science (OPSS), was entrusted in 1992 by the Prime Minister with a mission to extend this objective to the totality of the Government's activities. In principle, at least, the Charter and its clones in different service areas should provide a blueprint for a future in which concern for users will at last move decisively to the centre of the picture.

There are some difficulties in the way of establishing whether this objective is actually in the process of being achieved, as the Government is already claiming (Waldegrave, 1993b). First, there is the problem that the mission, though frequently presented as a homogeneous enterprise, actually takes substantially different forms in different areas – in particular, the relationship of service users to providers is differently structured so that in some situations the employment of the term 'user' itself can be actively misleading. Second, the nature of the mission is not completely clear. The term 'empowerment' has been freely used, but it is a contested one and it is not clear what the Government intends by it – whether it is the promotion of user control or merely greater responsiveness to 'wishes and needs' on the lines of common private sector assertions ('everything we do is driven by you'). Third, and more prosaically, many of the new devices have not yet had time to bed down. In one of the most important areas, community care (which is also one in which the centrality of users to the reforms has been especially clearly proclaimed), the new system has only been in place, in part, since April 1993 (see Lewis, this volume). Moreover, some of the most significant changes now taking place that affect the position of users are not the outcome of policies explicitly directed to promoting user choice; rather, they are the consequence of other government actions, mostly those 'Treasury-driven' policies intended to target or ration public spending. In addition, many of the positive developments that have tended to promote greater user involvement have much deeper and more diverse roots. A final irony: some of the key devices that have been adapted from the private sector are not in practice much used there for the purposes to which they are now being put in the public services. This is arguably so even in the case of contracts, to whose impact on the interests of users I now turn.

The impact of the introduction of contracts

The concept of contract has an apparent clarity about it, seen as a device for securing greater efficiency in service delivery. As Ian Harden puts it:

> contract provides a mechanism by which the supply of *private* services can be organised through the market. In so doing, it binds together individual legal rights and consumer sovereignty. The way in which private services are funded (that is by payments from those who choose to make them) resolves questions about who should be supplied and about who should get what (1992, p. 6).

So in terms of outcomes, it is legitimate to talk about consumers of private services as being 'sovereign'. But the situation is not at all the same in the public sector. Even the basic concepts associated with contracting do not transfer easily. As Sir Peter Kemp justly points out, 'the word "customer" is a very difficult and dangerous word to use in the context of public service' (HMSO, 1993; p. 390). This is because the environment in which users and providers of public services operate is fundamentally different. The demand for services, the rights of individuals to receive them and the means by which their needs are supplied all pose complex problems.

Individual participants in the contracting process can operate in a variety of capacities: as consumers of a service they have purchased as if they were taking part in a private sector transaction; as customers exercising an entitlement to delivery; as unwilling recipients of a service they have no particular wish to receive or as citizens helping to determine (through democratic processes) how and to whom a service is to be provided. In taking part in these transac-

tions, they may themselves be users or they may be acting on behalf of others, present (carers) or future (parents whose children
have not yet entered the grant maintained school). Others may be
acting for them (fundholding GPs for patients, for example). Their
access to the process that decides what service they receive and
when may be direct – or, in the case of 'compulsory' welfare (school-
children's experience of education, for example), effectively non-
existent (Lewis, 1993).

In this situation, the impact of the introduction of contracts should
be to enhance – at least initially – clarity in the definition of the
tasks that are to be performed (Common, Flynn and Hurley, 1993).
It ought to avert the excessive exercise of discretion and provide
the means by which standards of performance can be introduced
and assessments of achievement – comparative, where necessary –
made. But the actual users of the public service will not be the
direct beneficiaries of the process of change, even in broad principle. As Harden puts it, the new element introduced by contracts

> is not consumer sovereignty, however, nor greater rights for in-
> dividuals. Rather, it is the fact that the parties to the contract
> have separate interests. In this sense, 'competition' is inherent in
> the contractual approach; not competition between different pur-
> chasers, or different providers of services, but in the contractual
> relationship itself (Harden, 1992; p. 33).

This is because securing the public interest has ceased to be the
responsibility of a single organisation (the monopoly supplier of
Waldegrave's demonology) but is the outcome of a negotiated settlement between a variety of organisations, some of which may not be
in the public sector at all.

In this process, the users' interests are secondary: they depend
upon securing increased efficiency in service delivery as an outcome of negotiations in which they have played no direct part. Their
interests may even be harmed. The other side of the coin of clarity
is inflexibility, both in the definition of tasks and their discharge.
The need to monitor and continuously review the achievement of
service standards may result in the creation of new forms of bureaucracy as impenetrable and immutable as the older ones. The
penalties for failing to meet standards may inhibit innovation. 'Commercial confidentiality' may obstruct users' access to crucial items

of information about the service they wish to use.

As the evidence for the United States tends to show (Gutch, 1992; Richardson, 1994), the introduction of contracts may also encourage larger organisations at the expense of small community-based providers who may not yet have learned the rules of the game, or who cannot accept the level of risk which may be implied by entering into a contract relationship (this can be true for both for-profit and voluntary agencies). Purchasing organisations may fragment services by pursuing a strategy of maximum value for money through competitive contracting out of specialist services; or they may prefer to enter into relationships with agencies with whom they are familiar, or in extreme cases have created themselves (see Flynn and Common, 1992; Hoggett and Taylor, 1993). Such choice as has been created is therefore largely for agencies seeking suppliers, not for users choosing between products.

The result is that in general terms the patterns of contracting in quasi-markets like health and social services have often settled rapidly into dominance by large providers with a familiarity with the existing market (Le Grand and Bartlett, 1993). The outcome has so far been an absence of competition in the private market sense; and there is therefore no particular benefit for service users of the kind which the customer would expect to enjoy in the private market – though even there the evidence seems to be that contracts in themselves are not a particularly effective means of promoting competition (House of Commons Treasury and Civil Service Select Committee, 1993).

It is therefore not surprising that even in the field of community care, where users were explicitly intended to have direct access through the system of care management to the process of decision-taking, as laid down in the White Paper *Caring for People* (HM Government, 1989) the evidence of user involvement in contracting is extremely scanty. In the initial study undertaken by Flynn and associates, the evidence was that contracting 'had led neither to an increase in user choice nor to more user control' (Flynn and Common, 1992, p. 36). The investigators felt that at that stage (which was before the new community care procedures had been formally brought into operation) there was a real risk that 'the process of establishing the new market relationships between purchasers and providers may turn managers' and workers' attention away from the people who need the services' (ibid, 1992, p. 37). The following two reports showed little change in the pattern, the researchers reporting that

> we found that the choice of services had not been improved by
> the process of contracting, that services were either designed by
> the purchasers or the providers, with little user involvement and
> that services were managed by the providers and monitored by
> the purchasers, with little user control. There was some evidence
> of user feedback in the evaluation of services, but evaluation was
> generally done by professionals (Common, Flynn and Hurley, 1993;
> p. 28).

Taylor and Lewis, too, point to ways in which the introduction of
contracts is already having the effect of ironing out diversity among
providers; and observe that the potential benefits of the contract
system, in terms of improved access and choice, are not being carried over from the private sector (1993). Russell and colleagues, in
their review of the impact of new funding arrangements on voluntary organisations in the north-west of England (1993), refer to the
impact on one voluntary agency of entering a new funding contract
with the local Social Services department to provide family-based
short-term care, in which a clash of attitudes on user involvement
in decision-taking took a year to resolve.

Assessment

One possible way of assessing the overall impact that the introduction of contracts is having is to return to some principles for user
involvement defined before the Charter policies and the 'contract
culture' associated with them formally came into operation and see
whether they have been reflected in the new situation. These principles have evolved incrementally, based orginally on the National
Consumer Council's *Measuring Up* report (1986) and refined by
subsequent writers (Potter, 1988; Deakin and Wright, 1990; Grant,
1992). They suggest that the extent of success achieved in user (and
carer) involvement should be assessed on six criteria:

- information
- access
- choice
- representation
- redress
- accountability.

Measured in these terms, the Charter initiatives have considerable strengths in some areas and evident weaknesses in others. On information, some progress has been made; but there is still a tendency to confuse advertising (circulation of promotional material advocating use of a particular agency or service) with public service information setting out all options even-handedly and promoting informed choice by potential users as well as reinforcing accountability to the public at large. Improved access, in the sense of encouragement given to frontline staff to take personal responsibility for ensuring user satisfaction in the service they are delivering, has been one of the successes of the Charters. This has taken a variety of forms: for example, personal identification to callers, on the telephone or in person, by wearing badges – though sometimes this amounts to little more than saying 'no' nicely while wearing what Roy Griffiths once called the 'fixed white smiles of arctic winter'; and the problem of chronic medical secrecy has not yet been cracked. But access in the broader sense must remain problematic and is threatened by the emergence of systems that differentiate in the form of access they provide: prevent actual parents or tenants benefiting at the expense of potential future ones; or more immediately, fundholding GPs' patients being treated first.

Choice comes at the centre of claims made for changes; but it is unclear in practice whether diversity of providers has been achieved or indeed what the outcome for users would be if it were, since the enhanced value for money secured by purchasers is not necessarily passed on to users (Harden, 1992). The emergence of two-tier systems may also have the effect of excluding or restricting choice for users without adequate resources or with needs that are complex or expensive to meet, as providers 'cherry-pick' the better-off clients and more straightforward cases.

Strengthening of complaints procedures has been another area of concern under the various Charters; and links to the issue of effective redress for users. Here, too, claims of improvements secured or on the way (HM Government, 1994) have to be balanced against a number of problems apparently left unresolved: standards set too low and hence too easily met; rights not conferred and hence not justifiable; and public sector providers with budgets under acute pressure (for example London Transport) unable to afford to make financial compensation (Prior *et al.*, 1992).

But it is accountability that remains the chief area of weakness.

There is no significant evidence yet of involvement of users either directly or indirectly in decision-taking (compare experience of preparation of community care plans). For critics, this is one reflection of a wider process of loss of democratic accountability – the elevation by the Government of a 'New Magistracy' to replace democratically elected local government (Stewart, 1993). This, they assert, leads to the passing of local responsibility to a self-perpetuating oligarchy consisting of congeries of businessmen and retired major-generals (co-opted as 'non-execs') who view users as some kind of variant on the stroppy workers or bolshie other ranks with whom they are familiar in their 'real' lives.

For these critics, the essential flaw is that the Charter is not a citizen's but a consumer's charter. In order for users to exercise choice effectively (it is further argued), they need to be able to function as citizens – that is, to be able to help influence not only their own circumstances but the overall pattern of collective choices (Stewart, 1993). As it is, the 'democratic deficit' in the new system (Bogdanor, 1993) prevents them from doing so. William Waldegrave has strongly contested these assertions, arguing that there is no 'democratic deficit' because there never was any real accountability under the previous system – a proposition for which recent research provides some support (Day and Klein, 1987). He goes on to argue that issues of the exercise of control over a particular service are not, ultimately, what interest users; their main concern is with the efficiency with which the service is delivered and the extent to which it matches their needs (Waldegrave, 1993b). To extend the argument, users may even have little interest in which agency delivers the service and who manages it.

On balance, to talk of 'user empowerment' achieved through the group of initiatives summarised in the successive commentaries to the Citizen's Charter (HM Government, 1993, 1994) may seem not much more than hyperbole. It is probable (though not certain) that the extent of consumer knowledge of services being provided through the public sector may have been extended, as William Waldegrave claims (1993b); but knowledge by itself is still far from being power. His critics do not find this surprising. They argue that any 'empowerment' that may take place on the terms defined by the Charter has been strictly limited and confined to individual choices exercised in situations where the consumer of the services has some access to resources and a range of choices open to them. Many of the recent reforms do not have these characteristics (Prior *et al.*, 1992).

The future for users: agents or patients?

However, if there are deficiencies in the ways in which the Government's proposals have functioned, there may be a legitimate alternative which involves less sweeping claims but greater purchase on reality. It is possible to have intermediate objectives, to aim to secure not instant empowerment but changes in the character of the service provided, in order to make it more responsive to user preferences. As already implied, this is familiar territory for local government and (to a lesser extent) for the health service.

Two examples of such initiatives are the All Wales Strategy for the development of Strategies for Mentally Handicapped People (sic) (Grant, 1992) and the Birmingham Community Care Special Action Programme (Wistow and Barnes, 1993). Both of these programmes had as a central feature the involvement of service users. However, neither of these have depended directly upon the introduction of contracts; and their achievements (which are real and radical) pre-date the Citizen's Charter (would either of them have earned a chartermark?). And it remains true that the impact of the introduction of the 'contract culture' into the field of social care has caused much turbulence. In particular, the voluntary sector – which sees itself (not always justifiably) in the role of trustee for users of services it provides – has been plunged into a state of hyper-anxiety.

Might it be possible to cope constructively with some of the effects of the current turbulence promoted by a too-hasty move into the 'contract culture' if in future the objectives for public services were modified, from instant empowerment of users, reclassified by imperfect analogy with the private sector as customers, to a more realistic set of targets? The answer must have a good deal to do with the way in which the voluntary sector responds, since in social care, at least, their future involvement at a significant level is now prescribed.

Evidence from the vast haystack of gossip and data assembled for Knight's *Voluntary Action* (1993) shows how exercised voluntary organisations currently are about the implications of contracting and how uncertain they are about which direction to take. These responses reflect a very proper concern about values and objectives, together with a sense of a particular type of relationship between voluntary organisations and the users of their services, which is not necessarily justified in practice. At the same time, the Volunteer Centre's review of recent experience (Hedley and Davis Smith, 1993) suggests that some organisations, at least, see significant development opportunities – in addition to enhanced prospects for security – in the new situation.

These uncertainties are especially important at a time when there is such pressure on resources. Community care in particular was initially seriously underfunded. The result has been that rationing of resources has been introduced by the back door (that is, by departmental circular letter) and user choice risks being severely constrained as a result. This development has also had serious knock-on consequences for smaller independent providers. At the same time, the access of the voluntary sector generally to alternative sources of funds has shrunk dramatically. Recent evidence shows how far the funding pattern has become skewed in the direction of funding from government – either directly or through local authorities (Russell *et al.*, 1993; Charities Aid Foundation, 1993). This trend reflects the increased pressure on charitable trusts and the falling away of private sector support during the recession. The pattern is likely to continue in the immediate future (*Charities Aid Foundation*, 1994) and means that the small community-based organisations will be especially at risk (Williams, 1993). These changes will also affect self-help groups, operating on terrain where user and provider shade into one another and networking in order to do so. It is particularly important that this part of the sector should be protected as the likely 'seedbed' of future innovation (Hoggett and Taylor, 1993).

Some conclusions and reflections

Although the processes of change sketched in this paper are still far from complete, there are already signs that the new procedures that have been introduced over the past decade are developing their own momentum, which not even those who initiated the process – let alone those mainly affected by it – will be fully able to control. Although some large voluntary organisations have declared their intention of standing aside, most simply have no choice but to accept that they will have to participate in the contract culture and learn how to survive there, in a rapidly changing environment.

One response to this situation has been to call repeatedly for government to establish what is usually described as a 'level playing field'. That image is now almost exhausted by endless repetition; if it retains any meaning it must be that in circumstances where they will be closely accountable for their standard of performance to purchasing agencies voluntary organisations will need a full range of professional skills (as well as their distinctive strip) if they are to perform successfully on the pitch, in a potentially highly competitive environment. It should also be added that some of those for-profit bodies with whom the voluntary sector is now competing in social care have argued strongly that the pitch slopes the other way, against them.

This has led voluntary organisations to fall back on their traditional claims to embody values that are not found among their competitors – and to suggest that achieving change that benefits all citizens hinges on those values: trust, collaboration and mutual (non-monetary) exchange, whose importance is well established; all values which are exemplified by users-as-providers, but are not frequently to be found in the marketplace.

Certainly, it is arguable that the nature of transactions in the contract culture need not be adversarial and characterised by a lack of mutual commitment to common goals and limited sharing of risks or even information (Seko, 1992). There are other ways of constructing contractual relationships which recognise the particular strengths of many voluntary bodies and the multiplicity of accountabilities (and sometimes the diversity of goals) that characterise them.

The difficulty about making a special case for the voluntary sector in this way is not only the familiar one about its diversity, but also the strong suspicion that the users of the services provided by voluntary organisations may be less interested in values and traditions than in the quality of the service that they are receiving (see Taylor, this volume). Here the new relationships thrown up by the introduction of contracting may give users another point of entry: purchasers may be persuaded to act on their behalf either directly or by providing information and communicating with them through public consultation and research – processes that may by-pass voluntary sector providers (even those who profess to act as advocates for their clients).

To meet this challenge voluntary organisation contractors will need to be able to demonstrate exactly what it is that is distinctive about the character of the provision they make and how this benefits the users of their services, in minute particulars (to adopt William Blake's phrase). Meanwhile, the provisional conclusion might be that users have yet to secure much positive gain from the contract culture; that it has some potential, mostly in terms of efficiency gains providing better quality services for users-as-customers; but any benefits it might have had for users-as-citizens have not yet been realised. Which is yet another reason why the better aspects of postwar welfare (specifically, the public service tradition) should not be too lightly discarded. .

References

Arnstein, S. (1971) 'A ladder of citizen participation', *Journal of the Royal Town Planning Institute*, 57(4): 176–82.

Beveridge, Sir W. (1948) *Voluntary Action,* Allen & Unwin, London.

Bogdanor, V. (1993) 'When the buck doesn't stop here any more', *Guardian*, 14 June.

Cartwright, A. (1969) *Patients and their Doctors*, Routledge & Kegan Paul, London.

Charities Aid Foundation (1993) *Charities in Recession*, CAF, Tonbridge.

Charities Aid Foundation (1994) *Charity Trends, 1993,* 16th edn, CAF, Tonbridge.

Cole, G.D.H. (1943) *Planning for Britain*, Gollancz, London.

Common, R. , N. Flynn and D. Hurley (1993) 'Contracting for care, further developments' London School of Economics, mimeo.

Day, P. and R. Klein (1987) *Accountabilities*, Tavistock, London.

Deakin, N. (1987) *The Politics of Welfare*, Methuen, London.

Deakin, N. and A.W. Wright (1990) *Consuming Public Services*, Routledge, London.

Flynn, N. and R. Common (1992) *Contracting for Care*, Joseph Rowntree Foundation, York.

Gaster, L. (1993) *Organisational Change and Political Will*, School for Advanced Urban Studies, Bristol.

Gilmour, I. (1992) *Dancing with Dogma*, Simon & Schuster, London.

Gladstone, F. (1979) *Voluntary Action in a Changing World*, National Council for Voluntary Organisations, London.

Grant, G. (1992) 'Researching user involvement in mental handicap services' in M. Barnes and G. Wistow (eds) *Researching User Involvement*, Nuffield Institute for Health Care, Leeds.

Gutch, R. (1992) *Contracting Lessons from the US*, National Council for Voluntary Organisations, London.

Harden, I. (1992) *The Contracting State*, Open University Press, Buckingham.

Hatch, S. (1980) *Outside the State: Voluntary Organisations in Three English Towns*, Croom Helm, London.

Hedley, R. and J. Davis Smith (1993) *Review of Recent Trends in Volunteering*, Volunteer Centre UK, Berkhamsted.

Hills, J. (ed.) (1990) *The State of Welfare*, Clarendon, Oxford.

HM Government (1989) *Caring for People: Community Care in the next decade and beyond*, HMSO, Cm 849.

HM Government (1993) *The Citizen's Charter: Raising the Standard*, HMSO, London.

HM Government (1994) *The Citizen's Charter: Report Back*, HMSO, London.

Hoggett, P. and M. Taylor (1993) 'Quasi-markets and the transformation of the independent sector', paper presented to Quasi-markets Conference, Bristol, March.

House of Commons Treasury and Civil Service Select Committee (1993) *Interim Report*, HMSO, London.

Knight, B. (1993) *Voluntary Action*, Home Office, London.

Lawson, N. (1992) *The View From Number 11*, Bantam Press, London.

Le Grand, J. and W. Bartlett (1993) *Quasi-Markets and Social Policy*, Macmillan, Basingstoke.

Lewis, J. (1993) 'Developing the mixed economy of care', *Journal of Social Policy*, 22(2): 173–92.

National Consumer Council (1986) *Measuring Up: Consumer Assessment of Local Authority Services*, National Consumer Council.

Potter, J. (1988) 'Consumerism and the public sector: how well does the coat fit?' *Public Administration*, 66: 149–64.

Prior, D. *et al.* (1992) *Is the Citizen's Charter a Charter for Citizens?*, Local Government Management Board, Luton.

Richardson, J. (1994) *Reinventing Contracts*, Transatlantic perspectives on the future of contracting, NCVO, London.

Ridley, N. (1992) *My Style of Government*, Fontana, London.

Russell, L., D. Scott and P. Wilding (1993) '*Funding the Voluntary Sector: A Case Study from the North of England*,' Manchester University Department of Social Policy and Social Work.

Seebohm, F. (1968) *Report of the Committee on Local Authority and Allied Personal Social Services*, HMSO, London.

Seko, M. (1992) *Prices, Quality and Trust*, Cambridge University Press, Cambridge.

Skeffington, A. (1969) *Participation*, HMSO, London.

Stewart, J.D. (1993) *The New Magistracy*, European Policy Forum, London.

Stewart, J.D. and M. Clarke (1988) *The Enabling Local Council*, Local Government Management Board, Luton.

Taylor, M. and J. Lewis (1993) 'Contracting: What Does it do to Voluntary and Non-Profit Organisations?' paper presented to Conference on Contracting, London, July 1993.

Waldegrave, W. (1978) *The Binding of Leviathan: Conservatism and the Future*, Hamish Hamilton, London.

Waldegrave, W. (1993a) 'The Citizen's Charter', *Local Government Management*, Summer, p. 7.

Waldegrave, W. (1993b) *Speech to Public Finance Foundation*, London, July.

Williams, P. (1993) *Long-Term Funding and Support for Community Initiatives*, Gulbenkian Foundation and Save the Children Fund, London.

Wistow, G. and M. Barnes (1993) 'User involvement in community care: origins, purposes and applications', *Public Administration*, 71(3): 279–300.

9

What Kind of Leadership do Voluntary Organisations Need?

Richard Kay

Introduction

Writing in 1982, Mintzberg argued that management is what managers in the real world do, whereas leadership is an increasingly arcane concept, cultivated by academics and poorly related to any kind of practice. This view reflected widely held disillusionment of research into leadership at that time. Much of that research had been the study of the behaviour of those in leadership positions – the leader being identified as the person who had been formally designated as such. This research was usually based on positivist empiricist assumptions about how leadership can be known, and of how generalisable, lawlike relationships between variables are waiting to be discovered, for example the behaviour of the leader causing the attainment of organisational goals by followers.

Yet Kotter (1982), Bennis and Nanus (1985) and later Kouzes and Posner (1989) were arguing for a conceptual differentiation between leadership and management functions, thereby implicitly seeing both concepts as having use; whereas other writers used the concepts of management and leadership interchangeably. More recently Handy (1988) proposes that the concept of leadership is now being increasingly used in the organisational literature, rather than management, reflecting new ways of thinking about organisations – 'as societies or communities, rather than machines or warehouses' (ibid., p. 20).

Based on an interpretive approach, this chapter proposes a conceptualisation of leadership as a multi-dimensional *process* of social interaction, creating and sustaining acceptable meanings of issues, events and actions. Leaders are conceptualised as those who have involvement and influence in this leadership process. This conceptualisation differentiates the process of creating and sustaining the meanings, the interpretations, from the form and content of that meaning, which will vary. This differentiation makes sense of the varied uses of the concept of leadership by the chief executives identified in the research. Leadership as a concept is thus used in this chapter to depict a social interaction process, rather than the behaviour of a particular person, although particular skills are identified which are needed in order to participate in the leadership process. The account of leadership is developed from interpretive epistemological assumptions about the multiple, conflicting, contradictory and paradoxical meanings that can be used to make sense of our experiences, of events or issues and of the influence others can have on the creation of those meanings.

By conceptualising leadership as a multi-dimensional, sense-making, socio-political, cultural and enactment process, the concept of leadership can be separated off from *only* depicting the actions of a role-holder having formal authority, for example a manager; leadership can also be understood as involving individuals *and* teams or groups in the process of sense-making and the influencing of others over the meaning of events, issues and actions. By recognising the tentativeness and contingency of the meanings we give to our experience, since this can only be known through perspectives/conceptual frameworks, the importance of networks, both as sources of meaning and as the means of influencing the meaning others give to their experience, is pointed to. It is argued there needs to be a culture within the voluntary sector which recognises and values the multiple meanings of events, the diversity of perspectives and the development of skills, both to read these and to create order and community from this diversity.

Research into leadership

The academic approach to the study of leadership in organisations usually begins with a definition of leadership; however, as writers such as Stogdill (1974) and Yukl (1981) point out, there is a wide range of definitions. Yukl (1981) argues that the wide-ranging definitions reflect different perspectives on a multi-faceted phenomenon. Bryman (1986) points though to a measure of agreement amongst writers that leadership involves an intentional social influence process exerted by the leader over follower(s). This definition reflects the traditional focus of the research into leadership as usually the behaviour of people who hold hierarchical positions, despite some early work being undertaken on leaders who emerge in particular situations and had no formal authority.

Research into leadership in this century has followed a general pattern. There was an initial search for the personality traits of leaders; dissatisfaction with the results led to an approach which proposed that there are specifiable sets of behaviours which are the skills of leadership. Unsatisfactory results from this area of research led to the development of the contingency approach – based on the thesis that research had so far failed to reach generalisable conclusions because it did not take account of the particular circumstances within which leadership is undertaken. Disappointment with results from contingency theories encouraged Miner (1975) to propose that the concept of leadership had an uncertain future. He therefore proposed a model of influence processes which made no direct reference to leadership. Yet House wrote with more optimism, 'I would like to stress my belief that the study of leadership has yielded a number of empirically supported generalisations and a number of promising theories. I am optimistic about the future. I see promise and progress in leadership theory and research' (1988, p. 260).

Such optimism is held by Yukl (1981) who believes that over time it will be possible to reach some consensus on the definition of leadership (a true definition of leadership).

These statements by House and Yukl reflect a particular approach to social science, a positivist, empiricist approach (Burrell and Morgan, 1979).

As Hunt (1991) and Chell (1993) argue, research into leadership (including that of House (1988) quoted above) has generally assumed the positivist stance, objectifying reality (Yukl's (1981) comment about leadership being a complex, multi-faceted phenomenon follows this approach) and assuming causal connection between variables. 'Progress for these social scientists is the support of hypotheses with data systematically collected in order to measure key variables, and the identification of new relationships between variables so that further elaboration of the theory can take place' (Chell, 1993, p. 152). Leadership is thus conceptualised in deterministic and mechanistic terms, with an input of a particular behaviour of a leader influencing (causing) the output of a behaviour by followers, for example meeting organisational goals, taking account of objective contingencies.

The alternative interpretive approach is put forward by Dachler:

> The desire. . . . to evaluate scientific progress in leadership and management research takes on a different meaning within an epistemology that acknowledges explicitly the social and subjective processes of interpretation when observing reality. New leadership knowledge does not imply a search for new variables and new relationships among facts delivered by an observer independent and value free – that is, objective leadership reality. Rather it implies a search involving a systematic questioning of the processes by which we see and know (1988, p. 265).

For those writing from an interpretive perspective, no true definition of leadership is possible; the only consensus possible will be of convention of use.

Following such an interpretive approach, I argue in this chapter for an account of leadership that understands it not as some objective phenomenon, behaviour or trait external to the individual which can be measured, but as a social construct which has use to make sense of a social process, one that has use value rather than truth value. This approach recognises that not only is the researcher an interpreter of social reality, but also those depicted as leaders and followers are similarly interpreters, making sense of their reality through perspective/conceptual frameworks. As a result, the behaviour of leaders can have different meanings for the leader and followers; the leader's behaviour is made sense of subjectively by these followers. Such an approach recognises, as is argued by Rorty (1989) the contingency of our meanings, beliefs and perspectives, for 'the world is necessarily always a world under description, a world seen from a certain perspective' (Black; 1979, pp. 39–40). Paradoxically, social reality can be many things at once; an interpretive approach similarly recognises that the environment in which a leader (and others) operates is not given; the leader makes sense of her/his reality.

Thus paradoxically the leader both creates and discovers her/his reality by describing through the medium of language an object, a physical thing, an event or experience. Language is a tool to make sense of reality, rather than a mirror reflecting that reality. As Morgan (1986) argues, we engage objective reality, subjectively. Moreover the interpretive approach recognises that linguistic structures are also mental structures; we think through (by way of) language.

In line with positivist assumptions, leadership researchers have usually taken a very individualistic stance, seeing the influence of the leader as unidirectional from the leader to the followers, rather than as an interactive social influential relationship. Even Pondy's (1978) conceptualisation of leadership as the management of meaning, whilst based on an interpretive approach, can lead to an understanding of leadership only as a uni-directional, downward influencing process. This unidirectional approach ignores not only the different meanings followers can give to the behaviours of leaders, but also the part of influence in the sense-making process – how others in a network of social relations can influence the meaning others, even those in formal authority roles, give to their experience.

Studies of managers by Carlson (1951), Mintzberg (1973), Sayles (1979) and Kotter (1982) show them having contacts, dialogues and interactions with a wide range of people, particularly those over whom the manager has no formal authority, including lateral relations with people inside and outside their organisations. Interviews by Hosking and Morley (1988) with chief executives identified them as having established both external and internal relationships from whom they could gain information, to make sense of their experiences, to find out what was going on, obtain other points of view (a sense-making process) and also who could help them achieve influence (a political process). Hosking and Morley (1993) argue that making sense of a given context, in thought and action, is reflected in the relationship process between participants. Any account of leadership has to take account of this context of social relations; as well as the cultural context within which the meaning-making process is taking place.

Leadership in the voluntary sector

Methodology

The research involved interviews between 1988 and 1994 with chief executives/directors of national and regional voluntary organisations providing services directly or indirectly to children and/or young people. These were selected by nominators who occupied positions where judgements about the effectiveness of the management/leadership of voluntary organisations is required – experienced managers in the sector, members of charitable trusts or others who had extensive experience of working with chief executives of voluntary organisations. The aim of the research has been:

1. To study the sense-making of the chief executives – the interpretations they make of their experience and the metaphors used to structure those interpretations (Kay, 1992, 1994).
2. To study their conceptualisation of their effectiveness, recognising that effectiveness is a social construct and therefore can be conceptualised in many ways.
3. To develop an account of leadership in the voluntary sector.

The critical incident technique was used, with the chief executives being asked to describe two incidents where they had been particularly effective and two where they felt they had been particularly ineffective during the preceding twelve months. Not all the chief executives could recount four incidents; however a total of 148 critical incidents were recounted by the 34 chief executives (eight of these chief executives who were interviewed in 1988 were re-interviewed in 1993). All but two of the interviews were taped, and all interview transcripts analysed.

An account of leadership

Based on the research, it is argued in this chapter that leadership as a concept has use-value in describing a multi-dimensional *process* of social interaction of creating and sustaining acceptable meanings of issues, events and actions. Leadership is therefore depersonalised, as not being the property of a particular role-holder with formal position authority such as a chief executive, for leaders are conceptualised as those who are expected to have influence in this leadership process. By identifying the different dimensions of the leadership process, and the different conceptualisations of these dimensions, it is proposed that it is possible to identify the action and skills needed of the leader(s) in each dimension. It is therefore possible that paradoxically leaders may be followers, and followers may be leaders during the unfolding of this process.

The dimensions of the leadership process are conceptualised as:

1.   A social and cognitive sense-making process;
2.   A socio-political process;
3.   A cultural process;
4.   An enactment process.

1. Leadership – a social and cognitive sense-making process

A detailed analysis of the meanings the chief executives gave to their experience which influenced their actions showed a wide use of paradoxical sense-making. Examples from the statements by the chief executives are (the arrows are used as a means of depicting the complexity of the sense-making):

A   'It is about recognising people as employees, but also about recognising them as people'

  This, it is proposed, brings together two perspectives in tension shown in diagrammatic form as:

recognising people as employees ⟷ recognising them as people

B   'I agree in principle with the notion of the voluntary sector being caring people, but I have heard it all too often used as an excuse for not confronting something, nor challenging and not actually demanding efficiency'

  This, it is proposed, brings together three perspectives in tension:

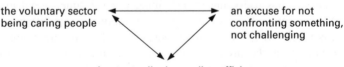

the voluntary sector being caring people ⟷ an excuse for not confronting something, not challenging

and not actually demanding efficiency

C   'Finding a way that had no resource implication, both progressing
    policy development work, and in a way that actually enhanced people's
    understanding of the issues and met an individual staff need at the
    same time – three dimensions which seemed to be economical'

Whilst the chief executive defines this as three perspectives, I would
propose it as four perspectives:

That had no resource
implications. . . .
which seemed economical

both progressing
policy development
work

enhanced people's
understanding of the issues

met an individual
staff need at the
same time

All the chief executives brought together two, three and four perspectives to make sense of their experience. The identification of
managers/leaders living with paradox is not new (see Morgan, 1986;
Vaill, 1989; Kouzes and Posner, 1989; Hickman, 1990). However,
writers tend to concentrate on managers/leaders living with only
two paradoxical perspectives. This research showed the chief executives bringing together three or four different perspectives (structured by language socially created) to make sense of their experience,
reflecting the complexity of that experience. However this sense-
making process was not carried out in individual isolation, for the
analysis of the interview transcripts shows the chief executives identifying themselves as in a network of social relations which included
the trustees, chair, staff, senior managers, project managers, service-
users, members, funders, government departments, members of the
community, local authorities, consultants and others; the actual composition of the social network varied with each incident. One of the
purposes of this network of social relations was to gain information
and others' views. Thus one chief executive said 'You can't rely
totally on your conventional management structure for your information system'; other quotations include 'the need to go round to
listen to what the prevailing issues and views are'; 'I think you
need to be looking in more than one direction to see how things are
being perceived, otherwise you are conning yourself that everyone
is with you; self-deceit is a sin in my book'; 'it is important to
have other perspectives'. It was seen as important that the perspec-
tives/meanings others in a network of social relations gave to the
event or issue were taken account of by the chief executives and

others. For example, one incident involved resolving these four perspectives:

People were saying 'We must do more health projects'	I thought that probably at a project level we were picking up health issues, but just in a sense weren't aware of it
There was a member of staff. . . . who was feeling under-used and marginalised	They had the traditional hang-ups about health professionals, which people coming from a social work background do.

It is suggested that one of the complexities of leadership in the
voluntary sector may be the wide range of different interests/per-
spectives that have to be taken into account and coped with. There
was much evidence in the research of the chief executives emphasising that one of the key things they had learned to do was to
listen to others, to take account of their views or perspectives; for
example, one chief executive said 'It would be very rare for *us*
(emphasising not just him involved in the listening, sense-making
process) to totally disregard what a manager at a lower level said'.

There was, however, also emphasis on the need to make judgements; which was often a synthesis of others' views. A number of
those interviewed made reference to the culture of the voluntary
sector being consultative, but emphasised that at the end of the day
a decision had to be made. As one chief executive said, 'If you just
listen, you are weak; if you just decide, you are autocratic'. Another
chief executive stated 'I had to say to them: I hear your judgement,
but I have to make judgements . . . I value your views and opinions
but I have to make a judgement'. The leader(s) had to create meaning of the issues or events from their own and others' multiple and
often contradictory meanings. The paradox is that the act of creating meanings involves the act of discovering, and taking account
of, the meanings others are giving to the event or issue; for leadership, it is argued, is not just creating an individual meaning but
also creating meaning acceptable to others from this diversity. To
create and sustain social order requires acceptance of meaning by
others. Thus the leader recognises the tentativeness and contingency
of her/his meaning, not only because it is a perspective but also
because it may not be a meaning acceptable to others. This reflects

the dilemma identified by the Hampden-Turner and Trompenaars (1994) 'Equality v. Hierarchy' which they argue is resolved by recognising that all potential sources of information and solutions are equal, but that there has to be a recognition of the judgement and authority of the hierarchy that is coaching and evaluating them. The emphasis on authority in this dilemma statement and the research study's focus on chief executives in formal hierarchical positions might be seen to place particular emphasis on the influencing process as an exercise of formal, downward influencing, authority. Yet the chief executives recognised the need for that meaning to be accepted by others. As one chief executive said, 'I think it was the first time I had very consciously weighed up the politics of the game, and really thinking to myself who is going to be giving my story . . . A deliberate policy of briefing the committee, the senior management team, to build a strategy with them for change in the organisation'.

2. Leadership – a socio-political process

The process just outlined supports the thesis of Smith and Peterson (1988) that the meaning-making process is a multiple-party process. The networks of social relations are seen not only as a means to gain information and knowledge of other viewpoints, but also as a means of influencing people or groups both inside and outside the organisation. Pondy (1978) argued that the dual capacity to make sense of things and put them into language meaningful to large numbers of people gives the person who has it enormous leverage. When networking is conceptualised as a political process, it is understood as being about creating and influencing commitment to particular descriptions/meanings of the person's experiences and to particular actions. Networking may again involve social relationships outside formal authority relationships.

An analysis of the transcripts of the interviews with the chief executives showed a range of images of this socio-political process; for example, 'get them to understand other people's viewpoints'; 'hearing lots of conflicting things and saying I judge we go in that direction'; 'to influence and encourage people to take a wider view'; 'selling it to our lay leaders'; 'to influence developments at the right moment when their minds are open'; 'I try to steer them towards a decision I believe sensible'; 'as a result of a lot of negotiation with the members'. This latter statement recognises that the meaning may change during the negotiation. It is therefore important to understand this political process as not always a uni-directional, downward influencing process, contrary to the dominant image in much writing of the chief executive as the single leader influencing subordinate followers. It is often a process involving a number of parties in a network of social relations influencing each other. Thus the leadership process dimension is conceptualised here as the process where one or more persons contribute to the influencing of others of the sense they make of their experience, issues and actions. Pondy's (1978) statement on making things meaningful to others also points to situations where there are not only conflicting meanings, but also the need to negotiate acceptable meanings, where there is ambiguity, uncertainty and misunderstanding.

The delicacy of this negotiation to influence the meaning of the situation and actions (and of the skills involved), are pointed to in this statement by a chief executive: 'It didn't seem as if it was going to be a success story most of the 4–5 months it took to resolve it; and at the end of the day if anybody had really dug their toes in, however much they respected what I was trying to do, if their interests looked as if they were going to be adversely affected. . . .' This statement also highlights the weakness of assuming those in authority positions always have acceptable influence over others. This was highlighted in another incident where a plan of senior managers was rejected by other managers as they stated 'We have no ownership of this, we have no understanding of this, we have no commitment to it, so you, the Director and the management team, just manage the whole thing, you must do it all yourself'.

The search is thus for a socially acceptable meaning, a meaning that will accommodate the different views/perspectives of the stakeholders involved, a negotiated order, to create order out of this diversity. The research showed a wide use of the concepts such as 'taking people with you'; 'getting people on board with you'; 'getting their commitment'.

Leadership has been differentiated from management by Kotter (1982), Kouzes and Posner (1989) and Bennis and Nanus (1985) as being about producing change, whilst management is conceptualised in terms of making organisations run smoothly, about order, predictability and constancy. In the research, all those interviewed used the journey metaphor, an image of change, as one of the metaphors they used to make sense of their experience. Kouzes and Posner propose the metaphor of the journey as the most appropriate for discussing the tasks of leaders. 'This is because the root origin of the word "lead" is "to go", denoting travel from one place to another' (1989, p. 32). Yet nearly all the chief executives, unsolicited, also emphasised the need to maintain what they described as 'the reason for being of the organisation', 'what we stand for', 'what we are about' and core process values, such as 'equality of opportunities', so emphasising constancy and stability. Depicting leadership as a *process* of influencing the creation and sustaining the meaning others give to their experience or actions enables a recognition that the form and content of the meaning created may differ as a result of the leadership process; leadership as a process may therefore paradoxically be both about change and stability. Yet there was also a recognition by a number of the chief executives that, whilst it was important to emphasise and hold on to 'the reason for being' and the 'core values' of the organisation, these were contingent and could be changed. Some of the voluntary organisations were undertaking exercises to review and change their purpose/mission statements.

There was a recurring theme in many of the chief executives' accounts of the relationship between the projects for young people, the centre and the organisation as a whole. The centre was depicted as maintaining the whole, through sustaining the core values, purpose and objectives of the organisation; while projects would look to how they could contribute to the implementation of these (work programmes to achieve these often being different). Leadership was being exercised at the centre (sustaining continuity) whilst the centre was enabling leadership to be exercised at the project level. As one chief executive said

> You needed to have a strong centre, which was about holding values and mission, what we are about; and then strong regions, who were about doing it, putting it into practice ... they both give real authority to the senior management team as leading the organisation, but they give space to people who want to be experimental, pursue particular value issues in practice and new work.

3. Leadership – a cultural process

Emphasis has been placed in this chapter on the creation and sustaining of a socially acceptable meaning. Taking a cultural perspective has value in identifying the context of the meaning-making process
and the socially acceptable means required to be undertaken to achieve
the acceptance of meaning. Thus one chief executive stated 'The
style of this organisation is one of not quite consensus but a lot of
time is spent on getting people alongside and on board with the
ideas, feeling that this is something that people would broadly welcome'. However, interviewed five years later, he recounted an incident, referred to earlier, of the rejection of a reorganisation by
managers; as he said, 'We would have shifted substantially the organisation's culture and values by just becoming rather domineer-
ing, by saying "this is it, this must be done".' Another chief executive
stated 'I had a particular role in saying we have a culture, a certain
approach; however difficult it is, we need to see it through. . . .'
There are also further examples of the sustaining of meaning, which
have been referred to earlier.

Taking a cultural perspective also points to the multiple meanings in organisation. Martin's (1992) work on cultures in organisations identifies three perspectives to study cultures: the Integrative
Perspective, with an emphasis on harmony and homogeneity; the
Differentiation Perspective that identifies different organisational
subcultures; and the Fragmentation Perspective that focuses on the
multiplicity of meanings within organisations created by 'webs of
individuals, loosely connected by their changing position on a variety of issues' (Martin, 1992, p. 153). The Fragmentation Perspective is consonant with the incidents and the meaning-making process
recounted by the chief executives in a network of social relations
loosely connected by those incidents/issues. The Integrative Perspective
points to the unsolicited theme running through many of the accounts of the chief executives of their *and* others' role in sustaining
the values/purpose/reason for being of the organisation. This sustaining of meaning introduces a fourth leadership dimension: the
Enactment Process.

4. Leadership – the enactment process

This dimension is the process of ensuring that the socially created
and accepted meanings are reflected in actions – that actions or

practices reflect the socially accepted meanings. Thus the incidents recounted included not only the negotiation of meaning, but also the negotiation and taking forward of action to reflect those meanings. The incidents also included the vetting of proposed action to see if it was consonant with the existing socially accepted meaning. Thus opportunities for new development were rejected as not being consonant with the reason for being of the organisations; and actions were challenged which were incompatible with the values of the organisation, such as equal opportunities.

The use of leadership by the chief executives

An apparent contradiction in the research was the multiple meanings given by the chief executives to the concept of leadership. The research did not involve immediately asking all the chief executives for their definition of leadership, on the grounds that these may be built on their implicit theories of leadership (McElroy, 1982). Furthermore, the research was also interested in whether the chief executives used the concept to make sense of their experience as Handy (1988) proposed is increasingly the case. However, where the chief executives did use the concept, they were asked to elaborate on their use of it in the context in which they were using it. Fifteen of the thirty-four chief executives used the concept without prompting. When asked to elaborate on their use of the concept, they differentiated leadership from management, but their definitions varied. Thus:

> 'Reinforcing the values, conveying the vision and trying to sort of shape things so they pick them up.'
> 'Setting the style, the ethos, the objectives of the project and taking people with you.'
> 'Leadership is being reasonably consistently successful in moving an organisation and teams of people in an agreed direction.'
> 'Obtaining commitment to ways of working.'
> 'Trusting you, believing in this overall vision and direction you are taking the organisation.'
> 'That group is the main leadership body contributing to the direction of the organisation and feeling some sort of ownership of it.'
> 'Setting the aims, getting ownership of them.'

The definition of leadership can be seen to be many things. These definitions, though, can be seen to contain:

1. Use of the concepts both of setting (creating) and reinforcing (sustaining);
2. The idea of taking people with you, commitment, gaining acceptance of the vision and so on;
3. The creation or sustaining of a number of meanings, that is, a vision, ethos, way of working, direction and so on;
4. The idea of leadership through a group as well as through individuals.

The apparent paradox of contradictory multiple-meanings of leadership amongst the chief executives can be resolved by accepting that:

1. Leadership as a process can be about creating *and* sustaining meaning;
2. Leadership can involve a number of people in the making and sustaining of meaning;
3. The leadership process can create multiple and varied meanings and that vision, direction and ethos are *forms* of meaning. (It has been argued elsewhere that these forms of meaning are structured by different metaphors (Kay, 1992, 1994).

A *commonality* of these definitions is the need to gain commitment, ownership, agreement to these meanings, consonant with the account of leadership in this chapter. Furthermore, the elaborations of leadership by the chief executives are, it is argued, consonant with the account of leadership developed here.

The implications for the voluntary sector

This research has focused on chief executives of voluntary organisations. Ironically, an account of leadership is developed which challenges the concept of leadership as an activity merely of an individual at the top of an organisation, for leadership is a social, not an individual activity, and involves a network of socially interacting individuals or groups. This account of leadership *does* recognise that an individual such as a chief executive of a voluntary organisation may have considerable influence in the meaning-making and sustaining process. It is also argued, however, that the meaning-making and sustaining process, the process of leadership, is a continuous process throughout and at all levels of the organisation; organisations are socially constructed, maintained and changed, and are, as this research identified, what Peckham (1985) argues to be a loose package of diversities. The weakness of the concept of leadership, a noun, is that it does not reflect this dynamic process, the word *'leading'* would be more helpful.

By conceptualising leadership as a process having four dimensions:

1. A social and cognitive sense-making process
2. A socio-political process
3. A cultural process
4. An enactment process

it is proposed that different people, conceptualised as leaders, can be involved and have influence in carrying out these four different process dimensions, the action needed to fulfil these dimensions requiring varied skills. Thus, paradoxically, during the process, leaders can be followers, and followers can be leaders.

This supports the proposal for the concept of leadership to be separated from depicting a process only involving a person in a position of formal authority, and from seeing the process only in individualistic terms – the image of the heroic leader. It is therefore seen as important that all staff and volunteer members at all levels of voluntary organisations, *and* service users, need to be enabled to exercise leadership and to develop the skills to participate in this process. For this to be effective, there will need to be an organisational culture which recognises that different meanings, perspectives, interests or values may be held by others; a non-oppressive and anti-discriminatory culture that values diversity of views, and a willingness to learn from others; yet also the recognition of the importance of a negotiated order and the creation of meanings acceptable to others. There needs therefore to be an understanding of the importance of social relations, informal and formal, within and outside voluntary organisations, to the leadership process.

Important leadership skills are seen as: reading situations from multiple perspectives; listening; managing the tensions and value of multiple viewpoints; being able to synthesise conflicting and contradictory meanings, yet also making one's own judgement when appropriate; negotiation skills; the ability to make sense to others, yet also to be prepared to be influenced by others; the need to be able to cope with flux and change, yet also recognising the value of continuity and stability. There is therefore a need to avoid a domination of the Western way of thinking of either-or to recognise the value of and-both thinking. The development of paradoxical thinking is therefore seen as important, with a move away from trying always to remove ambiguity – to learn to live with paradox. The development of paradoxical thinking can take place in formally structured training sessions, but also in individual or group supervision sessions.

Conclusion

This chapter answers the question 'What kind of leadership do voluntary organisations need?' by proposing the conceptualisation of leadership as a multi-dimensional process of social interaction, creating and sustaining acceptable meanings of issues, events and actions. It is hoped that this conceptualisation will be acceptable as a definition which has use-value, rather than truth value, and aids the understanding of the complexity and skills of the meaning-making processes within voluntary organisations. Such an account goes against the dominant theme at present in much recent organisational and management writing of the chief executive alone leading the organisation.

The emphasis in this chapter on the tentative and contingent nature of our sense-making is consonant with the values of the voluntary sector of equality of opportunity and the valuing of diversity. Yet, to develop organisations as 'societies or communities' (Handy, 1988, p. 20) requires the creation and sustaining of acceptable meaning whilst still valuing such diversity and difference. A measure of the leadership skills within the voluntary sector will be the resolving of this paradox.

References

Bennis, W.G. and B. Nanus (1985) *Leaders: The Strategies For Taking Charge*, Harper & Row, New York.

Black, M. (1979) 'More about metaphor', in A. Ortony (ed.) *Metaphor and Thought*, Cambridge University Press, New York.

Bryman, A. (1986) *Leadership and Organisation*, Routledge & Kegan Paul, London.

Burrell, G. and G. Morgan (1979) *Sociological Paradigms and Organisational Analysis*, Heinemann, London.

Carlson, S. (1951) *Executive Behaviour*, Stromberg, Stockholm.

Chell, E. (1993) *The Psychology of Behaviour in Organisations*, 2nd edn, Macmillan, Basingstoke, Hampshire.

Dachler, H.P. (1988) 'Constraints on the emergence of new vistas in leadership and Management science: an epistemological overview' in J.G. Hunt, B.R. Baliga, H.P. Dachler and C.A. Schriesheim (eds) *Emerging Leadership Vistas*, Lexington Books, Lexington MA.

Hampden-Turner, C. and F. Trompenaars (1994) *The Seven Cultures of Capitalism*, Piatkus, London.

Handy, C. (1988) *Understanding Voluntary Organisations*, Penguin, London.

Hickman, C.R. (1990) *Mind of a Manager, Soul of a Leader*, John Wiley, New York.

Hosking, D.M. and I.E. Morley (1988) 'The skills of leadership' in J.G. Hunt, B.R. Baliga, H.P. Dachler and C.A. Schriesheim (eds) *Emerging Leadership Vistas*, Lexington Books, Lexington MA.

Hosking, D.M. and I.E. Morley (1993) *A Social Psychology of Organising*, Harvester Wheatsheaf, Winchester.

House, R.J. (1988) 'Leadership research: some forgotten, ignored or overlooked findings' in J.G. Hunt, B.R. Baliga, H.P. Dachler and C.A. Schriesheim (eds) *Emerging Leadership Vistas*, Lexington Books, Lexington MA.

Hunt, J.G. (1991) *Leadership: A New Synthesis*, Sage, Newbury Park.

Kay, R.P. (1992) 'The metaphors of voluntary/non-profit sector organising', *Cranfield University School of Management Working Paper*, no.13/92.

Kay, R.P. (1994) 'The artistry of leadership', *Non-Profit Management and Leadership*, 4 (3).

Kotter, J.P. (1982) *The General Managers*, Free Press, New York.

Kouzes, J.M. and B.Z. Posner (1989) *The Leadership Challenge – How To Get Extraordinary Things Done in Organisations*, Jossey Bass, San Francisco.

Martin, J. (1992) *Cultures in Organisations: Three Perspectives*, Oxford University Press, New York.

McElroy, J.C. (1982) 'A typology of attribution leadership research', *Academy of Management Review*, 7: 413–17.

Miner, J.B. (1975) 'The uncertain future of the leadership concept: an overview' in J.G. Hunt and L.L. Larson (eds) *Leadership Frontiers*, Kent State University Press, Kent, Ohio.

Mintzberg, H. (1973) *The Nature of Managerial Work*, Harper & Row, New York.

Mintzberg, H. (1982) 'If you're not serving Bill and Ben, then you're not serving leadership' in J.G. Hunt, U. Sekaran and C.A. Schriesheim (eds) *Leadership: Beyond Establishment Views*, Southern Illinois University Press, Carbondale II.

Morgan, G. (1986) *Images of Organisations*, Sage, Beverly Hills, CA.

Peckham, M. (1985) *Romanticism and Ideology*, Penkeville, Greenwood, FI.

Pondy, L.R. (1978) 'Leadership as a language game' in M.W. McCall, Jnr., and M.M. Lombardo (eds) *Leadership: Where Else Can We Go*, Duke University Press, NC.

Rorty, R. (1989) *Contingency, Irony and Solidarity*, Cambridge University Press, Cambridge.

Sayles, L.R. (1979) *Leadership: What Effective Managers Really Do and How They Do It*, McGraw-Hill, New York.

Smith, P.B. and M.F. Peterson (1988) *Leadership, Organisations and Culture*, Sage, London.

Stogdill, R.M. (1974) *Handbook of Leadership : A Survey of Theory and Research*, Free Press, New York.

Vaill, P.B. (1989) *Managing as a Performing Art*, Jossey Bass, San Francisco.

Yukl, G.A. (1981) *Leadership in Organisations*, Prentice-Hall, Englewood Cliffs, NJ.

10

Do We Need Governing Bodies?

Margaret Harris

Raising the question

The idea that governing bodies may not be needed is now out in the open. The terminology may vary – management committees, executives, councils, trusts, boards and so on – but the underlying, provocative, question is being asked: do we really need our voluntary sector governing bodies?

Twelve years ago, when I first started doing research into management committees, the abolitionist argument could only be whispered in dark corners of pubs. I recall the shock I felt at the end of a research interview with a respected senior manager of a national voluntary agency; having answered all my questions with great seriousness, she grinned as I turned to leave and said, 'Let's face it – management committees are really bullshit.'

In research projects and workshops in the intervening years, I have heard versions of this opinion voiced on numerous occasions. Participants have argued that their agencies are dependent for their very survival on their paid staff; that governing bodies are not able to empathise with the agency's purposes or to understand its work; that they do not take seriously their responsibilities; that they are uninterested in their core policy-making task; and that their meetings are dominated by discussion of trivial issues.

These views are not confined to the staff of voluntary agencies. Members of governing bodies themselves can feel uncertain of their role, or even redundant, in the face of staff expertise, complex agency goals, and a rapidly changing environment. Recent social policy changes have exacerbated the problems experienced around the implementation of the governing body role (Billis and Harris, 1992).

Suggested responses to dissatisfaction with the performance of governing bodies vary. On the one hand, intermediary bodies and influential commentators have argued for clearer role prescriptions for governing bodies and appropriate training to raise awareness of responsibilities (NCVO/Charity Commission, 1992). Suggestions have also been made that paying board members, as in the commercial sector, would be an incentive to more effective performance (Cornwell, 1993). In the United States, the 'take your responsibilities seriously' viewpoint has given rise to a flourishing consultancy industry which includes a national advisory institute, specialist courses, publications, videotapes and satellite link-ups (Carver, 1990).

At the other extreme is the viewpoint included in Knight's (1993, p. 303) vision for the future of the new voluntary sector in the age of contracting:

> It would be possible to dismantle the voluntary management boards of many charities that appear . . . to be much more trouble than they are worth. . . . the notion of voluntary boards appears to be flawed, and it would be better to scrap them.

Between the extremes of the training and abolition arguments is a pragmatic response to the felt inadequacies of governing bodies; one which quietly marginalises governing bodies and excludes them in practice from meaningful participation in major decisions. A self-fulfilling cycle is set up in which staff do not share information with their governing bodies, who then lack the means to participate in debate or understand the agency's work. Staff take this as confirmation that there is no point in sharing information with their governing bodies and the cycle of governing body exclusion is reinforced (Harris, 1989).

The pragmatic response may be gaining ground at present, driven by staff professionalism and the impact of negotiating for contracts (Billis, 1993). Thus, I was recently consulted about a planned reorganisation of a national voluntary agency with active local members; the plans proposed that national committees elected by local branches should 'report to' senior paid staff. And in an exploratory study of the impact of contracting on local management committees (Harris, 1993a), we found voluntary sector staff who argued that contract negotiations should be conducted directly between themselves and their statutory sector counterparts, by-passing management committees who were seen as unable or unwilling to appreciate the issues and the opportunities. In some cases, statutory sector staff were actively encouraging voluntary sector staff in this.

In the face of such discontent and cynicism about the governing body role, and lack of consensus about how to respond to the difficulties, the assumption that we *need* voluntary governing bodies demands re-examination. This chapter, then, considers the fundamental issue: what purpose is served by voluntary governing bodies? It looks at the functions 'officially' allocated to governing bodies and suggests some reasons why governing bodies may in practice perform those functions inadequately. It argues that, rather than abolish or marginalise governing bodies, positive steps could be taken to explain and respond to the practical problems which surround the implementation of their role.

Since the 'voluntary sector' encompasses a mixed bag of organisations ranging from community associations and self-help groups to the big national charities, generalisations about voluntary governing bodies are inevitably open to challenge. All the same, the accumulation of negative sentiments about governing bodies suggests that we cannot avoid questions about the broad principles underlying their role.

The manifest functions of governing bodies

This part of the paper focuses on the functions 'officially' allocated to voluntary governing bodies in agency constitutions, in-house guidelines, handbooks, legal and governmental documents and so on. This is what Wilfred Brown (1965, p. 47) referred to as the 'manifest' organisational situation; the one 'formally described and displayed'.

Taking 'functions' to be broad, ongoing duties[1], and drawing on my own (Harris, 1989; Harris, 1993b) and other research in this country and in North America (Widmer, 1993), five key functions can be seen to be commonly prescribed for voluntary governing bodies.

First, the governing body is expected to be the point of final accountability for a voluntary organisation (Leat, 1988, and this volume); to take responsibility, for example, for the conduct of paid and voluntary staff and for the use of agency resources. External groups – including funders, donors, clients, purchasers of services, journalists, and regulatory authorities such as the Charity Commission – look to the governing body to 'answer for' the agency's conduct. The accountability function may entail a high public profile for one or more members of the governing body, especially if there is a crisis over, say, funding or quality of service provision. As voluntary agencies have expanded their role in welfare provision, the accountability expectations on their governing bodies have been highlighted (NCVO, 1992; Charity Commissioners, 1992). One reflection of this has been the new trend to refer to governing bodies as 'trustees' – irrespective of their formal titles or legal status (NCVO, 1994).

A second function – being the employer – is closely linked to the accountability function. As the employer of any paid staff, the governing body may be involved in performing a range of tasks including hiring and firing, discipline, monitoring of work, promotion and payment. In larger voluntary agencies many of these tasks may be delegated for day-to-day purposes to paid staff, with the governing body being closely involved only in the appointment and management of the Director. In voluntary agencies in which volunteers are involved in direct service provision, the governing body often carries an 'employer equivalent' function in relation to those volunteers.

A third function, and one to which great importance is attached in prescriptive handbooks (Carver, 1990; O'Connell, 1985), is the formulation of policy; determining how the mission, purposes and goals of the voluntary agency are set and, if appropriate, changing them in response to new circumstances. Carrying out the policy function may involve the governing body in setting priorities, developing plans and monitoring outcomes.

A fourth function is to secure and safeguard necessary resources; not only money but also premises, staff and equipment. This is a function which is particularly emphasised in North America (Houle, 1989; O'Connell, 1985), although small community groups and membership associations in this country also place emphasis on the personal involvement of governing body members in fundraising and maintenance of premises and equipment (Brophy, 1994). Responsibility for the continuity and very survival of a voluntary agency is thus placed with its governing body.

Finally, governing bodies are expected to provide a link and a buffer between a voluntary agency and its environment; a function referred to in North American literature as 'boundary spanning' (Harlan and Saidel, 1993). On the one hand, they are expected to represent the agency's activities and policies *to* the outside world; and, on the other, they are expected to bring in knowledge, pressures and opinions *from* the outside world. By occupying this unique position at the interface between an agency and its environment, it is thought that voluntary governing bodies can not only help their agencies to remain aware of need and demand in their field, but also to act as 'a mechanism that organizations can use to deal with uncertainties in their external world' (Middleton, 1987, p. 141).

Not all voluntary agencies prescribe all five of these functions for their governing bodies. And the five functions are not necessarily distinguished in this way in formal documents and training. Indeed, there is some overlap – both conceptually and practically – between the functions. For example, being the employer of agency staff may be seen as a prerequisite for performance of the accountability function. And the 'boundary spanning' function can be seen as a means through which the other four functions can be better executed[2].

The argument at this stage in the chapter, then, is not that these five functions are necessarily distinct in theory or practice, but that they can be seen as the principles underlying the 'official' or public statements of voluntary agencies about the role of their governing bodies. They constitute, in effect, the case *for* voluntary governing bodies.

This is a case which has been 'heard' well beyond the agencies themselves. The assumption that voluntary governing bodies perform these functions lies behind much of the rhetoric about 'active citizenship' (Kearns, 1992) and about the important contribution made by charity trustees to 'meeting society's needs' (Prime Minister's Office, 1991). It is also reflected in a range of legal requirements and obligations (George, 1989; NCVO, 1992).

The functions in practice

Comparing these five manifest functions of governing bodies with the dissatisfactions about their performance presented earlier, it seems

that much of the disillusion is rooted in perceptions that, *in practice*, many governing bodies do not perform the functions officially
prescribed for them, or do so in an inadequate fashion (Bradshaw,
Murray and Wolpin, 1992; Brophy, 1994; Harris, 1989; Kearns, 1990).
To use Brown's (1965, p. 48) terminology again, there is a lack of
'consistency' between the 'manifest' and the 'assumed' situation.
What, then, is the reason for this gap between official statements
and what happens in practice?

Sometimes the gap is due to ignorance. Members of governing
bodies can be unaware of functions which have been allocated to
them in official statements and in law (Ford, 1992; Siciliano and
Spiro, 1992). Or they can be misled by 'the lure of the corporate
model' (Hodgkin, 1993) into thinking that the paid Director or Chief
Executive Officer can be left to carry out all key functions. Or they
may assume that the functions officially allocated to the governing
body are no more than a 'ceremonial conformity' (Meyer and Rowan,
1991, p. 41); that the board members will never, in practice, be
called upon to implement them (Harris, 1989).

It is quite possible for governing bodies to remain ignorant of
their functions because in many voluntary agencies – particularly
those with professional paid staff, those which are members of a
strong national body, or those which have long enjoyed secure funding
– the importance of the functions may not be apparent on a day-to-
day basis. It becomes apparent only when a crisis occurs such as a
threat to funding, financial mismanagement, resignation of the paid
director, a shift in public policy, or a major failure in the quality of
service (Billis, this volume; Collins, 1993; Humphrey, 1991).

Another explanation for the gap between manifest statements and
practice emerges from studies of the way in which governing bodies
interact with paid and volunteer staff (Harris, 1993b). These studies
suggest that the governing body role is not susceptible to implementation in isolation from other organisational roles; rather the
role is better understood as being 'contingent' (Kramer, 1985) and
'interdependent' with the role of staff (Harris, 1989; Herman, 1989).
Thus the extent to which members of the governing body are aware
of their official functions may be dependent on the extent to which
staff see themselves as having a responsibility to 'develop' and inform
their own governing body (Feek, 1982). Similarly, the extent to which
they are able to perform their official functions may be dependent
on what staff are 'prepared to allow' (Platt *et al.*, 1985, p. 30).

A further corollary of the contingent nature of the governing body role is that the enthusiasm and competence with which the role is performed can change frequently. The relationship between governing bodies and staff – and particularly the relationship between the voluntary chairperson and the paid agency director – is by nature 'dynamic'; open to constant negotiation and renegotiation (Conrad and Glenn, 1983; Harris, 1993b; Middleton, 1987). The relationship can change not only as different persons with different organisational perceptions occupy the roles, but also in response to shifting environmental influences (Alexander, Fennell and Halpern, 1993). In these circumstances, the chances are increased that governing bodies – at least from time to time in an agency's history – will 'fail' to understand or execute functions which are 'officially' expected of them.

The accumulating body of research on governing bodies suggests a third possible explanation for the gap between practice and the manifest statements about governing body functions; an explanation which relates to the organisational structures of service-providing voluntary agencies and one which focuses on the power relationships established within voluntary agencies between governing bodies and other key groupings.

Governing body power

In this part of the chapter it is suggested that the ability of voluntary governing bodies (B) to carry out the functions prescribed for them may be affected by the power which they are able to exercise in relation to other key groupings in their agency. These groupings are:

- staff (paid and/or voluntary) (S);
- clients (beneficiaries) (C); and
- the 'guardians' of the agency (those who have a positive concern for the long-term survival of the agency and its purposes, who may include founders, funders, former members or former clients) (G).

Our research suggests that the 'pattern' or 'model' of interaction amongst these four groupings varies between voluntary agencies

(Harris, 1993c). Three examples of how different models may have different implications for the way in which a governing body is able to implement its official functions in service-providing voluntary agencies, are given here.

1. The traditional model

One model of interaction between the four key groupings is well established and well understood within the voluntary sector. In the Traditional Model, the groupings relate to each other in a simple linear fashion. There is a chain which begins with a vision of need and ends with the provision of a service which responds to that need via a group of staff (Billis, 1989).

Figure 10.1

The governing body (B) is seen as representing, or reflecting the views of, the guardians of the agency (G). The legitimacy of the governing body derives from the understanding that it has been 'entrusted' by the agency's guardians (Smith, 1992). At the same time, it is the employer of one or more members of staff (S). The staff, in turn, deliver services to consumers or beneficiaries (C) of the agency.

This model mirrors the form of charitable organisation established by nineteenth-century philanthropists and social activists, who had a desire to respond to a perceived social need, a vision of how to do so, and the ability to mobilise the necessary resources. Such people would appoint, elect, or themselves become, the governing body of an organisation which would, in its turn, recruit and control one or more service-delivering staff – paid or voluntary. These staff then provided services for 'patients', 'orphans', 'deserving poor' or other beneficiaries.

Although it is now relatively rare in the UK for agencies to be started by private philanthropists, it is not uncommon for new agencies to be started according to the Traditional Model, with old-style philanthropic 'guardians' being replaced by charismatic personalities: umbrella organisations which 'float off' projects as free-standing voluntary agencies; national federations which 'foster' new local groups; and local authority departments which encourage the development of agencies with whom they can enter into service-providing contracts.

Voluntary agencies which work according to this model – that is, agencies in which key groupings are in broad agreement that this is the way in which they are linked to each other – provide a framework which facilitates governing bodies fulfilling the functions officially ascribed to them. Thus, the governing body's position as the point of final accountability is emphasised by the linear chain. And the clear link it has with the agency's guardians gives the governing body credibility in policy discussions, in soliciting resources, and in representing the agency to the outside world.

2. The membership model

A second model, the Membership Model, differs from the Traditional Model in an important respect: the chain forms a closed circle. There is a clear and intentional link between the agency's consumers (C) and its guardians (G). As in the Traditional Model, the governing body appoints staff to deliver a service. However, the beneficiaries are not 'third parties', but the 'guardians' themselves. This is a model which frequently operates in membership associations, mutual aid groups and consumer-led voluntary welfare agencies.

Figure 10.2

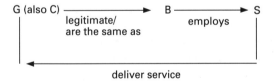

The comparative clarity of the linear links in the Traditional Model, which imply a high degree of governing body power and therefore the ability to execute prescribed functions, do not apply in Membership Model agencies. Beneficiaries have a direct link to the governing body, and thence to control of the staff.

This situation might be expected to strengthen the power of the governing body, since it is in a position to monitor and evaluate the quality of the work done by its staff through direct experience. However, trained staff, such as social workers and nurses, may resent the threat to their ability to exercise professional judgements which is implicit in a situation in which 'clients' are also employers and managers. Such staff may confront their governing bodies over who has the right to determine what is in the best interests of beneficiaries, or what is an 'authentic' interpretation of the agency's purposes.

A second possible counter-influence to governing body power lies in the close link in the Membership Model between guardian/beneficiaries on the one hand and staff on the other hand. Where the two groups are in close and frequent contact, they can find ways of working which meet their own needs satisfactorily, but in which governing body involvement is perceived as unnecessary or intrusive. If both the staff and the beneficiaries are contented, what need is there to consult the governing body?

Thus, in agencies working according to a Membership Model, governing bodies may find it difficult to perform their prescribed functions. If they cannot control staff, they are not in a position to take final responsibility for the quality of the agency's work or the safeguarding of its resources. And if other key groups in the agency feel that the governing body is redundant and make a collective effort to exclude it from policy-making and other aspects of the agency's work, the ability of the governing body to act as a credible boundary spanner is diminished.

3. The entrepreneur model

Newer voluntary agencies may work with a pattern which is closer to a third model, the 'Entrepreneur Model'. As in Traditional and Membership Model agencies, the guardians have a vision of an agency responding to an identified social need. Also as in the Traditional Model, there is a linear link between the guardians, the governing body and the staff. The crucial difference is that the guardians comprise entrepreneurial practitioners who are personally employed in delivering the agency's outputs. Thus, as in the Membership model, guardians have a dual role in the agency. In this case, they are not only 'sponsors', but also agency staff.

Figure 10.3 indicates how the ability of governing bodies to influence, manage or control staff in agencies operating according to

Figure 10.3

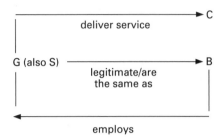

the Entrepreneur Model can be even more circumscribed than in Membership Model agencies. Their employees are also the agency's guardians: the people to whom they owe their very existence as a governing body. Moreover, the ability of the agency to attract outside funding may be largely dependent on the energies and public relations efforts of the guardian/employees (Rock, 1988).

In such circumstances, the power of the governing body to perform its prescribed functions can be radically curtailed. The fundraising capacity and root enthusiasm for the survival of the agency is located in the guardian/staff group. The governing body cannot, therefore, act as an effective resource procurer or boundary-spanner. Since it has limited control over the staff, it can perform neither the employer nor the accountability functions effectively. The extent of its involvement in policy will be determined by the guardian/employees.

Two comments from research with staff of Entrepreneurial agencies illustrate the difficulties faced by governing bodies in such circumstances. One member of staff, a paid manager who was also one of the small group who founded the agency, thought that

The staff just don't need the management committee.

Another senior manager summarised the role of his governing body as follows:

The committee has difficulty in defining its role.... They don't own the organisation.... It's dominated by staff.... It's like a support group for the staff.

These views can be contrasted with the perspective of a former trustee of an Entrepreneurial Model agency who reflected how the governing body had been

> prickly and defensive and lacking any real willingness to be accountable ... we, the trustees, had no control. ... [The staff] resisted any attempts to control or supervise their work. ... Not surprisingly trustees got bored and de-motivated.

Some implications for practice

In this paper, five key 'official' functions of voluntary governing bodies have been identified. It has been suggested that the question of whether governing bodies are needed is grounded in the observation that, in practice, they may fail to perform those functions adequately.[3] Drawing on empirical research studies, three explanations have been offered for this gap between manifest statements and practice: ignorance and optimism about prescribed functions; the contingent nature of the governing body role in relation to staff; and the fact that the power of governing bodies in relation to other key agency groupings can vary because voluntary agencies operate according to different organisational models.

If voluntary governing bodies fail to perform the functions we expect of them, we can take a passive approach and connive in their marginalisation and even abolition. However, the five key functions are sufficiently weighty to justify a more positive, developmental approach. Moreover, the three research-based explanations provide a starting point for such a pro-active approach; an approach which seeks to respond to the complex practical problems which governing bodies face in the implementation of their role.

In this context, training and education are relevant; where members of governing bodies are unaware of their prescribed functions, training could be useful. However, research suggests that the 'target group' for such training needs careful consideration.

Up to now, training advocates have generally focused on members of governing bodies themselves. But research evidence suggests that voluntary and statutory sector staff, as well as politicians, can also be ignorant about the functions of governing bodies and that they can contribute to the practical difficulties which arise in the implementation of the governing body role. Moreover, the implementation of that role is, in practice, interdependent with the role of other key groupings. Thus training which focuses on the role of governing bodies in isolation from other roles is likely to have limitations. Courses attended by 'pairs' of staff and governing body members, for example, may provide a better forum for open discussion and encourage a 'partnership' approach to tackling problems.

The content of training also needs careful consideration. Training which concentrates on the technical aspects of being a member of a governing body – running meetings, conforming with employment law, monitoring service quality, keeping accurate accounts, and so on – is unlikely to be effective unless it is also rooted in an explanation of the important broader functions of governing bodies. It is the understanding of these distinctive functions which can motivate people to serve on a voluntary governing body in the first place (Harris, 1990) and encourage them to undertake training.

Research also suggests that sensitivity is needed in approaching governing bodies about training. Since members of voluntary sector governing bodies give their time freely, we cannot lose sight of the fact that they have a choice about how they use their leisure time. As Davis Smith argues elsewhere in this volume, the fact that people are volunteers has important practical implications. For example, insistence that members of governing bodies attend courses, or an authoritarian approach to how they 'must' perform their functions, could de-motivate them (Harris, 1993a; Hedley and Rochester, 1992) or encourage them to commit their time instead to the increasing number of boards in the governmental and quasi-governmental sector; the 'governors' and 'trustees' of schools, hospitals and other public services.

Thus, training – provided it is sensitive and appropriate with respect to target groups, content and approach – would be one appropriate response to the practical problems surrounding the implementation of the voluntary governing body role. But it cannot provide all the answers. As the presentation of the power models demonstrates, when governing bodies fail to perform expected key functions, the cause may be deeper than ignorance about formal responsibilities. The underlying structure of some voluntary agencies may be such that governing bodies just do not carry the power necessary to perform prescribed functions (Harris, 1993c).

In such cases, organisational consultancy of a non-judgemental, collaborative kind, involving all the key groupings within the agency, may facilitate discussion within voluntary agencies about available organisational choices and the implications of each. The experience of the Centre for Voluntary Organisation suggests, for example, that members of governing bodies and their staff can often work together productively in tackling questions about the boundaries of their respective roles, when they are offered a framework which recognises the interdependence of their roles and does not imply that there is one 'best' answer (Harris, 1993b).

Finally, we can speculate that the efficacy of both the training and consultancy responses to the practical problems surrounding the governing body role would be enhanced if greater public recognition were given to the valuable role which can be played by members of voluntary governing bodies. In fact, the question of whether we *need* our governing bodies opens up the much broader question of what value we attach to our voluntary sector. Do we wish to preserve the distinctive features for which the sector has been traditionally valued (Young, 1991); or are we prepared to accept what Billis (1993) has described as a 'slide into change', in which key features of voluntary agencies, including their governing bodies, are devalued and eroded?

Notes

1. In this paper, the term 'functions' is used to refer to duties 'prescribed for a particular position within an organisation' (SSORU, 1974, p. 257). Functions are broad 'ends or purposes' (p. 59) which are ongoing and open-ended, 'in contrast to "tasks" which imply some specific objective and time limit' (p. 257). It is argued that the five functions distinguished in this paper are commonly ascribed to voluntary governing bodies. The tasks which may be entailed in the performance of any one function will, however, vary between voluntary agencies.
2. I am grateful to Winifred Tumin who contributed this insight during discussions at the CVO 15th Anniversary Conference. She explained: 'I am a "better" trustee if I bring knowledge and experience of the wider world to bear on my "core" duties.'
3. I do not intend to overstate the case. There are, as the Anniversary Conference participants emphasised, numerous examples of energetic and creative voluntary governing bodies who perform their expected functions and who are not subject to criticisms of the kind discussed in this paper.

References

Alexander, J., M. Fennell, and M. Halpern (1993) 'Leadership instability in hospitals: the influence of board–CEO relations and organizational growth and decline', *Administrative Science Quarterly*, 38: 74–99.

Billis, D. (1989) *A Theory of the Voluntary Sector: Implications for Policy and Practice*, Working Paper no. 5, Centre for Voluntary Organisation, London School of Economics, London.

Billis, D. (1993) *Sliding into Change: The Future of the Voluntary Sector in the Mixed Organisation of Welfare*, Working Paper no. 14, Centre for Voluntary Organisation, London School of Economics, London.

Billis, D. and M. Harris (1992) 'Taking the strain of change: UK local voluntary agencies enter the post-Thatcher period', *Nonprofit and Voluntary Sector Quarterly*, 21(3): 211–25.

Bradshaw, P., V. Murray and J. Wolpin (1992) 'Do nonprofit boards make a difference? An exploration of the relationships among board structure, process and effectiveness', *Nonprofit and Voluntary Sector Quarterly*, 21(3): 227–49.

Brophy, J. (1994) 'Parent management committees and pre-school playgroups', *Journal of Social Policy*, 23(2): 161–94.

Brown, W. (1965) *Exploration in Management*, Penguin, Harmondsworth.

Carver, J. (1990) *Boards that Make a Difference*, Jossey Bass, San Francisco.

Charity Commissioners (1992) *Charities – The New Law: A Trustees' Guide to the Charities Act 1992*, Charity Commissioners for England and Wales, London.

Collins, C. (1993) *Struggling to Survive: Four Voluntary Organisations' Experience of Losing Funding*, Case Study no. 6, Centre for Voluntary Organisation, London School of Economics, London.

Conrad, W. and W. Glenn (1983) *The Effective Voluntary Board of Directors*, Swallow Press, Ohio.

Cornwell, A. (1993) 'Not a Job for Amateurs?', *Third Sector*, 4 November, p. 6.

Feek, W. (1982) *Management Committees – Practising Community Control*, National Youth Bureau, Leicester.

Ford, K. (1992) *Trustee Training and Support Needs*, National Council for Voluntary Organisations, London.

George, P. (1989) *Making Charities Effective: A Guide for Charities and Voluntary Bodies*, Jessica Kingsley, London.

Harlan, S. and J. Saidel (1993) 'Nonprofit boards of directors in third-party government', paper presented to the *Association for Research on Nonprofit Organizations and Voluntary Action*, Toronto, Canada.

Harris, M. (1989) 'The governing body role: problems and perceptions in implementation', *Nonprofit and Voluntary Sector Quarterly*, 18(4): 317–23.

Harris, M. (1990) 'Voluntary leaders in voluntary welfare agencies', *Social Policy and Administration*, 24(2): 156–67.

Harris, M. (1993a) 'Voluntary management committees: the impact of contracting', paper presented to the Conference *Contracting – Selling or Shrinking*? London, NCVO / South Bank University.

Harris, M. (1993b) 'Exploring the role of boards using total activities analysis', *Nonprofit Management and Leadership* 3(3): 269–82.

Harris, M. (1993c) *The Power and Authority of Governing Bodies*, Working Paper no. 13, Centre for Voluntary Organisation, London School of Economics, London.

Hedley, R. and C. Rochester (1992) *Understanding Management Committees*, Volunteer Centre UK, Berkhamsted.

Herman, R. (1989) 'Board functions and board–staff relations in nonprofit organizations: an introduction', in R. Herman and J. Van Til (eds) *Nonprofit Boards of Directors*, Transaction, New Jersey.

Hodgkin, C. (1993) 'Policy and paper clips: rejecting the lure of the corporate model', *Nonprofit Management and Leadership*, 3(4): 415–28.

Houle, C. (1989) *Governing Boards*, Jossey Bass, San Francisco.

Humphrey, R. (1991) *Closed Down*, Case Study no. 4, Centre for Voluntary Organisation, London School of Economics, London.

Kearns, A. (1990) *Voluntarism, Management and Accountability*, University of Glasgow, Centre for Housing Research, Glasgow.

Kearns, A. (1992) 'Active citizenship and urban governance', *Transactions of the Institute of British Geographers, New Series*, 17: 20–34.

Knight, B. (1993) *Voluntary Action*, Home Office, London.

Kramer, R. (1985) 'Towards a contingency model of board–executive relations', *Administration in Social Work*, 9(3): 15–33.

Leat, D. (1988) *Voluntary Organisations and Accountability*, National Council for Voluntary Organisations, London.

Meyer, J. and B. Rowan (1991) 'Institutionalized organizations: formal structure as myth and ceremony', in W. Powell and P. Dimaggio (eds) *The New Institutionalism in Organizational Analysis*, University of Chicago Press, Chicago.

Middleton, M. (1987) 'Nonprofit boards of directors: beyond the governance function' in W. Powell (ed.) *The Nonprofit Sector: A Research Handbook*, Yale University Press, New Haven.

NCVO (1992) *The Charities Act 1992: A Guide for Charities and Other Voluntary Organisations*, National Council for Voluntary Organisations, London.

NCVO (1994) *The Good Trustees Guide*, National Council for Voluntary Organisations, London.

NCVO/Charity Commission (1992) *On Trust: Increasing the Effectiveness of Charity Trustees and Management Committees*, National Council for Voluntary Organisations, London.

O' Connell, B. (1985) *The Board Member's Book*, The Foundation Center, New York.

Platt, S., J. Powell, R. Piepe, B. Paterson and J. Smyth (1985) *Control or Charade?* Portsmouth Polytechnic, Portsmouth.

Prime Minister's Office (1991) 'Text of a speech made by the Prime Minister the Rt Hon John Major to the *Charities Aid Foundation* at the Queen Elizabeth II Conference Centre on Tuesday 5 November 1991', Press Office, Downing Street, London.

Rock, P. (1988) 'On the birth of organisations', *LSE Quarterly*, Summer: 123–53.

Siciliano, J. and G. Spiro (1992) 'The unclear status of nonprofit directors: an empirical survey of director liability', *Administration in Social Work*, 16(1): 69–80.

Smith, D.H. (1992) 'Moral responsibilities of trustees: some first thoughts', *Nonprofit Management and Leadership*, 2(4): 351–62.

SSORU (Social Services Organisation Research Unit) (1974) *Social Services Departments*, Heinemann, London.

Widmer, C. (1993) 'Role conflict, role ambiguity, and role overload on boards of directors of nonprofit human service organizations', *Nonprofit and Voluntary Sector Quarterly*, 22(4): 339–56.

Young, K. (1991) *Meeting the Needs of Strangers: Voluntary Action in a Changing World*, Gresham College, London.

11

Are Voluntary Agencies Really More Effective?

Martin Knapp[1]

Introduction

> Why should we be in such a desperate haste to succeed, and in such desperate enterprises? If a man does not keep pace with his companions, perhaps it is because he hears a different drummer (Henry David Thoreau, 1817–1862).

Are voluntary agencies really more effective? The breadth of this question demands immediate clarification. First, voluntary agencies are defined here as formally constituted, self-governing, private entities, not distributing profits to any owners, and benefiting from voluntarism. These criteria define a sector which includes registered, exempted and excepted charities in England and Wales (and their equivalents elsewhere in the UK), plus many non-charity bodies (such as self-help groups, housing associations, universities and friendly societies), but excludes co-operatives and those 'not-for-profit' agencies which are merely extensions of public authorities.[2] Second, the chapter works with a catholic interpretation of *effectiveness* – including equity and efficiency – and seeks to bring a number of perspectives to bear. Third, for the good reasons of familiarity and comparative advantage and the bad reason of pressure on space, most examples and evidence are drawn from community care.

Community care – framework for effectiveness

It is helpful to use the mixed economy of care framework, both to describe community care and, more importantly, to introduce issues concerning effectiveness. Cross-classification of provider and purchaser types – producer (or supply) and funder (or demand) types – produces a multi-celled schema which can be employed to locate service configurations and transaction types (Table 11.1), and to identify policy options (Table 11.2).[3] This chapter obviously concentrates mainly on the *voluntary sector*. The definitions of the provider types should be self-evident; the definitions of purchasing routes will become clear later. Although it is a stylised description of the myriad inter-relationships between supply and demand, the matrix reminds us of the broader practice and policy contexts within which voluntary organisations operate. In its three-dimensional hologram version – not available in this book because of technical difficulties – the mixed economy matrix also incorporates a dimension representing the mediating links between providers and purchasers, including brokerage, health insurance, care management and regulation.

The voluntary sector's contributions to health and social care are dissimilar. In social care there are a number of large, long-established, highly respected charities. They are particularly active in the direct provision of care, and in some locales they are the main providers of, for example, services for abused children, and people with physical, learning and sensory disabilities. Provision of some services – such as for people with multiple sensory impairments – is dominated *nationally* by the voluntary sector. Many voluntary organisations have impressive networks of local branches.

Many of these organisations are heavily dependent on government funding. For the UK as a whole, the proportions of total income coming from government in 1990 were high for each main user group sub-sector: children and families (43 per cent), elderly people (40 per cent), people with physical or sensory impairments (40 per cent), people with learning disabilities (73 per cent) and multiple user groups (59 per cent) (Kendall and Knapp, 1995). These percentages exclude demand-side social security payments to service users. In addition, central government funding of health and social services voluntary organisations amounted to £363 million in 1990, equivalent to 8 per cent of total income.

Many community care voluntary organisations are deeply embedded

Table 11.1 *The mixed economy matrix social care examples*

Purchase, demand or funding	Provision or supply of services			
	Public sector	*Voluntary sector*	*Private sector*	*Informal sector*
Coerced collective demand	Local authority field social work services	Contracted-out day care	Publicly funded placements in private residential homes	Foster family care for children funded by SSD
Uncoerced or voluntary collective demand	Voluntary organisation payments for public sector training programmes	Self-help group paying for expert advice from larger voluntary organisation	Purchases of goods and services by Mind or Age Concern	Foster family placements arranged and funded by Barnardo's
Corporate demand	Private residential home payments for LA registration and inspection	Corporate donations to charities	Private nursing home purchases of food, electricity, etc.	Employers' payments for employees' childminding
Uncompensated individual consumption	User charges for LA home help support	Parental payments for pre-school day care	Payment for private residential care by family or resident	Private childminder services
Compensated individual consumption	LA residential home fees backed up by pensions	Board and lodging payments to voluntary homes	Housing benefit and other user subsidies for private housing	Purchases from community care grants
Individual donation (for use by others)	Volunteers working in LA intermediate treatment unit	Donations to the Children's Society or Mencap	Volunteers in private residential homes	Intra-family transfers of resources and care

169

Table 11.2 *The mixed economy matrix: policy examples*

Purchase, demand or funding	Provision or supply of services			
	Public sector	*Voluntary sector*	*Private sector*	*Informal sector*
Coerced collective demand	Welfare state	Contracting out		Support for carers
Uncoerced or voluntary collective demand	National lottery			
Corporate demand		Encouragement of corporate philanthropy		
Uncompensated individual consumption	User charges for public services		Textbook markets	
Compensated individual consumption		User-financed long-term care insurance		
Individual donation (for use by others)		Tax incentives for charitable donations		Reinforcement of the family

in local statutory decision-making networks, both overtly (through community care planning) and otherwise (via overlapping committees or boards). Some local authorities continue to express reservations about them (Wistow *et al.*, 1994), while others allocate significant sums in grants or contracts to the voluntary sector (Taylor *et al.*, 1993). Many voluntary social services organisations are widely perceived by users and carers to be part of the community care mainstream, yet most would hope that they are also perceived by the donating public to have retained an ability to pioneer new service developments and to campaign for change. Alongside the large, national bodies are the many small, local social care organisations, running just one or two facilities.

By contrast, the voluntary sector is a comparatively minor provider of mainstream health care. The establishment of the National Health Service (NHS) sounded the death-knell for many voluntary hospitals, and others were absorbed into the public sector. Today, the sector's major contributions can be seen in hospice provision and other care for terminally ill people, health promotion, alternative medicine, medical research, and nursing home and other long-term care. The sector receives a comparatively small proportion of its income from statutory sources. In Liverpool, for example, 73 per cent of the annual income of social services organisations in 1990 came from central or local government, compared to 58 per cent for mental health organisations and 28 per cent for 'other health' organisations (Shore *et al.*, 1994). Nationally, about a quarter of the voluntary health care sector's income in 1990 came from government (Kendall and Knapp, 1995).

There have been many important changes to the mixed economy of community care over the last forty years, but none is as significant as those introduced by the 1990 NHS and Community Care Act (see Lewis, this volume). Health and social care were identified by the 1979 Thatcher Government as in need of reform, but were among the last of the major areas of public policy to receive legislative attention. The 1990 Act might justifiably be seen as introducing some of the most interesting and threatening challenges for the voluntary sector for some years. On the health side, the Government's commitment to health gain provides opportunities for many voluntary organisations to move from a somewhat marginalised position to centre stage. But there are few voluntary sector hospitals; the demand for private health insurance supplied by BUPA and other voluntary sector bodies has reached a plateau, albeit perhaps only temporarily; and there do not appear to be long queues of private sector firms waiting for opportunities to develop acute care provision.

In social care, it is the new 'enabling' and co-ordinating roles for local government which raise the greatest challenges. The mixed economy is also increasingly dominated by market forces, with local authority support for voluntary bodies more likely to be routed through tightly specified contracts than through general grant aid (Taylor *et al.*, 1993; Osborne and Waterston, 1994). Voluntary sector complaints about the new 'contract culture' have rather confused the move from grants to contracts with the promotion of competition. The former is much less threatening than the latter, for the private sector has shown its ability to respond quickly to new market opportunities in its rapid expansion in residential and nursing home provision in the 1980s. Nevertheless, the introduction of more specific contracts and local government realisation that it has enormous bargaining power in some service areas could leave some organisations vulnerable to loss of autonomy (Forder and Knapp, 1993; Lewis, 1993; and the chapters by Deakin, Lewis and Taylor in this volume). A second relevant trend is the move away from reliance on residential and nursing home provision to domiciliary care, in the anticipated interests of economy and user welfare, coupled with various short-term requirements (such as the '85 per cent rule' governing the Special Transitional Grant: Wistow *et al.*, 1994). This trend offers opportunities to voluntary organisations specialising in, or diversifying into, day, domiciliary or respite care, and in supporting carers.

After a comparatively lean period in the 1950s and 1960s, therefore, the UK voluntary health and social care sectors have more recently received considerable encouragement from central government, and from some local authorities. The relative contribution of the sector to gross domestic product and its 'market share' in some parts of the economy have grown significantly, but have also brought problems. In particular, they pose questions about effectiveness.

The production of welfare and effectiveness

The discussion of voluntary sector effectiveness has often been tackled by examining a number of supposed benefits which the sector confers. For example, a number of 'rationales' have been given for government funding of the sector, including assumed comparative advantages in terms of cost-effectiveness, choice, flexibility, innovation, participation by users and other citizens, campaigning and advocacy.[4] Examination of UK evidence concerning the assumptions behind these rationales a few years ago uncovered relatively little empirical support beyond the anecdote (Knapp *et al.*, 1990; and see below). What was clear, however, was that increases in government funding for the voluntary sector, especially in the form of contracts, could well threaten the very advantages which central and local government either assumed or sought to promote. Thus, a cost-effective service may become relatively less cost-effective if more public funding is received; a flexible response to a social problem may be less flexible once public authorities try to purchase that flexibility through contracts; and diversity, autonomy and specialisation could be reduced by the standardising tendencies of formalised contractual links between the sectors.

Discussions or assertions of this kind demand some unpacking of the definition of effectiveness. There are a number of ways to 'deconstruct' effectiveness, and the context within which this is undertaken will have some bearing. It is helpful to concentrate on community care, and to use the *production of welfare* framework. We can distinguish: the *resource inputs* to community care, mainly staff (paid and volunteer); capital and consumables; *costs*, the resource inputs expressed in monetary terms; the *non-resource inputs*, which are those influences on outcomes which do not have an identifiable price or are not currently marketed; the *intermediate outcomes*, which are services of a given quality, weighted for user characteristics or 'casemix', produced by combinations of resource and non-resource inputs; and the *final outcomes*, which are changes in the health, welfare and quality of life of service users and their carers, relative not only to their circumstances at the start of care but preferably also relative to some comparison group or norm (Davies and Knapp, 1981; Knapp, 1984).

Based on the production of welfare framework, we can define effectiveness broadly to mean the achievement of goals specified in terms of each of these input, cost and outcome dimensions. Different goals will probably be chosen by different actors in the care system: carers may have different aims from users, who in turn may have different priorities from care agencies (see Deakin in this volume). Health and social services authorities may disagree quite fundamentally on strategic policy aims. Policy and practice goals could also be expressed in terms of the linkages between component elements of this framework. Retaining a broad front, effectiveness can be interpreted to encompass different interpretations of efficiency and equity (justice), as well as criteria such as autonomy, liberty and diversity.

Alternative perspectives on effectiveness

Effectiveness in its broader or narrower sense is in the eye of the beholder. There are numerous stakeholders within and surrounding the voluntary sector, each with their own criteria of effectiveness – each hearing their own different drummers, in Thoreau's terms. If we return to the mixed economy matrix, we can see a number of (overlapping and interdependent) perspectives on voluntary sector effectiveness, in particular those of the public sector, the voluntary sector itself, users and volunteers.

Coerced collective demand – the public sector perspective

Coerced collective purchasing or demand involves the government as purchaser on behalf of individuals or groups of citizens, mandated by the electoral process. Central government and most local authorities are increasingly seeing the voluntary sector as an important instrument or vehicle of community care policy. NHS purchasers, on the other hand, are not so likely to view the voluntary sector in this light, although the advent of the internal NHS market makes it more likely that *external* markets will develop.

Central government's main objectives for community care are threefold: easing the transition to the new arrangements; promoting independent living outside of institutional settings; and encouraging private and voluntary sector providers. Overlaying these aims are various political, social and economic agenda, not necessarily mutually consistent (Wistow *et al.*, 1995). The encouragement of the non-statutory sectors is linked to the government's core aims of greater choice, flexibility, innovation and cost-effectiveness (Secretaries of State, 1989a). Similar sentiments prompted the health service reforms, with the government arguing that the 'independent sector' brings the advantages of wider choice for patients and general practitioners, cost-effectiveness, and a flexible and rapid response to patients' needs (Secretaries of State, 1989b).

But is there evidence to support these government assumptions about the comparative effectiveness of the voluntary sector? It is clear that rhetoric has run ahead of reality. Consider, for example, the core aims of choice, flexibility and cost-effectiveness.

1. Choice

The voluntary sector is first-choice provider for many people because of its distinctive orientation, ideology or quality of service, a consequence in part of its autonomy and opportunity to tailor services to satisfy different preferences or needs. Central government certainly encourages provider pluralism in the belief that choice confers benefits on service users, and specialist roles for the voluntary sector are promoted when central or local government is the purchaser. There are numerous examples of this specialist role in community care (Kramer, 1981; Blakemore, 1985; Ettorre, 1987; Hills, 1989). But the encouragement of specialisation and choice has drawbacks, for it risks pushing up public sector purchasers' transactions costs, and creating market niches and associated market power for some providers. In other words, there is a potential tension between provider pluralism (and therefore choice) and the kinds of efficiency gain which the government expects from social care markets (Forder *et al.*, 1995).

The *potential* for the voluntary sector to offer a distinctive service is clear. But is choice encouraged or narrowed by the contractual links being introduced? Some characteristics of the new community care arrangements leave one unsure of the effect of choice: local authorities retain their funding monopoly; competition can reduce rather than increase product variability; regulation can create so-called 'coercive isomorphism' – increasingly similar provision (DiMaggio and Powell, 1983); localised contracting can operate against open access (important with, for example, services for people with HIV/AIDS, drug or alcohol problems); and block contracts can constrain provider variety. The mechanisms by which public authorities encourage pluralism will determine whether this voluntary sector potential is realised.

2. Flexibility and innovation

Are voluntary organisations 'the living laboratory of aesthetic, spiritual, and intellectual innovation' (Nielson, 1979, p. 5) or is their ability to develop new services or configurations of support partly 'based on invidious organisational stereotypes whereby government is perceived as intrinsically rigid, riddled with bureaupathology, and offering mass standardised services that are dehumanising' (Kramer, 1987, p. 241)?

Many community care developments offer evidence of voluntary sector innovativeness (Osborne, 1994), but whether the sector is *more* innovative than the government or private sectors is another matter. Some writers have argued that the voluntary sector is no more innovative than the public (Rodgers, 1976; Kramer, 1981; Brenton, 1985; Moore and Green, 1985). However, the voluntary sector can act as conduit, incubator or developer of ideas for the public sector to adopt and adapt. Many of the innovative practices of voluntary agencies uncovered by Kramer (1981) in his four-country study were initiated from within the public sector. If a public agency 'wishes to avoid being locked into long-term delivery' (Judge and Smith, 1983, p.218), arm's-length innovation or experimentation may be ideal. This may not gel with the contracting culture, since local authorities may find it hard to specify contracts for innovative work. However, the risks associated with innovation may be reduced, for public officials in Britain may recognise, as have their US counterparts, 'that they can change programme direction with relative impunity and can cut back on services more easily than they could if public employees were involved' (Lipsky and Smith, 1990, pp. 636–7).

It may be the case that a multiplicity of agencies and energetic managers maximises the potential for innovation. The pertinent questions for public policy are, however, rather different, and would include questions about the opportunities to innovate, the routing of public sector initiatives through non-statutory agencies, the ability to purchase innovative services, and the chances of the wider exploitation or application of service improvements.

3. Cost-effectiveness

The claim for voluntary sector cost-effectiveness is conventionally based on arguments about its style of governance, less bureaucratic administration, ready supply of volunteer labour, greater staff commitment, lower wages, fewer constraints from trade unions, ability to recoup some costs from users, multiplier funding effects from donations, and simple economies of scale (Reid, 1972; Hatch and Mocroft, 1979; Judge, 1982). Again, however, the evidence is less striking (and sometimes rather shaky) and more complex than the policy assertion.

Before pronouncing on comparative cost-effectiveness or efficiency, checks should be made: that the public, voluntary and private sectors are delivering equivalent services or supporting equivalent user groups (or adjustments should be made for differences); that the salient characteristics of the sectors are measured consistently (for example, including accurate capital and overhead costs, with some public sector overheads being transactions costs arising from the need to monitor the non-statutory sectors); and that there may be a need to move beyond the immediate future to a longer-run view of performance. By these criteria, some arguments for comparative cost-effectiveness cannot be accepted. In fact, evidence from research at the Personal Social Services Research Unit (PSSRU) suggests that – once costs are standardised for user differences, exogenous cost-raising factors and effectiveness – the voluntary sector advantage may disappear (Knapp and Missiakoulis, 1982; Knapp, 1986). On the other hand, Beecham *et al.* (1991) found that the private and voluntary sectors could provide community care services for former long-stay psychiatric hospital in-patients more cost-effectively than could local authorities, which in turn were more cost-effective than health authorities.

The three 'effectiveness aims' – choice, flexibility and innovation, and cost-effectiveness – underpin central government's encouragement of the voluntary sector, but they also characterise some local authority perspectives. Ongoing research on the mixed economy of care at the PSSRU and the Nuffield Institute includes interviews with officers and politicians in 25 local authorities (Wistow *et al.*, 1994, 1995). One of our questions in 1993 elicited their views on possible supply-side developments. *Inter alia*, one in six authorities had discouraged and two-thirds had encouraged the setting up of new services in the voluntary sector. A majority of authorities expressed a clear preference for the voluntary sector over the private, based on: perceived similarities in values with the public sector (especially when services had been floated off from the authority);

long track records and long-standing public–voluntary sector relationships; and voluntary sector representation on joint planning
machinery, together with often quite widespread ignorance and suspicion of the private sector.

It would be misleading to leave this brief discussion of the public sector perspective with the impression that there is widespread
agreement between central and local government. There is, for example, the practice of one tier of government using the voluntary
sector to by-pass or undermine another. Local authorities for their
part have long provided financial support for voluntary agencies
which actively lobby against central government policy, for example in relation to environmental issues. In contrast, central government aimed to reduce the size of local authority housing provision
by shifting responsibility to housing associations via voluntary transfers
introduced by the 1988 Housing Act.

Uncoerced collective purchasing – the voluntary perspective

Uncoerced collective demand is an inelegant but convenient term
for the purchasing of provision by voluntary organisations from
voluntarily donated funds from individuals, companies and foundations. Together, these donations can account for sizeable proportions of total voluntary sector income, for example for a third or
more of the income of UK organisations working with children and
families or in the support of people with physical or sensory disabilities (Kendall and Knapp, 1995).

Charitable support from trusts and foundations grew, particularly
after 1900, with rapid industrialisation enabling some individuals to
amass vast personal fortunes. In previous centuries the wealthy had
funded welfare activities, especially churches, schools and hospitals, and some had formed trusts to pursue their philanthropic wishes.
Many trusts were established in the early years of this century to
address fundamental social problems and to encourage more systematic giving. Today, only a small part of voluntary sector funding comes from uncoerced collective purchasing, that is from
foundations and other voluntary bodies.

From a foundation's perspectives, the criteria for the assessment
of effectiveness would be shaped in large measure by trust instruments. It may or may not be able to pursue broad social objectives,
although 'social worth' is arguably assumed implicitly in the exten-

sion of tax advantages to foundations. Salamon (1987) pulled together a number of related questions concerning voluntary collective funding, suggesting four sources of what he called 'philanthropic
failure' or doubts as to the ability of the voluntary sector *on its
own* to meet society's needs: philanthropic insufficiency (collective
provision inadequate in scale), particularism, paternalism and amateurism. Particularism (specialism) allows the voluntary sector to
meet the needs of particular groups in the population, and is a valued
characteristic of the sector. But this same feature could also mean
inequitable, wasteful provision and marginalisation. Have voluntary
agencies historically favoured the middle classes, leaving the lower
income groups for public agencies (Benton *et al.*, 1978; Gibelman,
1980; Webb, 1981; Wedel, 1986)? In social care, the voluntary sector's contribution to meeting needs has been unevenly spread
(Packman, 1968; Hatch and Mocroft, 1977). Some of this variation
results from uneven local government support and encouragement,
but voluntary services develop in part out of local, autonomous action and will almost inevitably be piecemeal and particular. Even if
voluntary agencies subscribe wholeheartedly to the equitable provision of social services, their constitutions or charitable objects may
prevent them from making the appropriate contribution. Paternalism
is linked to the danger of *noblesse oblige*. Governing bodies or elites
may constitute 'a self-selected and self-perpetuating minority . . . more
representative of their philanthropic origin than of their clientele'
(Kramer, 1981, p.266). Middle-class values may dominate aims and
practices and reinforce the damaging idea that welfare is something
which is done to the working class by their social superiors (Holman,
1981).

Finally, Salamon and others have argued that uncoerced collective demand leaves the voluntary sector open to amateurism: unlikely to develop a sufficiently professional, well-informed approach
to the alleviation of social problems. The amateurism hypothesis is
as least as contentious as the other charges of philanthropic failure
and obviously begs questions about the real efficiency of
professionalisation, the identification of needs and the underlying
nature of production relations. Nevertheless, there is the danger that
agencies dependent on the caprices of donations or on volunteers
and low paid, highly motivated staff, perhaps drawn from a narrow
social band, may be poorly informed about the need for more skilled,
technical or up-to-date 'professional' approaches. On the other hand,

amateurism may be the source of innovation and the encouragement for volunteerism, as well as the only feasible means (in some circumstances) to involve users in decision-making.

Clearly we have here another illustration of Thoreau's 'different drummer', for the voluntary sector's own perspective on its effectiveness may consciously be at variance with the government's or the general public's perspective. Even when differences of perspective are not deliberate, a voluntary organisation must not be fooled into believing that 'management by objectives', quality assurance, performance indicators or other tools of the new managerialist approach constitute a full set of effectiveness measures. These are merely tools for internal management. Perhaps they are very useful for that purpose. But often they are rather naive and inadequate tools plucked from an MBA course or a consultant's toolkit, and certainly they will not produce the kinds of effectiveness measure needed for public policy debate.

Compensated and uncompensated individual purchasing – the user perspective

The voluntary community care sector has long championed the cause of the user, notwithstanding occasional charges of paternalism or particularism. This emphasis is most obvious in relation to citizen advocacy, and is associated with organisations such as Citizens' Advice Bureaux, law centres and legal advice centres, and many of the national organisations active in the social care field. Also of relevance is advocacy interpreted as campaigning or lobbying, which, if we are wanting a neat categorisation, could be characterised as supporting *groups* of users as well as those people who may be users at some future time.

Citizen advocacy can support and empower vulnerable people who may particularly benefit from assistance and advice, if only because they have not been encouraged in the past to take decisions for themselves. More generally, the participative structure of many voluntary organisations can be an important localised, democratic, consumerist vehicle for allocating resources and changing priorities (Arnstein, 1969; Johnson, 1981; Brenton, 1985). When the public sector is providing the services, the transaction costs of user participation in decision-making may be too high for both parties. The majoritarian, categorical and size constraints on government, to use

Douglas's (1983) theoretical framework, make it costly for decision-makers to involve citizens; the costs of inconvenience, access and acquiescence – to name but some – may make it unattractive for citizens to try to participate in government. Under these circumstances, voluntary bodies offer a less costly route to participation and active citizenship.

The voluntary sector might be better attuned to the needs of users. (This is readily revealed in the actions of those people who freely purchase voluntary sector services.) There has not been a thorough review of the evidence on responsiveness to need, but two findings provide some support for voluntary sector effectiveness. The closure of two large psychiatric hospitals in North London has allowed hundreds of people to establish new lives in the community, almost always successfully in terms of quality of life (Leff, 1993). People who move to voluntary sector accommodation in the community appear to be more likely to move on to other (planned) accommodation better suited to their changing needs. Weisbrod and Schlesinger (1986), in a study of Wisconsin nursing homes, found greater compliance with input and intermediate output regulations by private (for-profit) homes when compared with voluntary (non-profit) facilities, but a greater frequency of resident complaints in the former sector. These two findings obviously do not prove that voluntary organisations are comparatively more effective from the user's perspective, but they should certainly prompt further consideration of this feature of the sector.

Policy advocacy, campaigning or lobbying is an increasingly visible aspect of UK voluntary sector activity. Whether or not it is true that policy advocacy groups have been 'far more effective in raising issues and shaping the political agenda than in developing solutions and forcing compromises' (Jenkins, 1987, p.312), the quintessential campaigning role of the voluntary sector provides us with an effectiveness criterion for which it would be hard to find a comparator. If we are looking for more debate, we might argue that the better endowed or more vociferous lobbyists achieve more than their poorer, meeker colleagues, thus raising again the particularism issue.

Giving – the volunteer perspective

More than one in twenty people interviewed for the 1991 Volunteer Centre UK national survey of voluntary activity had volunteered regularly (at least once a month during the past year) through an organisation dealing with health and social welfare and/or the support of elderly people (Lynn and Davis Smith, 1991). People volunteer for a host of reasons, including altruism, social adjustment aims (to fit some normative expectation of behaviour, to gain prestige or social approval for participation, or to expand their social circle), for therapeutic reasons (to help cope with inner anxieties and uncertainties about personal competence and worth, to feel needed), to gain knowledge and intellectual enrichment, and for instrumental reasons (to acquire specific new experiences or skills which might later generate career opportunities, or to provide an opportunity to display those skills to potential employers). More than one motivating factor is usually at the root of volunteering (Van Til, 1988; Qureshi *et al.*, 1989 and Davis Smith, this volume). Ranged against these potential benefits are the individual costs of volunteering, both pecuniary and psychic, tangible and intangible. Implicitly, volunteers weigh up the benefits and costs of volunteering, although actual participation will also inevitably be influenced by organisations' demands for volunteers (Steinberg, 1990; Knapp *et al.*, 1994a, b). Thus individual motivations or rationales for volunteering, and the constraints which individuals encounter or perceive, would provide us with another set of criteria for adjudging voluntary sector effectiveness, for volunteers will have views about the abilities of organisations to meet their own personal expectations and needs (Lynn and Davis Smith, 1991, chs 9, 10).

Conclusion

The voluntary sector's contribution to British society and to the British economy is substantial, but despite its size relatively little is known about its effectiveness. This chapter examined a number of perspectives which bear on the effectiveness question. We needed to explore each of them because voluntary organisations are resourced from a number of sources, because they get public support and tax breaks, and because – quite simply – they are fundamentally important to millions of volunteers and users.

The potential for developing a much clearer picture of the comparative achievements and weaknesses of the sector remains unexploited. Some of the criteria for assessing voluntary sector effectiveness ought to be readily amenable to the standard approaches of social science research, and – trite though it undoubtedly sounds – more research is needed. However, some of the criteria for effectiveness which would be suggested by stakeholders in the voluntary sector will be much harder to operationalise. As Nielson has written:

> Size ... is the least measure of the Third Sector: the more important is what it does and what it represents. The direct functions which the component institutions and associations perform are plain and familiar; they teach, they cure, they engage in the search for new knowledge, they entertain, they preach, they agitate for reforms. They operate in that large sphere of life which does not centre on power and authority or the production and acquisition of material goods and money. ... They therefore exist in a sense in the interstices of the structure of authority and materiality, and most of their products are essentially intangible, as unmeasurable as compassion, inspiration, or dissent (Nielson, 1979, pp. 4–5).

Notes

1. Parts of this chapter benefit from my work with Jeremy Kendall, and some evidence and insights come from work with Jules Forder, Gerald Wistow, Brian Hardy and Rob Manning. Comments on an earlier version by Justine Schneider, Pat Warren, Perri 6 and participants at the CVO 15th Anniversary Conference helped to improve the arguments and examples. Responsibility for the contents is still mine alone.

2. These criteria constitute the so-called *structural/operational definition* suggested by Salamon and Anheier (1992) and used in the 13-country study which they are directing, although definition of the sector from first principles and employing very similar criteria predates their application. Brenton (1985), Hatch (1980) and Johnson (1981), for example, offer such an approach in the UK. The relevance of this particular set of criteria in the UK context and its links with the policy and legal frameworks are discussed in Kendall and Knapp (1994, 1995).

3. A simpler version of this matrix was first suggested by Judge (1982). It was subsequently broadened in, for example, Knapp (1989). See also Wistow *et al.*, (1994, ch. 3) and Knapp and Wistow (1995) for discussion of some of the issues raised by or within this representation of the mixed economy today.

4.   These rationales are reviewed by, for example, Hatch (1980), Kramer (1981), Judge and Smith (1983), Douglas (1983), Brenton (1985), and others. Beatrice and Sydney Webb (1912) crystallised a number of views with their distinction between *parallel bars* and *extension ladder* roles.

References

Arnstein, S.R. (1969) 'A ladder of citizen participation', *Journal of the American Institute of Planners*, 35: 216–24.

Beecham, J., M.R.J. Knapp and A. Fenyo (1991) 'Costs, needs and outcomes', *Schizophrenia Bulletin*, 17(3): 427–39.

Benton, B.B., T. Field and R. Millar (1978) *Social Services: Federal Legislation vs. State Implementation*, Urban Institute, Washington, DC.

Blakemore, K. (1985) 'The state, the voluntary sector and new developments in provision for the old of minority racial groups', *Ageing and Society*, 5: 175–90.

Brenton, M. (1985) *The Voluntary Sector in British Social Services*, Longman, London and New York.

Davies, B. and M.R.J. Knapp (1981) *Old People's Homes and the Production of Welfare*, Routledge & Kegan Paul, London.

DiMaggio, P. and W. Powell (1983) 'Institutional isomorphism', *American Sociological Review*, 48: 147–60.

Douglas, J. (1983) *Why Charity? The Case for a Third Sector*, Sage, Beverly Hills.

Ettorre, B. (1987) 'Drug problems and the voluntary sector of care in the UK: identifying key issues', *British Journal of Addiction*, 82: 469–76.

Forder, J. and M.R.J. Knapp (1993) 'Social care markets: the voluntary sector and residential care for elderly people in England', in S. Saxon-Harrold and J. Kendall (eds) *Researching the Voluntary Sector*, vol. 1, Charities Aid Foundation, Tonbridge.

Forder, J., M.R.J. Knapp and G. Wistow (1995) 'Competition in the mixed economy of care', *Journal of Social Policy*, forthcoming.

Gibelman, M. (1980) 'Title XX purchase of service: some speculations about service provision to the poor', *Urban and Social Change Review*, 13.

Hatch, S. (1980) *Outside the State*, Croom Helm, London.

Hatch, S. and I. Mocroft (1977) 'Factors affecting the location of voluntary organisation branches', *Policy and Politics*, 6: 163–72.

Hatch, S. and I. Mocroft (1979) 'The relative costs of services provided by voluntary and statutory organisations', *Public Administration*, 57: 397–405.

Hills, J. (1989) 'The voluntary sector in housing: the role of British housing associations', in E. James (ed.) *The Nonprofit Sector in International Perspective*, Oxford University Press, Oxford.

Holman, R. (1981) 'The place of voluntary societies', *Community Care*, 12, 16–18 November.

Jenkins, J.C. (1987) 'Nonprofit organisations and policy advocacy' in W.W. Powell (ed.) *The Nonprofit Sector: A Research Handbook*, Yale University Press, New Haven and London.

Johnson, N. (1981) *Voluntary Social Services*, Martin Robertson, Oxford.

Judge, K. (1982) 'The public purchase of social care: British confirmation of the American experience', *Policy and Politics*, 10: 397–416.

Judge, K. and J. Smith (1983) 'Purchase of services in England', *Social Services Review*, 57: 209–33.

Kendall, J. and M.R.J. Knapp (1994) 'A loose and baggy monster: boundaries, definitions and typologies', in J. Davis Smith, R. Hedley and C. Rochester (eds) *An Introduction to the Voluntary Sector*, Routledge, London.

Kendall, J. and M.R.J. Knapp (1995) *Moving Frontiers: The UK Voluntary Sector*, Manchester University Press, Manchester, forthcoming.

Knapp, M.R.J. (1984) *The Economics of Social Care*, Macmillan, London.

Knapp, M.R.J. (1986) 'The relative cost-effectiveness of public, voluntary and private providers of residential child care', in A. Culyer and B. Jönsson (eds) *Public and Private Health Services*, Basil Blackwell, Oxford.

Knapp, M.R.J. (1989) 'Private and voluntary welfare', in M. McCarthy (ed.), *The New Politics of Welfare*, Macmillan, London.

Knapp, M.R.J. and S. Missiakoulis (1982) 'Inter-sectoral cost comparisons: day care for the elderly', *Journal of Social Policy*, 11(3): 335–54.

Knapp, M.R.J. and G. Wistow (1995) 'The developing mixed economy of care in England: successes and failures', PSSRU Discussion Paper 1035, University of Kent at Canterbury.

Knapp, M.R.J., E. Robertson and C. Thomason (1990) 'Public money, voluntary sector: whose welfare?' in H. Anheier and W. Seibel (eds) *The Nonprofit Sector: International and Comparative Perspectives*, de Gruyter, Berlin and New York.

Knapp, M.R.J., V. Koutsogeorgopoulou and J. Davis Smith (1994a) 'Volunteer participation in community care', Discussion Paper 1032, PSSRU, University of Kent at Canterbury.

Knapp, M.R.J., V. Koutsogeorgopoulou and J. Davis Smith (1994b) 'The economics of volunteering', PSSRU Discussion Paper 1060, University of Kent at Canterbury.

Kramer, R.M. (1981) *Voluntary Agencies in the Welfare State*, University of California Press, Berkeley.

Kramer, R.M. (1987) 'Voluntary agencies and the personal social services', in W.W. Powell (ed.) *The Nonprofit sector: a Research Handbook*, Yale University Press, New Haven and London.

Leff, J. (1993) 'The TAPS project: evaluating community placement of long-stay psychiatric patients', *British Journal of Psychiatry*, supp. 19, p. 162.

Lewis, J. (1993) 'Developing the mixed economy of care: emerging issues for voluntary organisations', *Journal of Social Policy*, 22(2): 173–92.

Lipsky, M. and S.R. Smith (1990) 'Nonprofit organisations, government and the welfare state', *Political Science Quarterly*, 104: 626–48.

Lynn, P. and J. Davis Smith (1991) *The 1991 Survey of Voluntary Activity in the UK*, Volunteer Centre UK, Berkhamsted.

Moore, J. and J.M. Green (1985) 'The contribution of voluntary organisations to the support of caring relatives', *Quarterly Journal of Social Affairs*, 1(2): 93–130.

Nielson, W.A. (1979) *The Endangered Sector*, Columbia University Press, New York.

Osborne, S.P. (1994) 'The role of voluntary organisations in innovation in social welfare services', *Joseph Rowntree Foundation Findings*, no. 46.

Osborne, S.P. and P. Waterston (1994) 'Defining contracts between the state and charitable organisations in national accounts: a perspective from the UK', *Voluntas*, 5(3): 291–300.

Packman, J. (1968) *Child Care Needs and Numbers*, Allen & Unwin, London.

Qureshi, H., D. Challis and B. Davies (1989) *Helpers in Case-Managed Community Care*, Gower, Aldershot.

Reid, P.N. (1972) 'Reforming the social services monopoly', *Social Work*, 17: 44–54.

Rodgers, B.N. (1976) *Cross-National Studies of Social Service Systems*, United Kingdom Reports, vol. 1, School of Social Work, Columbia University, New York.

Salamon, L.M. (1987) 'Partners in public service: the scope and theory of government-nonprofit relations', in W.W. Powell (ed.) *The Nonprofit Sector: A Research Handbook*, Yale University Press, New Haven and London.

Salamon, L.M. and H.K. Anheier (1992) 'In search of the non-profit sector. I: the question of definitions', *Voluntas*, 3: 125–51.

Secretaries of State (1989a) *Caring for People: Community Care in the Next Decade and Beyond*, Cm 849, HMSO, London.

Secretaries of State (1989b) *Working for Patients*, HMSO, London.

Shore, P., M.R.J. Knapp, J. Kendall and S. Carter (1994) 'The voluntary sector in Liverpool', in S. Saxon-Harrold and J. Kendall (eds) *Researching the Voluntary Sector*, vol. 2, Charities Aid Foundation, London.

Steinberg, R. (1990) 'Labour economics and the nonprofit sector: a literature review', *Nonprofit and Voluntary Sector Quarterly*, 19: 151–69.

Taylor, M., J. Kendall and A. Fenyo (1993) 'The survey of local authority payments to voluntary and charitable organisations', *Charity Trends*, 78–82.

Van Til, J. (1988) *Mapping the Third Sector*, Foundation Center, New York.

Webb, A.L. (1981) 'Collective action and welfare pluralism', ARVAC Occasional Paper no. 3, Association of Researchers in Voluntary Action and Community Involvement, London.

Webb, S. and B. Webb (1912) *The Prevention of Destitution*, Longmans, Green, London.

Wedel, K. (1986) 'Privatising social services in the USA', *Social Policy and Administration*, 20: 14–27.

Weisbrod, B.A. and M. Schlesinger (1986) 'Public, private, nonprofit ownership and the response to asymmetric information: the case of nursing homes', in S. Rose Ackerman (ed.) *The Economics of Nonprofit Institutions, Studies in Structure and Policy*, Oxford University Press, New York.

Wistow, G., M.R.J. Knapp, B. Hardy and C. Allen (1994) *Social Care in a Mixed Economy*, Open University Press, Buckingham.

Wistow, G., M.R.J. Knapp, J. Forder, B. Hardy, J. Kendall and R. Manning (1995) *Social Care Markets*, Open University Press, Buckingham, forthcoming.

12

Should Volunteers be Managed?

Justin Davis Smith

Introduction

'Should the salt of the earth be managed?', asked the first edition
of the Management Development Unit Bulletin of the National Council
for Voluntary Organisations in 1983. The response from the volunteering world has been a resounding yes. In line with the trend over
the past decade towards greater formalisation and professionalisation
of voluntary agencies, organisations have begun to develop ever more
formal systems for the involvement and management of their volunteers. These systems have been largely based on those in place
for paid staff. Thus the language of interviews, references, job descriptions, appraisals, and grievance and disciplinary procedures have
become a common part of the vocabulary of volunteering.

The developing management orthodoxy, however, has not gone
unchallenged. Critics have argued that the new management culture
imported from the paid workplace is inappropriate and at odds with
the culture and values of volunteering. Moreover, the heavy emphasis on formal management processes has been held to deter volunteers from marginalised groups from coming forward, thereby working
against efforts to open up volunteering to a broader cross-section of
society. The time is ripe to take stock and review developments
over the past decade. Is the management culture which has grown
up appropriate for volunteer agencies? Has it, as its supporters would
argue, led to a more efficient use of volunteers and to greater satisfaction on the part of the volunteers themselves? Or is it at odds
with the spirit and values of volunteering, threatening to bring an

187

over-formalised and stylised structure to an activity for which informality and flexibility is its very lifeblood? Should organisations reject altogether the concept of the management of volunteers? Or should they be devising new models of management which are more in keeping with the values of the movement?

This essay is an attempt to explore some of these issues. The first section looks at the growth of managerialism in the volunteering sector and argues that with the onset of the 'contract culture' it is a trend that is likely to continue. The second section looks in more detail at the critiques of managerialism which have been advanced, and raises the possibility that the blurring of boundaries between paid and unpaid work may not only undermine the values of volunteering, but may bring into question the very existence of volunteering as a distinctive social force. The final section asks whether or not it is possible to 'square the circle' between the managerialists and the dissenters and develop a management style in keeping with the values of volunteering.

A word on definitions. For volunteering, the definition used is that adopted by The Volunteer Centre UK for its 1991 National Survey, namely an 'activity which involves spending time, unpaid, doing something which aims to benefit someone (individuals or groups), other than or in addition to close relatives, or to benefit the environment' (Lynn and Davis Smith, 1991). Defining management is a more complex task, and a full examination of the mountainous literature on the subject is beyond the scope of this chapter. Nevertheless it is necessary to make a stab at defining terms. Peter Drucker (1970) has argued that there are but three functions of management: to produce economic performance; to make a productive enterprise out of human and material resources; and to manage workers and work. Other writers have come up with longer lists of the defining characteristics of management with perhaps more relevance for volunteering. For example Brech (1967) identified four functions of management: planning, co-ordination, control and motivation, whilst Hicks (1972) settled for six: creating, planning, organising, motivating, communicating and controlling. The management literature on volunteering is on the whole consistent with these definitions.

The growth of managerialism

The issue of the management of volunteers was not of course discovered by the Management Development Unit (MDU) of NCVO
in 1983. During the charitable boom of the last century, organisations such as the Charity Organisation Society (COS) and the housing projects of Octavia Hill put great store by the training and
management of their volunteers. In the case of the COS an experiment at the end of the century to introduce paid staff at regional
level was defeated on the grounds that paid staff had been shown to
be less effective than volunteers. However, in more recent times it
was the Aves Report of 1969 that brought the issue of the management of volunteers to the fore.

The Aves Report came at a time of growing interest in the contribution volunteers were playing in the social welfare field. The
importance of management in the future development of volunteering was spelt out very clearly in the Report:

> It is very necessary in any service using volunteers that there
> should be some form of organisation of their work. By organ-
> isation we mean the provision of a system within and through
> which volunteers are enabled to carry out their work, as far as
> may be possible, effectively, smoothly and with satisfaction to
> their clients, themselves and the services which need their help
> (Aves, 1969, p. 93).

For Aves the management of volunteers was essential both to ensure an effective and efficient service and to ensure that the volunteers themselves were gaining satisfaction from their involvement.
It is worth noting that reconciliation of the needs of the organisation with the needs of the volunteer (which do not always coincide)
has been identified as a major challenge in the management literature (for a good review of this literature see Hedley, 1992). Aves
also drew attention to another issue that was to become important
in the debate over the management of volunteers – the terminology
used. 'Unfortunately', the Report notes, 'the word [organisation or
management] conveys to many people an impression of regimenta-
tion or of pushing people around' (p. 93), but despite the search for
a more 'convenient' term it was unable to find one. Fifteen years
later Charles Handy, the management guru of the voluntary sector,

made the same point. Writing for the same MDU Bulletin in 1983 he commented that 'management is an ugly word with ugly connotations, particularly in the voluntary world. It smacks of hierarchy, of commanding and controlling, even of manipulation' (Handy, 1983, p. 8). The current anti-management backlash in the volunteering sector was therefore to some extent anticipated by Aves and Handy, although neither were querying the principle of managing volunteers – they were simply searching for a more acceptable terminology.

Aves's drive for better management of volunteers was given impetus with the setting up of the Volunteer Centre in 1973. But the real push did not come until the 1980s, fuelled by the changing social policy environment in which volunteering was now operating. The development of a pluralist approach to welfare provision, enshrined in the community care legislation, and the renewed emphasis on contract funding of voluntary groups, meant that volunteers began to take on an increased role in service delivery. Gone were the days when volunteers could afford to be treated as well-meaning amateurs. With volunteers being expected to play their part in the mixed economy of welfare, a new professional approach to their organisation and management was required. The emphasis within government on efficiency, effectiveness and value for money, symbolised as far as the voluntary sector was concerned by the Efficiency Scrutiny of Government Funding of the Voluntary Sector (HMSO, 1990), further increased the pressure on agencies to organise their volunteers in a professional manner.

Interest in the management of volunteers has not been confined to the voluntary sector. Similar developments have taken place in the statutory sector. At the same time as Aves, the Seebohm Report recommended that volunteers should play a larger role in the work of the statutory social services. In 1967 there were only fourteen voluntary service coordinators in the National Health Service. By 1973 there were over 200 in place. But despite the innovative work of some statutory bodies in involving volunteers, their performance overall has been patchy, reflecting both financial stringency (in a time of retrenchment for local and health authorities, putting money into the development of volunteering has been seen as a low priority), and professional suspicion of the value of volunteers.

Moves towards welfare pluralism have not always been translated into support for volunteering. A study by Community Service Volunteers of a sample of community care plans found that only a small proportion made any reference to the contribution to be made by volunteers in implementing the plans (CSV, 1993). Similarly a study by The Volunteer Centre UK of contracts negotiated between local authorities and voluntary agencies found that only one in five made any reference at all to the work of volunteers. There is some evidence that contracting, whilst expanding the work of voluntary agencies (and hence perhaps volunteering), may have led to a reduction of support for volunteering within the local authorities themselves (Presland, 1993).

The drive for managerialism was not thrust upon a reluctant volunteer sector. To many it was welcomed as a good thing, an indication that volunteering was at last being taken seriously and that volunteers were finally receiving the recognition and support that they deserved. Liz Burns, the director of Volunteer Development Scotland, speaking at the 1991 annual conference of The Volunteer Centre UK, argued that 'meaning well is not enough – although it is a useful starting point. The real key to success is successful management. Our organisations deserve it, our customers deserve it, and our volunteers deserve it. Above all, volunteering is too important and too strongly rooted not to be worth it' (Burns, 1991, p. 4). For Burns, management of volunteering was essential, both because 'the voluntary sector is having to carry an increasing share of the load in many fields', which demands that volunteers have 'new skills, and sustainable levels of competence and stability' (p. 3); and because volunteers are demanding better support and organisation. In the 1990s people are more conscious of the need to spend their spare time well. This means that 'volunteers will have higher expectations of the agency that has recruited them; they will not be prepared to hang around waiting to be given something to do' (p. 3).

The same view has been expounded by Peter Drucker (1989). Writing in the Harvard Business Review, he has argued that 'the steady transformation of the volunteer from well-meaning amateur to trained, professional, unpaid staff member is the most significant development in the non-profit sector' (p. 91). The push for this has not only come from the agencies, looking to ensure an effective and efficient delivery of services; volunteers themselves are demanding greater support from, and involvement in, the organisations they work for. Demographic and economic changes mean more and more volunteers are 'educated people in managerial and professional jobs'. These people, says Drucker, are not satisfied with being helpers. 'They are knowledge workers in the jobs in which they earn their living, and they want to be knowledge workers in the jobs in which they contribute to society – that is, their volunteer work' (p. 92). If organisations want to attract and hold these people they need to offer them 'meaningful achievement' (p. 92). And how will they do this? Drucker offers a list of demands that knowledge volunteers will want met. These include: responsibility; participation in decision-making; opportunities for advancement; yearly appraisals of their performance, leading to weeding out of 'under-achievers'; and crucially 'training, training, and more training' (p. 92).

Evidence from the European Values Study provides support to Drucker's argument. This far-reaching survey of changing social attitudes and values across Europe argues that individuals in the workplace and by implication in the 'volunteerplace' too are becoming less quiescent and more demanding of their rights. David Barker (1993) argues that these shifting attitudes will have implications for the way in which volunteers are organised and managed. 'The management of the voluntary contribution', he writes,

> is likely to become more complex. Those who invest their free time and energy in voluntary organisations will seek greater involvement in the decisions that determine the work of the agency and their participation within it. They may well demand improved access to strategic information, more scope for personal achievement and greater activity in the way they discharge their responsibility (p. 23).

The logic of the managerialist case advanced by Drucker and others is that volunteers should be treated as unpaid professionals. Some would go even further and argue that volunteers should be treated the *same* as paid members of staff. Christopher Spence, the director of the HIV/AIDS charity, London Lighthouse, speaking at the 1993 Aves Memorial Lecture, argued that the key issue facing volunteering in the 1990s is the issue of parity: how to ensure that an organisation through its management structure treats its volunteers in the same way that it treats its paid staff. 'This principle of parity', Spence claimed, 'is fundamental.

> It asserts that volunteers are entitled, except in pay, to all the same terms and conditions of service as paid workers: in other words, a full range of work opportunities, proper recruitment and induction procedures, clear job descriptions, managerial super-

vision, training and personal support, and the same say as paid staff in the affairs of the organisation. It also means, of course, that they are subject to the grievance and disciplinary policies (Spence, 1993, p. 8).

The drive towards formalisation of the volunteer role looks set to continue as welfare pluralism becomes a reality. Whilst empirical evidence about the effect of contracting on volunteers is scant, it seems likely that one consequence will be to accelerate the process of the professionalisation of voluntary work. Voluntary agencies, under pressure from funders to tie themselves more closely to specified outputs, will be forced to impose tighter controls on their volunteers to ensure that they do not default on the contract (see Lewis, this volume). Individual contracts will be offered to volunteers and overall a more formal, controlled environment will be created. The formalisation process may go further than tighter management controls; contracting may result in a squeezing out of volunteers as organisations take on more paid staff to deal with the increasing complexity and responsibility dictated by contract funding. The recent study on contracting carried out by The Volunteer Centre UK provides some evidence to support this argument. About one in eight organisations who had entered into contracts said that they had tightened up their procedures with volunteers as a consequence, although few reported the squeezing out of volunteers. Organisations which had taken a more formal approach to volunteering did not necessarily see this as a regrettable step. Rather they pointed to the fact that the increased funding available under contract had allowed them to pay more attention to the needs of volunteers, to provide them with appropriate training and support (Hedley and Davis Smith, 1994).

Contracting may also be changing the nature of volunteering in a more profound way. A study of paid volunteering carried out by the University of Exeter found that an increasing number of agencies are turning to payment of their volunteers (over and above expenses) as a means of dealing with the increased commitment and responsibility demanded of voluntary workers under contracts. The suggestion is made that paid volunteers are a hybrid, a halfway house between unpaid volunteers and paid staff, brought about as a direct consequence of the formalising pressures at work in the voluntary sector (Blacksell and Phillips, 1994).

Challenging the management orthodoxy

The managerialists have not had it all their own way. The trend towards a formalisation of the volunteer role has been attacked on the grounds that it runs counter to the spirit of volunteering and reinforces the current exclusion from volunteering of certain marginalised groups. Volunteering, it is argued, is about freedom of action and of choice, values that sit uneasily with formal management tools such as job descriptions, appraisals and disciplinary and grievance procedures. Volunteers are not the same as paid members of staff and should not be treated in the same way. To do so runs the risk of alienating volunteers from their work. Volunteers will rebel against formal managerial procedures and may leave the organisation as a consequence.

Paul Ilsley in *Enhancing the Volunteer Experience* sets out to 'challenge the trend towards professionalism that can be seen in many large volunteer organisations today and the related 'workplace model' on which the management of most such organisations appears to be based' (Ilsley, 1990, p. xii). He argues that 'instead of treating volunteers as if they were employees of a business, we recommend that managers give them the maximum opportunities to learn and to participate in the organisation's functions and even decision making processes' (p. xiii).

He continues:

> Metaphors are spawned by assumptions and in turn spawn models of action . . . the 'workplace metaphor' – the viewing of volunteers as equivalent to employees – has produced the workplace model, a very popular management strategy that requires volunteer organisations to be run like businesses. Both metaphor and model are based on certain assumptions (incorrect ones, actually) about what motivates volunteers, how they can be inspired, and how they should be supervised (p. 4).

Peter Tihanyi (1991), in an interesting study of volunteers in Jewish voluntary organisations' day centres, provides some empirical support for the view that over-formalisation can be off-putting to volunteers. He cites one volunteer as saying: 'I was given a terrific job description. I tore it up. I love to welcome people, take their names and addresses, take money, answer telephone calls, check on people who owe subs etc. It becomes apparent and you use your common sense' (p. 15). Recognising the inappropriateness of formal management systems, the day centre organisers had developed informal ways of supporting their volunteers; they gave little attention to 'induction, training, formal systems of supervision, and officially sanctioned "rewards"' (p. 4).

Not only is an overemphasis on formal procedures held to be at odds with the spirit of volunteering, it may also result in the exclusion from volunteering of marginalised groups. David Obaze of the Resource Unit for Black Volunteering has argued persuasively that the management practices in place in many of the larger volunteer organisations are off-putting to some prospective volunteers from the black community (Obaze, 1992). The use of formal management tools such as official application forms, references, job descriptions and appraisals are held to be inimical to many black people who see volunteering as firmly in the tradition of 'helping' rather than as unpaid work. Unemployed people and people on very low incomes may also find an overemphasis on formal procedures such as interviews and references off-putting, and there is evidence to suggest that ex-offenders are being screened out of volunteering through over-rigorous use of police checking as a routine part of the selection process (Unell, 1992).

The formalisation of volunteering may have more far-reaching implications. Employment law is a complex area but it is by no means certain that the absence of pay alone is sufficient to prevent a volunteer from being regarded in law as an employee and thus entitled to the protection of employment and anti-discrimination legislation. An article in *SCOLAG*, a journal of the Scottish Legal Action Group, cites the case of a volunteer with the Welfare Rights Office who had brought a complaint to the Industrial Tribunal in Scotland under the Sex Discrimination Act. Although in this instance the Tribunal decided that the volunteer was not an 'employee', and therefore not covered by the provisions of the Act, the case raises important issues regarding the desirability of formalising the volunteer role. The author of the article notes that difficulties could arise as a result of the movement 'within the voluntary sector towards issuing workers with handbooks or contracts (however called)', which typically 'cover such matters as discipline and grievance procedures and outline other main terms and conditions' (Tough, 1992, p. 43).

Of course those in favour of parity might well argue that allowing

volunteers the same protection as paid staff in terms of unfair dismissal, maternity rights, sickness pay, and the like is to be welcomed. But the implications in terms not only of resources (how
could this be afforded?) but also in terms of the fundamental distinctiveness of volunteering are enormous and appear not to have
been considered by the managerialists.

Squaring the management circle

Is it possible to reconcile these two sets of views? Can organisations involve and support their volunteers without over-formalising
the process? Can a management style be developed in keeping with
the values and ethos of voluntary action?

The challenge is a difficult one. The complexity of the task arises
out of the ambiguous position occupied by voluntary agencies –
which, as Billis (1989) has argued, inhabit both the world of the
association, with its emphasis on informality, membership and co-
operation, and the bureaucratic world of systems and processes.
Learning to cope with this ambiguity is a major challenge for volunteer involving agencies.

Elaine Willis has argued that it is possible 'to devise a management style that supports values most of us would recognise as "voluntary"'. Not only is it possible, it is essential for the future
development of volunteering. Whilst 'professionalism', she argues,
'is not automatically the kiss of death for the voluntary ethos. . . .
unmanaged and undirected volunteering usually is' (Willis, 1993,
p. 3). The research evidence would tend to bear this out. Volunteers *demand* support and organisation in their work. The 1991
National Survey of Volunteering found that the major disadvantage
cited by volunteers was poor organisation. Over two-thirds of volunteers said that 'things could be much better organised' (Lynn and
Davis Smith, 1991, p. 94). A study in the States (Pollard, 1977)
found that the main reasons why volunteers left their organisation
were: inadequate social support, lack of opportunities to make meaningful inputs to involvement and decision-making, lack of intrinsic
satisfactions, and, what is termed, an 'unexpected volunteer role
expectation'. The European Values System material suggests that
an increasing number of volunteers in the future will join with
Drucker's 'knowledge volunteers' in demanding more and more from

their organisation. So an unsupported, unmanaged volunteering 'free for all' is not an option: volunteers will not accept it. The issue is not whether volunteers should be managed but what form this management should take.

The weakness of the argument advanced by Drucker and the managerialists is to act as if volunteers are a homogeneous group with the same motivations and management needs. Drucker realises that this is not the case, admitting that in the States knowledge volunteers comprise probably no more than 10 per cent of all volunteers. Yet he fails to acknowledge that the changes in management style and process necessary to accommodate the demands of this small minority may well act as a turn-off to the majority of volunteers. No one would doubt the importance of enabling volunteers to take more responsibility for their work, to influence the nature of that work and to move on to more challenging roles if they so desire. The body of literature around the motivation of volunteers points to the necessity for organisations to try to meet individual needs and aspirations if they are to successfully recruit and retain volunteers (Hedley, 1992; Omoto and Snyder, 1993). But formal appraisals, contracts, job descriptions and a heavy emphasis on training may, as Tihanyi has shown, be off-putting to many. The challenge for organisations is to devise styles of management and support that meet the needs of all volunteers, not just the 10 per cent of knowledge volunteers.

Elaine Willis (1993) argues that it should be possible 'to find some common ground' around the essential elements of the management of volunteers, appropriate for all settings. The tools of management will be different, but the underlying principles will remain the same. A management ethos which is supportive of the values of volunteering would be 'accountable, learning, listening, person-centred as well as task-orientated, pro-active (solves problems, seeks opportunities, takes risks), purposeful and visionary' (p. 3). Liz Burns (1991), whilst arguing that the basic principles of management are the same in whatever setting – commercial or voluntary – argues that different styles need to be developed to take account of different types of voluntary work; the different size, nature and culture of the organisation in which the volunteering takes place; and, crucially, the different motivations and expectations of the volunteers.

Formal workplace models are not the only ways of organising volunteering. As Pearce (1993) has argued: 'Volunteers' efforts can be effectively spurred and encouraged through either informal social contracts or explicit bureaucratic ones' (p. 179). Organisations need not to abandon management altogether but to choose a style most suitable to the culture and ethos of the agency. For some this will mean the workplace model of individual job descriptions and the like; for others it will mean a much more informal and flexible approach. In the Tihanyi study the 'essential ingredient' identified by the day centre organisers was the definition of the volunteer's role. However, this was done not by issuing individual job descriptions but by assigning the volunteer to a particular department with specific functions and issuing the department with a job description. 'This way of defining the role', it was argued, 'gave direction to the work and limited personal responsibility without subjecting volunteers to the kind of detailed supervision they found irksome. And, for some, it offered room to develop their own interpretation of the role' (Tihanyi, 1991, p. 4).

As Ilsley (1990) has commented:

> Managing professionalism in a way that allows organisations to reap its benefits without having the spontaneity and life checked out of them by its rigidifying force is likely to be one of the greatest challenges that volunteer managers will face in the coming years (p. 89).

References

Aves, G. (1969) *The Voluntary Worker in the Social Services*, Bedford Square Press and Allen & Unwin, London.

Barker, D. (1993) 'Values and volunteering', in J. Davis Smith (ed.) *Volunteering in Europe: Opportunities and Challenges for the 90s*, Volunteer Centre UK, Berkhamsted. (See also D. Barker, L. Halman and A. Vloet (1992) *The European Values Study 1981–1990*, Gordon Cook Foundation, London.)

Billis, D. (1989) *A Theory of the Voluntary Sector: Implications for Policy and Practice*, Working Paper no. 5, Centre for Voluntary Organisation, London School of Economics, London.

Blacksell, S. and D. Phillips (1994) *Paid to Volunteer*, Volunteer Centre UK, London.

Brech, E.F.L. (1967) *Management, Its Nature and Significance*, Isaac Pitman.

Burns, L. (1991) 'Management: "Meaning well is not enough"', *Volun-*

teers, no. 88, Volunteer Centre UK, Berkhamsted, pp. 3–5.

Community Service Volunteers (1993) *Volunteers: A Forgotten Resource?* CSV, London.

Drucker, P. (1970) *The Practice of Management*, Heinemann, London.

Drucker, P. (1989) 'What business can learn from nonprofits', *Harvard Business Review*, July–August, pp. 88–93.

Handy, C. (1983) 'Organisations in search of a theory', *MDU Bulletin*, no. 1, NCVO, London.

Hedley, R. (1992) 'Organising and managing volunteers', in R. Hedley and J. Davis Smith (eds) *Volunteering and Society: Principles and Practice*, NCVO Publications, London.

Hedley, R. and J. Davis Smith (1994) *Volunteers and The Contract Culture*, Volunteer Centre UK, London.

Hicks, H.G. (1972) *The Management of Organisations: A Systems and Human Resources Approach*, McGraw-Hill, Maidenhead.

HMSO (1990) *Efficiency Scrutiny of Government Funding of the Voluntary Sector*, HMSO, London.

Ilsley, P. (1990) *Enhancing the Volunteer Experience*, Jossey-Bass, San Francisco.

Lynn, P. and J. Davis Smith (1991) *The 1991 National Survey of Voluntary Activity in the UK*, Volunteer Centre UK, Berkhamsted.

Obaze, D. (1992) 'Black people and volunteering', in R. Hedley and J. Davis Smith (eds) *Volunteering and Society: Principles and Practice*, NCVO, London.

Omoto, A.M. and M. Snyder (1993) 'AIDS volunteers and their motivations: theoretical issues and practical concerns', *Nonprofit Management and Leadership*, 4(2): Winter: pp. 157–76.

Pearce, J. (1993) *Volunteers: The Organisational Behaviour of Unpaid Workers*, Routledge, London.

Pollard, C.A. (1977) 'The challenge of volunteer commitment: why volunteers drop out and some suggestions for prevention', in A.W. Stubblefield, T.M. Sherman and W.L. Saunders (eds) *Proceedings: Roles of Colleges and Universities in Volunteerism*, Virginia Polytechnic Institute and State University.

Presland, T. (1993) *Volunteering in Social Services Departments*, Volunteer Centre UK, Berkhamsted.

Spence, C. (1993) 'Parity: practice or pretence?', *Volunteers*, no. 109, Volunteer Centre UK, Berkhamsted, p. 8.

Tihanyi, P. (1991) *Volunteers: Why They Come and Why They Stay*, Case Study no. 1, Centre for Voluntary Organisation, London School of Economics, London.

Tough, V. (1992) 'Rights for voluntary workers', *SCOLAG Journal*, March, p. 43.

Unell, J. (1992) *Criminal Records Checks Within The Voluntary Sector: An Evaluation of the Pilot Schemes*, Volunteer Centre UK, Berkhamsted.

Willis, E. (1993) 'How to manage volunteers and maintain your values as well', *Volunteers*, no. 102, Volunteer Centre UK, Berkhamsted.

13

What Kind of Training does the Voluntary Sector Need?

Stephen P. Osborne

Introduction

This paper addresses the question of the type of training required within the voluntary sector in the UK today and the extent to which this need is currently being met. It will begin by outlining the key challenges facing the contemporary UK voluntary sector. It will then review the existing literature on training needs in the voluntary sector, and report the findings of the research carried out by the author and his colleagues into training needs and provision within the sector. It will conclude by considering how training to meet the needs of the sector might best be facilitated in the future.

The challenges facing the British voluntary sector

The first issue to be addressed when considering the training needs of the voluntary sector is the changing environment and context of this sector. This chapter will concentrate on seven issues in this environment which, it is argued, pose important, though differing, training needs for the sector. The first two of these issues are general ones, concerning the context of the sector, whilst the others are more specific ones.

The changing pattern of social and community needs

One of the key concerns of the late twentieth century has been the fragmentation of family and community life and the most appropriate way in which to encourage social and community integration. For many, voluntary organisations are an essential component of this process of social integration (Emmanuel, 1993). This essential role requires nurturing and support, particularly through education and training. Emmanuel pointed to the lack of a proper training infrastructure as one of the key constraints to an effective British voluntary sector.

The diversity and distinctiveness of the voluntary sector

This diversity and distinctiveness are certainly not new factors in the sector; they are inherent characteristics of it, but no less important in the contemporary debate for this. The diversity of the sector is found in the range of activities it is involved with, the variety of sections of society that are represented by voluntary organisations, the number of its multiple constituencies (such as staff, trustees, members, volunteers and funders) and the confusion of roles carried out by people working within the sector. Moreover, as Harris (1990a) has noted, the state of our knowledge of the sector is poor, and this is itself a further difficulty. If we do not know what is happening in the sector, then it is hard to plan training for it. (See Taylor, this volume, for further discussion of these issues.)

Despite this diversity, there is agreement about the distinctiveness of the sector. American commentators have well documented the distinctive nature of non-profit (sic) organisations (for example, Cyert, 1988; O'Neill and Young, 1988), concentrating on the role of volunteers in the sector, the distinctive nature of its financial arrangements and the nature of its management. Studies in Britain have also delineated the voluntary from both the governmental sector (URBED, 1988) and the for-profit sector (Rooley and White, 1989). This distinctiveness poses questions about the type and source of training needed specifically for voluntary organisations, as opposed to more generically orientated training.

The rise of the contract culture and the growth of managerialism

The last decade has seen voluntary organisations move from the periphery to the centre stage in the provision of public services in the UK. This movement has its roots in the pluralist tradition of the voluntary sector (Gladstone, 1979), which has in recent years gained support from the British government as part of its determination to reduce the role of the state in public services. A particular feature of the changing environment is the growth of the 'contract culture' in the provision of public services (see Lewis, this volume). There has been an almost notorious distrust of management within the voluntary sector (Landry, 1985). This is now being challenged by the increasing need of voluntary organisations to be seen to manage and to be accountable as they take on an enlarged role in service delivery, as part of the contract culture. Locke (1993, p. 4) summarised well the dilemma that this poses for voluntary organisations:

> the problem is that whilst there is no lack of vision or commitment in most voluntary organizations, the ability to express this in terms of a contractual negotiation requires a high level of analytical skill. In the new environment, you have to be able to transcribe your lifelong conviction and heart of gold into a five line mission statement, six objectives and a four page business plan.

This contractual environment poses major challenges for the managerial skills of voluntary sector managers. The sector is beginning to respond (Belman, 1993; Singh, 1993), but this response requires further co-ordination.

The importance of equal opportunities and anti-discriminatory practice

British society is now a multi-cultural and multi-racial one. Because of their key roles in community development and service delivery outlined above, it is vital that voluntary organisations are able to respond to and reflect this diversity. However, the sector as a whole is being as slow to respond to this challenge as are the governmental and for-profit sectors (Jackson and Field, 1989; Connelly, 1990). Initiatives are emerging, such as the establishment of a national intermediary organisation for Black groups (Sia), as is awareness of the needs of Black and other ethnic minority groups in the voluntary sector (Johnson, 1990; West, 1991). Such initiatives need to be built upon and incorporated into the lifeblood of the sector.

The impact of the Charities Act on trustees

The Charities Act 1992 clarified existing and imposed new duties on the trustees of voluntary organisations. However, training support for trustees continues to be limited. In a major report, the National Council for Voluntary Organisations (NCVO, 1992a) argued that many trustees were ignorant of their real responsibilities, and recommended that training be made an important priority for this group. These findings in themselves were not necessarily new (see for example Locke *et al.*, 1990; Radcliffe, 1990), but the publicity that this report gave to the issues was. It has been backed up by subsequent research and by independent commentators (Hazell, 1992; Harrow, 1993).

The changing national framework for vocational training

The framework of vocational training has undergone a tremendous overhaul in the last decade. Training and Enterprise Councils (TECs) have taken a central role in co-ordination of training at a community level, including with voluntary organisations (Hedley and Keeley-Huggett, 1992). The British Government has also supported a move to competency-based education, with the development of National Vocational Qualifications (NVQs).

In principle, this move should be welcomed by the staff of the voluntary sector. Until recently, the sector had expected its paid staff to get by on commitment to a cause alone (Harris, 1990b). Recent American research, however, has suggested that there may be a growing recognition within the sector of the importance of training and career development, if the sector is to fulfil its potential (Mirvis, 1992). The NVQ structure could enable staff in the sector to build on and gain recognition for their existing learning and experience (Garner, 1992). Yet this is not a reality accepted by all individuals and organisations in the sector, some of whom are distrustful of the motives behind the initiative:

NVQs are being sold on the basis of equal access and good equal opportunities . . . [but] NVQs give voluntary sector employers an opportunity to continue to opt out of their responsibilities, while looking good, because they can get their employees training on the cheap . . . NVQs are a scam (Abse, 1993, p. 11).

The Europeanisation of British society

British membership of the European Community (EC) poses challenges and opportunities for our society as a whole, including the voluntary sector. A range of new regulations and structures need to be understood, whilst the possibility of trans-European trade amongst voluntary organisations poses particular challenges (Perri 6, 1992). An examination of the implications of this process for just one part of the voluntary sector, the Arts, is found in Mulder (1991), whilst research is also under way about the harmonisation across the EC of training qualifications for important parts of the voluntary sector (Ludwin *et al.*, 1993).

Summary

This section has reviewed the key challenges facing the British voluntary sector. It has found them many and varied, and requiring an infrastructure of training if the sector is to be able to respond to them in a positive manner. The extent of our knowledge of actual training needs of people in the voluntary sector, and the range of existing provision, will be examined next.

Training needs in the voluntary sector

The training needs of workers in the voluntary sector will be examined in three parts. These relate to the needs of volunteers and volunteer co-ordinators, the paid staff of voluntary organisations, and managerial staff.

(a) Volunteers and volunteer co-ordinators

Despite the fact that volunteers comprise an important resource of the voluntary sector, the lack of research about their training needs is stark. By far the largest body of knowledge is that in relation to the trustees and management committees of voluntary organisations. The key needs here relate to the financial and strategic management of their organisations, as well as to managing the relationship with their paid staff (for those with such staff).

Beyond this area, information is scarce, and mostly American based. Clary *et al.* (1992) and Pearce (1993) have both asserted the importance of training in the motivation and retention of volunteers, but are no more specific. Buckley (1990) has also sounded a warning note, suggesting that increased training opportunities may make volunteers prey to recruitment into the commercial sector (though Janey *et al.* (1991) saw this as a positive factor in encouraging people to volunteer in the first place). No other research dedicated to the training needs of volunteers could be identified by the author.[1]

A few studies have examined the training needs of volunteers, as an (invariably small) part of larger studies of the voluntary sector. Locke, 1993 (see also Locke *et al.*, 1993, and Sussex Rural Community Council, 1993) argued that the tasks that volunteers carry out in voluntary organisations are indistinguishable from those of the paid staff and so they have similar needs.

Very little is thus known about the needs of volunteers. What research there is must be treated with caution. The samples concerned are highly partial and often concentrate on volunteers working in service delivery, to the exclusion of those involved in campaigning or fundraising, for example; and on certain parts of the sector, such as social welfare.

In the field of volunteer co-ordination, there is more, mostly American, research. This has found that such staff have only a limited amount of dedicated training available to them and would want more; that there is a need for basic training in the management of volunteers and the operational management of their services; and that there is a need for more advanced training, concentrating on deepening their management skills (Stubblefield and Miles, 1986; Appel *et al.*, 1988; Brudney and Brown, 1990; Brudney, 1992).

(b) The paid staff of voluntary organisations

This study identified a number of recent substantial studies of the training needs of the paid staff in voluntary organisations. The most significant ones were Coopers & Lybrand, 1989; Fordham Associates, 1992; Williams, 1993; Dorset Initiative in Social Care, 1993; Locke *et al.*, 1993; Sussex Rural Community Council, 1993; Walker-Smith and Williams, 1993; and Partnership at Work, 1994.

There was remarkable agreement between these studies about the training needs of the staff in voluntary organisations. These fell into three clear areas:

- counselling skills, for use in their relationships with the users/ members of their organisations (these could be generic skills or more specialist ones, as in the case of child-care organisations);
- operational management skills, for the day-to-day running of their organisations (such as computer skills, typing, fundraising and first aid);
- management skills, for the overall management of their organisations (such as planning, evaluation, and inter-agency liaison).

Williams did dissent somewhat, arguing that it was not possible to generalise about the training needs of the staff of voluntary organisations. A larger national audit of their training needs was required for this to be done, based on the model of Training Needs Analysis.

In addition to this near unanimity on training needs there was also a clear consensus about the blocks to training which existed in the voluntary sector. These were:

- the availability of time to attend training courses, including job cover;
- low levels of resources available to support training initiatives;
- variable information availability about the range of courses and training support available;
- the lack, both of recognition of the need for training and of strategic policies on training and staff development, within voluntary organisations;
- poor accessibility of courses, in terms both of the prerequisites required for attendance and of their geographic spread.

(c) Management staff of voluntary organisations

Of all the areas, this is the one with the greatest depth of research, even spawning a conference and a book in America (O'Neill and

Young, 1988). Indeed, specialist management training for non-profit organisations in America is in advance of the UK; Wish (1990) detailed sixteen specialist courses available at universities, with a further five in developmental stages. The UK is catching up, however. NCVO (1993) listed seventeen courses which either included components dealing with management in the sector or were devoted to this topic alone.

Out of the studies on paid staff referred to previously, four of them (Coopers and Lybrand, 1989; Dorset Initiative in Social Care, 1993; Locke, 1993; and Sussex Rural Community Council, 1993) also covered management staff. In addition to these, six studies have addressed management training needs in more detail: Batsleer, 1988; URBED, 1988; Campbell, 1989; Paton & Hooker, 1990b; Harris *et al.*, 1991; and Bruce and Leat, 1993.

To an extent, the findings of these specialist studies were contradictory, and the samples concerned were often highly partial and/ or self selected. Yet four points do stand out.

First, there was a definite demand for management training in the sector, though many were distrustful of the traditional forms in which this came, with an emphasis on skills and values which were alien to the sector. The ideal appeared to be programmes which took the best practice from this tradition and integrated it into a voluntary sector context.

Secondly, there was an expressed need both for externally provided courses and for on-the-job training, and for both to recognise and build upon the existing experiences of practising managers.

Thirdly, there was a concern that such training should be integrated, rather than a series of 'ad hoc' short courses, and ideally should offer some form of qualification to the course participant. To be of optimum use to the organisations themselves, this also required a strategic approach to be taken to the whole issue of staff development.

Finally, constraints to training existed at the management level, as they did elsewhere, particularly in terms of time availability and finance.

Overview of training needs

Four points arise from the foregoing review. First, that our knowledge of training needs is partial. In some sectors (such as volunteers), this knowledge is almost nil. In others (such as management staff), the range of studies can be contradictory or based on questionable sampling frames. Moreover, training needs, where they are detailed, are usually posed in terms of the micro-skills required, rather than in terms of the wider learning outcomes required.

Secondly, what research is available demonstrates a clear demand for training by staff within the voluntary sector, and in particular for training related to managing their organisations at both the strategic and operational levels. Thirdly, there are significant obstacles to training and skills development within the sector, including the lack of strategic thinking about it, the 'voluntary' ethos, and the time and financial constraints.

Finally, the consensus is that this training and education, whilst building on the best practice in the other sectors of society and having recognition outside the voluntary sector, should recognise the distinctive features and needs of this sector. There is rather less consensus, however, about what these 'distinctive features' actually are.

The Aston survey of job roles and training needs in the voluntary sector

The Aston survey was based on a sample of 432 voluntary organisations, stratified by income and sector of work. The response rate was 53 per cent. The findings of the study have to be treated, therefore, with a degree of caution. Against this, it was the first national study, to our knowledge, to examine either job roles or training needs in the sector in such a systematic way.

The details of the sample are to be found in Table 13.1 in the Statistical Appendix to this chapter. In the text, the following 'shorthand' will be used:

- Small organisations   annual income under £10,000;
- Small/medium organisations   annual income between
                                  £10,000–£100,000;
- Medium organisations   annual income between
                                  £100,000–£1 million;
- Large organisations   annual income between
                                  £1 million – £10 million;
- Very large organisations   annual income over £10 million.

Employment in the voluntary sector

This research team has previously estimated that, in 1990, the medium to very large organisations comprised only 9 per cent of the voluntary sector. However, this 9 per cent accounted for 89 per cent of its total income (Clare and Scott, 1993). This skewed nature of the sector was not surprisingly reflected in its employment patterns:

- 52 per cent of small and small/medium organisations employed between 1.5 and 2.5 staff;
- 50 per cent of medium organisations employed between 6 and 25 staff;
- 67 per cent of large organisations employed between 11 and 100 staff;
- 64 per cent of very large organisations employed over 250 staff (though 5 per cent of these organisations employed no staff at all).

The job roles found within the voluntary sector were classified using the nine divisions of the Standard Occupational Classification. The study found 72 per cent of voluntary organisations employing some paid staff, and 45 per cent as having volunteer involvement (excluding their management committee members and trustees). Of those employing paid staff, the most common job roles were clerical (85 per cent) and managerial (81 per cent). Small organisations tended to employ only clerical or cleaning staff, whilst small/medium and medium-sized organisations were most likely to employ a mix of clerical and managerial staff. Large organisations were more likely to supplement these categories by a range of professional and technical staff, and very large organisations employed the widest range of staff (Table 13.2 in the Statistical Appendix provides the detailed breakdown of the sample).

Where information about job content was available, the thesis about the distinctiveness of the voluntary sector was at least partially confirmed, with job content falling into one of three categories:

- Jobs in the sector which were common to the public and private sectors (such as cleaning);
- Jobs in the sector which were common to the other two sectors, but possessed significant contextual differences (such as

managing volunteer-based staff groups);
- Jobs which were specific to the voluntary sector (such as fundraising).

Further work is required to specify and quantify these differing job roles and categories in more detail.

Training in the voluntary sector

This study received conflicting messages about training within the voluntary sector. On the positive side, it found 78 per cent of organisations spending part of their budget on training. This figure rose to 94 per cent for the large organisations, but was only 66 per cent for the small to medium organisations. Of those providing training, 89 per cent provided at least part of this in the form of generic training for all staff, on subjects such as equal opportunities. Voluntary organisations asserted that they were becoming more proactive in their approach to training. Moreover, there were now a wealth of sources of information about the availability of training provision (including directories and the providers themselves), and these were actively consulted by voluntary organisations.

However, there were also some more negative aspects to the study. Despite the growth of training provision, 23 per cent of organisations still spent nothing on it and 51 per cent spent 1 per cent, or less, of their annual budget. Even of the large organisations, 4 per cent spent nothing on training and 70 per cent spent less than 1 per cent of their annual budget. Only 13 per cent of voluntary organisations spent 2 per cent, or more, of their annual budget on training. The impact of this pattern was demonstrated in the information obtained on the constraints to training, with the lack of availability of funds being cited as the most common one.

The distribution of training provision was also skewed, with the associate professional, sales and managerial staff of voluntary organisations being the most likely to benefit. However, more than half the organisations surveyed provided some training for their professional, clerical and personnel staff (see Table 13.3 in the Statistical Appendix). Finally, the concerns about the NVQ framework evidenced elsewhere were also found here. These focused in particular on its bureaucratic nature and its cost.

The range of training available in the sector

The foregoing review of relevant literature, our own survey, and an *ad hoc* 'trawl' of training organisations revealed four sources of training in the sector:

- *In-house courses*, run either by the training section of an organisation, usually the large ones, or brought in from elsewhere. What evidence there is (for example Sussex Rural Community Council, 1993) suggests that this comprises the bulk of the training in the sector.
- *Short external courses.* There are a tremendous variety of such courses from a range of sources. Although there is some documentation and cataloguing of these courses (such as Flynn, 1994), their provision is *ad hoc* and uncoordinated.
- *Training manuals.* As a halfway house between the above two sources, there are distance learning materials intended to frame in-house courses. Some of these cover the process of creating a training programme (Paton and Hooker, 1990a; Hillyard-Parker, 1993). Others comprise actual course materials (National Extension College, 1993).
- *Integrated courses.* These are available either as courses of professional training which might be of relevance to voluntary sector staff (such as the Diploma in Social Work), specialist post-qualification courses in advanced studies (such as in community care) or as courses of management training and education.

However, despite the feeling within the sector that there were now a range of sources of information about training available, there continued to be a lack of any overview of training provision in its entirety, and of how it related to the expressed needs both of the sector and of its staff.

Conclusion: what kind of training does the voluntary sector need?

This chapter began by outlining the challenges which the voluntary sector faces in the UK today, and which it was argued pose significant issues for it, in terms of the training and development needed to respond positively to them. It then went on to explore our existing knowledge both of training and developmental needs in the sector and of the extent of training and educational provision to meet these.

From the above, it is clear that the issue for the voluntary sector in the approach to the twenty-first century is not necessarily the availability of training; there is actually a great deal on offer. Rather the challenge is to ensure that training relates to the needs of the sector and that ways are found to deal with the constraints to training.

Six points need to be addressed. First, the voluntary sector needs training related to its needs. Part of the problem at present is that we do not have a true picture of these needs on which to plan training provision, at a time when the sector is facing massive changes in its role and function in UK society. The result is the present *ad hoc* range of courses. Whilst some of the intermediary agencies might legitimately argue that they have an appreciation of the needs of their members, and other providers might argue that the market is dictating provision, it is clear that there are real gaps.

Secondly, and as a prerequisite to the first point, the sector needs a clearer picture of the training needs of its staff. Even where they have been asserted, these needs are frequently posed in terms of what courses are indicated ('a need for computer training'), rather than in terms of the learning outcomes desired ('the ability to use information systems to enhance financial management'). A shift of focus to the outcomes, rather than the inputs, of training and development is required in the future.

Thirdly, there is a tension between the expressed need for training which recognises the distinctive features of the voluntary sector, rather than simply treating it as an impoverished for-profit sector; which recognises the overlaps, and which also has recognition outside the sector. This latter point is most easily resolved where training leads to a recognised qualification, but further work is required on the former issue.

Fourthly, staff in the voluntary sector suffer from especial constraints in undertaking training. Because of the small size of many organisations, time-off is hard to organise, and finance is a genuine difficulty. Even in the larger organisations, problems exist where senior managers will not recognise the importance of training or where they see it as antithetical to the voluntary ethos of the sector (though there was some evidence in our survey that this attitude was beginning to shift, at least in relation to certain categories of staff).

Fifthly, there is a lack of a strategic approach which links training and staff development, in its widest sense, to the needs both of the organisations and of the people who make up the sector. In many organisations, short in-house courses are all that are ever likely to be available for large sections of the staff of voluntary organisations. A range of courses is therefore essential, as is a framework within which to integrate and recognise such training. The NVQ framework could provide this, but further work needs to be undertaken, in terms of the NVQ process itself, the resourcing of the framework, and marketing it to the staff and organisations of the voluntary sector. Whatever training is available, however, a strategic approach to its utilisation is required, at both the organisational and sectoral level, if maximum impact is to be achieved.

Finally, and perhaps as the key thread through all of the above, is the need for integration: integration of available courses with the needs of the sector, integration of course content with the special features of the sector, and integration of available courses into meaningful career packages for the people who make up the voluntary sector.

There are three possible ways to achieve this integration. The first is to rely on the local development agencies (such as Rural Community Councils (RCCs) and Councils for Voluntary Service) to take on this role. Many are doing this to an extent already, and probably have most idea of need at the local level. A number are also undertaking systematic reviews of training needs in their areas (such as Devon RCC and the London Voluntary Service Council). However, they are limited by resource constraints and their ability to deal with issues which might need a national response. The coverage of these agencies can also be partial, leaving them open to charges of being unrepresentative of their local voluntary communities.

A second way could be through the network of Training and Education Councils (TECs). These certainly have the potential and facilities to undertake such work. Initially, there was a disappointing response from them to the needs of the voluntary sector. However NCVO (1992b) has been working actively to combat this inertia, and latterly there have been encouraging signs of TECs taking a more pro-active role in relation to the voluntary sector, particularly in terms of funding training needs surveys of voluntary organisations in rural areas.

The final option would be a national organisation to promote and coordinate training for the voluntary sector in the UK. A possible model for this could be that of the Industry Training Organisation, or ITO (an example of which is the Local Government Management Board in relation to local government staff). The core roles of these bodies have been defined as:

- Defining, monitoring and reviewing future skill requirements and training needs for their sector;
- Providing a lead in establishing standards and competencies for key job roles in the sector, and arranging for the accreditation of learning;
- Advising the government and training providers about sectoral developments and their implications for training and education (O'Connell, 1990; Berry-Lound *et al.*, 1991).

To an extent, this might look an ideal solution. Such a body would have the profile to influence both training providers and the governmental infrastructure of training, and be able to integrate provision at a national level.

There are, however, disadvantages to this approach:

- As was discussed at the outset of this paper the voluntary sector is a large and amorphous sector of society and not a discrete industry. It also overlaps in many areas with other sectors of society. Such a national co-ordinating body might find it hard to clarify its sectoral boundaries, to encompass the heterogeneity of the sector, or to prevent itself overlapping with other (industry based) co-ordinating bodies, causing more, not less, confusion. Alternatively the result could be the creation of unnecessary and artificial boundaries between the voluntary and other sectors of society.
- The voluntary sector itself would need to meet the majority (if not all) of the cost of such a body. Given the lack of a strategic commitment to training in the sector, and its resource constraints, it is not clear whether such a will exists.
- It could lose out on the local detail which a more localised system could provide.

This latter disadvantage, at least, could be redressed by organisational arrangements which built upon existing networks. There is an argument for a national co-ordinating organisation which would link into and support the established training networks for the voluntary sector, at the sectoral level (other national co-ordinating bodies which covered part of the work of the voluntary sector), the community level (the system of local development agencies) and the locality level (TECs being particularly important here).

Indeed the example of the work of ITOs in other areas of the economy might provide a good model of just how such a co-ordinating body might link into and co-ordinate these networks (HOST Consultancy, 1991), though these bodies relate to clearly defined industries, rather than a sector of society.

What is clear is that, unless the sector does take action to integrate its training provision in a more meaningful manner, then its potential contribution to UK society will be significantly less than it might be. In these circumstances, the sector may not get the training that it needs, but it will get the training that it deserves.

Note

1. This picture is confirmed in a personal communication (20.12.93) to the author from Justin Davis Smith, Head of Research and Information of the Volunteer Centre UK. He records that the Volunteer Centre was 'not aware of any studies which have examined the training needs of volunteers'.

Acknowledgements

This chapter is based on research carried out by the author on behalf of the National Council for Voluntary Organisations and the Department of Employment. The author also acknowledges the contributions of the other members of the research team: Les Hems, Julie Green and Piers Waterston of the Public Sector Management Research Centre of Aston Business School; and Angus McCabe of the Birmingham Settlement. The content of this chapter is the responsibility of the author alone, however, and does not necessarily reflect the views of any of the above parties.

Statistical appendix

Table 13.1 *Sample elements and response rates*

Sample element	Estimated population	Gross sample	Completed Returns	
	N	n	n	%
Less than £10,000	64,000	68	40	59
£10,000 – £100,000	25,000	67	45	67
£100,000 – £1 million	7,500	67	40	60
£1 million – £10 million	1,500	67	28	42
Over £10 million	87	87	35	40
Housing organisations	2,000	76	40	53
Total	100,000	432	228	53

Table 13.2 *Job roles across the sample elements*

SOC high-level categories	Housing assoc. %	Less than £10,000 %	£10,000 – £100,000 %	£100,000 – £1 million %	£1 million – £10 million %	Over £10 million %	Total %
Managers	95	–	48	84	92	100	81
Professional	55	–	26	34	67	88	52
Associate professional & technical	86	–	25	36	52	85	56
Clerical & secretarial	92	17	67	81	100	100	85
Craft & related	44	–	–	19	35	36	27
Personal/protective service	61	–	29	38	25	50	41
Sales	3	–	3	9	8	34	11
Plant & machine operators	–	–	3	10	17	25	10
Other occupations	45	83	32	36	46	75	48

Table 13.3 *Provision of training by job role category*

SOC high-level categories	Housing association %	Less than £10,000 %	£10,000 – £100,000 %	£100,000 – £1 million %	£1 million – £10 million %	Over £10 million %	Total %
Managers	93	–	69	56	68	87	77
Professional	81	–	87	40	71	65	69
Associate professional & technical	96	–	100	73	55	86	84
Clerical & technical	81	0	33	63	62	85	68
Craft & related	18	–	–	17	75	78	47
Personal/protective service	78	–	50	56	50	57	62
Sales	100	–	0	67	100	75	73
Plant & machine operators	–	–	0	50	50	33	46
Other occupations	25	0	0	18	18	20	18

References

Abse, D. (1993) 'The great NVQ swindle' in *Voluntary Voice*, London Voluntary Service Council, London, November: 11.

Appel, M., R. Jimmerson and N. MacDuff (1988) 'Northwest volunteer managers, their characteristics, jobs, volunteer organizations and perceived training needs', *Journal of Volunteer Administration*, 7(1): 1–8.

Batsleer, J. (1988) 'Adult education, management training and the voluntary sector', *Adult Education*, 61(3): 227–33.

Belman, J. (1993) 'Inroads into rural training', *Contracting In Or Out?*, Autumn/Winter: 4.

Berry-Lound, D., M. Chaplin and B. O'Connell (1991) 'Review of industry training organisations', *Employment Gazette*, October: 535–42.

Bruce, I. and D. Leat (1993) *Management for Tomorrow*, VOLPROF, City University Business School, London.

Brudney, J. (1992) 'Administrators of volunteer services, their needs for training and research', *Non Profit Management and Leadership*, 2(3): 271–82.

Brudney, J. and M. Brown (1990) 'Training in volunteer administration', *Journal of Volunteer Administration*, Fall: 21–8.

Buckley, S. (1990) 'Training for community radio', *Radio*, June: 39.

Campbell, P. (1989) 'Management development and development management for voluntary organizations', *Transnational Associations*, 1: 2–12.

Clare, R. and M. Scott (1993) 'Charities' contribution to gross domestic product', *Economic Trends*, 482: 134–41.

Clary, E., M. Snyder and R. Rudge (1992) 'Volunteers' motivations', *Non Profit Management and Leadership*, 2(4): 333–350.

Connelly, N. (1990) *Between Apathy and Outrage*, PSI, London.

Coopers & Lybrand (1989) *Training for Community Enterprises*, Action Research Centre, London.

Cyert, R. (1988) 'Place of non profit management programmes in higher education' in N. O'Neill and D. Young (eds) *Educating Managers of Non Profit Organizations*, Praeger, New York.

Dorset Initiative in Social Care (DISC) (1993) *Training Needs of Voluntary Organizations in the Health and Social Care Spheres*, Dorset Community Council, Winchester.

Emmanuel, D. (1993) *Strengthening Citizens' Action in Local Communities*, Loughlinstown House, Dublin.

Flynn, P. (1994) *The Training Directory – Courses for London's Voluntary Sector*, London Voluntary Service Council, London.

Fordham Associates (1992) *Strengthening Local Organisations in the Inner Cities*, Inner Cities Unit of the DTI, London.

Garner, J. (1992) 'NVQs and the voluntary sector', *Voluntary Voice*, October: 12–14.

Gladstone, F. (1979) *Voluntary Action in a Changing World*, Bedford Square Press, London.

Harris, M. (1990a) 'Constrained commitment: challenges in developing education and training for voluntary sector workers' in *Towards the 21st Century, Proceedings of the 1990 Conference of the Association of Voluntary Action Scholars*, vol. I, London School of Economics, London.

Harris, M. (1990b) 'Working in the UK voluntary sector', *Work Employment and Society*, 4(1): 125–40.

Harris, M., G. Davies and C. Lessof (1991) *Education and Training for the Voluntary Sector: The Needs and the Problems*, Working Paper no. 9, Centre for Voluntary Organisation, London School of Economics, London.

Harrow, J. (1993) *Charity Managers and Charity Trustees*, NCVO, London.

Hazell, R. (1992) 'Trustees and training', *Association of Charitable Foundations Newsletter*, 12(1): 8–9.

Hedley, R. and B. Keeley-Huggett (1992) *Making the Right Connections?* Department of Employment, Sheffield.

Hillyard-Parker, H. (1993) *How to Manage your Training*, National Extension College, Cambridge.

HOST Consultancy (1991) *Review of Industry Training Organisation Network*, HOST Consultancy, Horsham.

Jackson, H. and S. Field (1989) *Race, Community Groups and Service Delivery*, Home Office, London.

Janey, J., J. Tuckwiller and L. Longquist (1991) 'Skill transferral benefits from volunteer experience', *Non Profit and Voluntary Sector Quarterly*, 20(1): 71–80.

Johnson, L. (1990) *Contracts for Care: Issues for Black and Ethnic Minority Groups*, NCVO, London.

Landry, C. (1985) *What a Way to Run a Rail Road*, Comedia, London.

Locke, M. (1993) *Managing in the Contracting Environment: Training Needs and Professionalisation*, paper presented to the NCVO/Gulbenkian Foundation Conference, '*Contracting – Selling or Shrinking*', University of the South Bank, London.

Locke, M., L. Down and J. Griffith (1990) *Review of Bureaux Management Committees*, NACAB, London.

Locke, M., J. Griffith, A. Jiwani, T. Hayman and N. Richards (1993) *Training for the Voluntary Sector in Newham*, University of East London, London.

Ludwin, L. *et al.* (1993) *In Search of a Profession: Training Needs of Development Workers in Local Community Economic Development*, Cooperatives Research Unit of the Open University, Milton Keynes.

Mirvis, P. (1992) 'Quality of employment in the non profit sector', *Non Profit Management and Leadership*, 3(1): 23–41.

Mulder, P. (1991) *European Integration and the Cultural Sector*, Arts Council, London.

National Extension College [NEC] (1993) *Organising in Voluntary and Community Groups*, National Extension College, Cambridge.

NCVO (National Council for Voluntary Organisations) (1992a) *On Trust: Increasing the Effectiveness of Charity Trustees and Management Committees*, NCVO, London.

NCVO (1992b) *The Local Audit Pack*, NCVO, London.

NCVO (1993) *Voluntary Sector Management Qualifications*, NCVO, London.

O'Connell, B. (1990) 'Training infrastructure – the industry level', *Employment Gazette*, July: 353–9.

O'Neill, M. and D. Young (1988) (eds) *Educating Managers of Non Profit Organizations*, Praeger, New York.

Partnership at Work (1994) *Department of Health/NCVCCO Voluntary Child Care Sector Training Initiative*, Consultants' Report (draft copy).

Paton, R. and C. Hooker (1990a) *Developing Managers in Voluntary Organizations*, Department of Employment, Sheffield.

Paton, R. and C. Hooker (1990b) 'Managers and their development in voluntary organizations: trends and issues in the UK', in *Towards the 21st Century: Proceedings of the 1990 Conference of the Association of Voluntary Action Scholars*, vol. II, London School of Economics, London.

Pearce, J. (1993) *Volunteers*, Routledge, London.

Perri 6 (1992) 'European Competition policy toward the non profit sector', *Voluntas* 3(2): 215–46.

Public Sector Management Research Centre (PSMRC) (1991) *Managing Social and Community Development in Rural Areas*, Aston University, Birmingham.

Radcliffe, R. (1990) 'Let's have trustees who are trained', *Charity*, 7(11): 8.

Rooley, R. and J. White (1989) *Management Development Needs of Voluntary Organizations*, Cranfield Institute of Technology, Bedford.

Singh, G. (1993) 'Consolidating links with specialist groups', *Contracting In or Out*? Autumn/Winter: 10.

Stubblefield, H. and L. Miles (1986) 'Administration of volunteer programs as a career: what role for higher education?', *Journal of Voluntary Action Research*, 15(4): 4–12.

Sussex Rural Community Council (1993) *Training Provision and Needs of Voluntary Organizations in East and West Sussex*, Sussex Rural Community Council, Lewes.

URBED (Urban and Economic Development Limited) (1988) *Managing Urban Change*, HMSO, London.

Walker-Smith, A. and J. Williams (1993) *Staff in the Voluntary Sector of the Personal Social Services*, NISW, London.

West, A. (1991) *Supporting Black Voluntary Action*, NCVO, London.

Williams, K. (1993) *Training Needs of Small Voluntary Organizations*, Kew Consultancy, London.

Wish, N. (1990) 'University and college based non profit management programs in the United States' in *Towards the 21st Century: Proceedings of the 1990 Conference of the Association of Voluntary Action Scholars*, Vol. II, London School of Economics, London.

14

Who Cares Whether Your Organisation Survives?
David Billis

Introduction

Looking back over many years of work with voluntary agencies, the main problems they have posed have rarely been expressed in terms of 'survival'. Naturally, agencies have fallen by the wayside, but growth rather than decline has more often than not been the main leitmotif. This remains the case today. For example, in recent research with housing associations the management of growth was one of the dominant themes raised by association directors and chairs (Billis, Ashby, Ewart and Rochester, 1994). (Another, which will come as no great surprise, was the role of governing bodies.)

If growth, and the opportunities presented by the new policy focus on the voluntary sector, are the order of the day, it may seem rather perverse to raise the issue of survival. Nevertheless, even if 'survival' – if defined as avoiding agency closure – is not on today's agenda of most agencies, there is another, more worrying, situation in which the question of agency survival may be raised. In other words, agencies may find themselves in such dire straits that, at the time, their survival does not appear at all certain. In a period of policy upheaval caused by contracting, with its threat to independence and original mission (Common and Flynn, 1992, p. 37; Lewis, 1993), we may expect an increase in states of crisis in which survival appears doubtful.

This chapter builds on the author's UK and US research to present a five-system model of change, and suggests that agency survival – whether it be closure or crisis – depends on compatibility *within* and *between* these systems. After brief comments on organisational change, the paper presents the model and illustrates through a case study the way in which central parts of the agency interact. The emphasis in this model is on elements that are susceptible to control by agency leaders. The paper closes with a discussion of implications for practice. I would also like to acknowledge the helpful comments on this paper made by Jane Skinner which I have referenced and incorporated into the text.

A five systems approach to change and survival

In voluntary sector studies it is hard to find any studies of survival and, notwithstanding a handful of exceptions (Young, 1985; Powell and Friedkin, 1987; Kramer, 1990; Wilson, 1992 and this volume), even the allied topic of organisational change has not emerged as an important theme. The position is different in the 'generic' literature which does not differentiate between the sectors, and in which organisational change has become a major research topic often linked to survival. For example, one important textbook repeats with approval the definition of change as 'the alteration and transformation of the form so as to survive better in the environment' (Hage, 1980, p. 262; Hall, 1987, p. 198).

A significant part of the vast generic literature might be regarded as rather 'deterministic' – change sometimes appears to lie outside the control of the organisational actors. Thus some authors claim that organisations can be identified at distinct stages in an evolutionary process, or life cycle, associated with their age of formation (Quinn and Cameron, 1983; Kimberly, Miles *et al.*, 1980; Stinchcombe, 1965). Others, such as the influential resource dependency and allied theories (Levine and White, 1961; Aldrich, 1976; Pfeffer and Salancik, 1978; McCarthy and Zald, 1977) suggest that organisations respond to those groups that control resources. Theories of isomorphism (DiMaggio and Powell, 1983; DiMaggio, 1983) are open to similar criticism, although Powell (in Powell and DiMaggio, 1991, p. 194) has later demonstrated sensitivity to this point by suggesting that earlier formulations presented 'organizations too passively'.

In contrast, this chapter follows a rather different research tradition (Jaques, 1976; Rowbottom, 1977; Billis, 1984) according to

which an understanding of the nature of social institutions can facilitate 'enacted change' (Rowbottom, 1977; p. 21). That tradition
is itself part of a much broader group of writers who believed in
the possibility of what was called 'planned change'. The essential
elements in this approach can be tracked in the seminal work by
Bennis, Benne and Chin (1970). They saw planned change as 'the
application of systematic and appropriate knowledge in human affairs for the purpose of creating intelligent action and change'
(p. 4). However the effective utilisation of knowledge for change is
not regarded as a one-way process from the academic or change
agent, and the client system or practitioner. They stressed, as we
attempted to do in the introduction to this book, the collaborative
nature of the enterprise. They urge caution in words which serve
this chapter well:

> We seem, quite often, to become lost at the crossroads of a false
> dichotomy; the purity and virginity of theory on the one hand
> and the anti-intellectualism of some knowledge-for-what adher-
> ents on the other. This division oversimplifies the issue (p. 4).

My objective here can be therefore now be laid out. It is to offer
organisational actors some ideas which may assist them in understanding and controlling issues of survival and change. These particular ideas have themselves emerged as a result of a lengthy period
of collaborative work with many agencies.

In keeping with this approach I propose that organisational change
and survival in voluntary agencies can be explained by examining
the way in which five major systems (Explanatory, Governance,
Human Resources or Work, Funding and Internal Accountability)
interact. Although interactions occur both (*a*) *within* and (*b*) *between* the five systems (see Figure 14.1), the brief presentation of
the theory in this section discusses only (a) *the intra-system* activity. Also, although the environment can permeate and influence
any of the systems, we shall assume that together they form one
larger 'closed' system since we are concerned with factors that are
more amenable to agency control.

By way of background to the theory I should also note that it
has been developed and utilised primarily in voluntary organisations that employ paid staff. These are my prime concern and they
will for the remainder of this paper be referred to as 'agencies'.

Figure 14.1

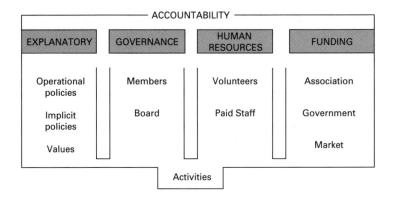

First, I would like to suggest that we consider that there is something which might be called the *Explanatory System*. This is the least tangible of the five systems, but it could be argued that this is a distinctive element of voluntary organisations, and one that is rarely given its due weight. We might consider this system as containing various levels of explanation for ever broader ranges and complexities of problem. So, we can begin with fairly detailed explanations and move on to more general answers.

I suggest therefore that it might be helpful to consider three possible levels of explanation. At one extreme we can find *operational explanations* which can be thought of as explicit statements of distinctive agency responses to problems. *Implicit policies* are at a broader level than operational explanations. Although they still relate in a general fashion to the activities of the organisation, they do not by themselves offer specific solutions. *Values* lie beneath implicit policies and are deeper views about the world and the nature of life which extend far beyond specific organisational boundaries. Some examples may help to illustrate the different levels of explanation and their interaction.

Interactions within the system could be observed in a project in a pregnancy advice agency where research (Billis, 1991) revealed that participants held very different values regarding the nature of human life: could abortion be permitted under any circumstances? These different values were reflected in the differing views held amongst staff, volunteers and committee regarding who should really be held accountable for resolving the question of an unwanted pregnancy. Should it be the individual herself? The state? Or a Voluntary Association? In other words there were different implicit policies with respect to what might be called welfare accountability. Most publicly obvious, and most damaging to the agency, were the difficulties in producing operational policies regarding 'non-directive counselling'. Two sets of policies were produced for different funders (Church and Local Government).

Another example is provided by Skinner (1994) who traces the way in which the debate in her agency over poverty echoes these three levels. Thus at the sharp end of operational policies there are debates about the balance to be struck between campaigning work, policy and change work and direct help to individuals. At successively deeper levels these debates may reflect implicit agency policies about who should be responsible for poverty and even deeper beliefs about the nature of 'poverty' itself which go well beyond the boundaries of agency activity.

Second, there is the *Governance System*, which in this paper will be taken as the Board and its committees, and is mainly responsible for the formal production of the mission and key operational explanations. This system can also include key groups such as members, headquarters bodies, and advisory groups. This is a simplified view of governance in voluntary organisations where (because of their ambiguous, hybrid nature) there is often considerable overlap in the roles of governing bodies and paid staff. A striking example of this is provided by the Pre-school Playgroups Association (Brophy, 1994, p. 162)

> From their inception playgroups were organised by mothers, some groups employed a paid leader but most were dependent on (unpaid) mothers working alongside the paid leader. Thus, the providers of the service, the users of the service and its managers were all mothers and frequently the same mothers doing all tasks.

There is a growing body of research literature devoted to the role of governance and governing bodies in voluntary, non-profit agencies. This is generally seen as a major problem area (Harris, 1993). Little effort has, however, been devoted to the relationship of governance to organisational change and survival, or indeed to the study of the relationships between the various parts of the governance system. What is clear is that those relationships, especially between headquarters and local groups, are often tense and uneasy (Young, 1989; Billis and Harris, 1992). Local groups often resent the 'interference' of regional and national bodies, who in turn can regard local bodies as parochial and narrow minded.

The third of the five systems is the *Human Resource System* or *work system* which essentially comprises paid staff and volunteers undertaking operational and supporting work. Looking at the American experience, Smith and Lipsky (1993, p. 111) suggest that what they call 'the direct service role' is 'most characteristic of organisations providing emergency help and crisis intervention', whereas the support role 'is more widespread, including activities such as fundraising, serving on boards, helping with mailings and political lobbying'. Although I am not convinced that this division of activities fits the reality of all agencies, the authors' further contention that government funding 'tends to shift volunteers out of direct service and into support roles', is one deserving British research attention. What limited evidence we do have certainly indicates that human resources can justifiably be considered to be a system within which the different elements interact in an important fashion for agency futures.

Fourth is the *Funding System* which has traditionally received considerable attention from American non-profit scholars. According to Weisbrod (1988) non-profits are associated with collective/ trust goods and donations; for-profits with private goods and sales revenue; and governmental organisations with collective goods and taxes. Gronbjerg (1993), in a study of non-profit funding adopts a somewhat different classification and divides resources into (*a*) self-generated income or earned resources which involve direct market transactions, and (*b*) subsidy revenue from donors and public agencies. The funding of welfare is put in a wider context by Glennerster (1992).

My own approach is to regard different parts of the system as being typically associated with different sectoral origins. Thus (*a*) fees are associated with the market sector, (*b*) donations, legacies, appeals, membership dues and so on, with the association sector, and (*c*) the tax and allied forms of revenue with the governmental sector. Following this approach, certain changes within the funding system (for example from donations to fees) may be more important than others since they indicate changes in agency relationships with different sectors.

Fifth, the *Internal Accountability System or Structure* defines the nature of the relationship, the rules and procedures that hold the other systems together and that govern the relationships within each system. The accountability structure enables activities to be undertaken by the agency. In 'bureaucracies', which I shall take to mean organisations that employ paid staff (Jaques, 1976) the accountable managerial hierarchy is the basic principle of organisation. It is the overwhelming principle of organisation for undertaking large-scale work in the public and private sectors.

Elsewhere (Billis, 1989) I have described voluntary agencies as 'ambiguous' or 'hybrid' organisations, by which I mean that they share the fundamental structural characteristics of bureaucracies (since they employ paid staff) and also of 'membership associations' (formal groups that come together to tackle some problem). The prime principles of organisation in membership associations are different from that in bureaucracies and rest upon the notion of elections and voting, ideas which are foreign to even the most 'democratic' of management hierarchies. The accountability system of voluntary agencies is consequently complex (Leat, 1988) and internal tensions are a familiar feature.

In this presentation the work and activities of the agency are seen to result from the interaction of the five systems, but primarily from the efforts of the Governance and Human Resource (work) Systems.

In summary, therefore, this theory suggests that there are five major systems, each of whose internal components interact in important ways. An understanding of those interactions is essential for the study and control of major organisational change and eventual survival. However, this is only part of the story; we turn now to examine the inter-system relationships and tensions.

Dynamic equilibrium and inter-system tensions

Underlying the argument so far has been the implication that agencies can usually be considered to be in a state of what might be called 'dynamic equilibrium'. This can initially be defined as a state in which the internal components of the five systems are continually changing and adjusting to each other without either changing the core mission or resulting in a crisis. Subtle changes in values lead to changes in agency public relations policies and the way in which clients and users are portrayed. Governance functions previously performed by national bodies may be delegated lower down the constitutional structure. The allocation of work between paid staff and volunteers can slowly change. A loss of funding of one sort may lead to efforts in other directions. The system of accountability may become more or less 'bureaucratic' or 'democratic'. All these interactions can be part and parcel of a normal voluntary agency process of more or less planned change within each system. It should be noted in passing that the notion of 'equilibrium' has been utilised by other authors, and has also been linked to the question of organisational survival. However, the focus has been on the *motivation* of participants to remain with the organisation and 'hence ensure its survival' (March and Simon, 1993; p. 103).

Now let us turn to examine the inter-system position. It is possible to describe a rather unlikely situation in which members of the Governance System (management and other committees, members) and Human Resource System (paid staff, volunteer service workers, fundraisers, and so on), consist of people who share common values and thrash out operational policies in an open fashion. Current funding stakeholders (government, foundations, other donors) have a good knowledge of the activities of the agency and are in tune with its basic policies. Past funding stakeholders can rest easy that their wishes have been translated into acceptable activities. The agency has adopted a system of accountability that is in tune with its values, that controls work in an effective fashion, and is acceptable to governing bodies, staff and funders. A balance has been struck between bureaucracy and democracy.

This is of course so far a static and idealised model of agency life. A more realistic description is to postulate (as with the intra-system description) a 'normal' state of dynamic equilibrium *between* the systems. Changes and readjustments that we noted inside each system also take place between the systems. It is not difficult to demonstrate how changes in any one system can have an immediate knock-on effect on other systems. Thus, although most attention is usually given to the impact of funding changes on other parts of the agency, and these are the most tangible and visible, it is no means certain that changes in the other systems are less influential. Often, for example, one of the most far-reaching changes is that of chair or director. A new director (or chair) may wish to introduce a more 'businesslike' approach. A new member with financial skills is encouraged to join the committee; he or she in turn begins to question the cost-effectiveness of certain programmes, funding sources are scrutinised, adjustments are made in the traditional rather 'easy going' accountability procedures, less emphasis is placed on the need for volunteers, and so on. Supporting evidence regarding the relative significance of resources and other systems is provided by Skinner (1994, p. 16). She points out:

> Certainly the experience here at the Settlement is that change of Chair, change of Chief Executive and change in who manages major parts of activity are more important in explaining and understanding the change and growth that have occurred here over the last four years than direct study of resources.

In a state of dynamic equilibrium, inter-system changes are absorbed without too much pain and have been planned or at least discussed. However there are times when 'equilibrium' is a far from adequate word to describe the situation. Tensions erupt between the systems which no amount of fire-fighting and minor adjustments can resolve. Often, these tensions become visible to the outside world. Staff are at loggerheads with management committees; resignations and dismissals are commonplace; committees are split over basic policies, volunteers leave in droves; funders have no faith in the committee or chair or perhaps the director; disagreements over 'bureaucratic' versus 'democratic' systems of accountability bring the agency to a stage of guerrilla warfare. In short, the core activities and fabric of the agency appear endangered. It is unclear who cares whether the agency survives.

Inequilibrium and crisis: definition and a case study

The main argument of this chapter can now be displayed. It is that imbalance within and between the systems leads to a situation in which agency survival is questioned. The state of dynamic equilibrium has tipped over to a state of crisis. If the model is to be of use to agency leaders and others concerned with the sector, some additional explanation is necessary. This section draws on the author's research on change and crisis in American non-profits (Billis, 1993) in order to define 'crisis' and provide a case study example.

We shall follow the suggestion of Weitzel and Jonsson (1989, p. 105) who suggest that at a state of organisational 'crisis' stakeholders begin: 'to dissolve or restrict their relationship with the organization'. In this chapter, in order to avoid situations where the withdrawal by stakeholders might be part of an orderly exit, only examples where the exit or restriction of stakeholders is unplanned and seen to be harmful to the agency will be taken to indicate a state of crisis.

I suggest therefore it might be fruitful to consider agencies where there is the unplanned withdrawal of a crucial part of different types of stakeholders, as being in a state of 'crisis'. Thus *a combination* of any of these unplanned events would result in an agency falling within the definition, for example:

- resignation of chair or key committee members;
- resignation or dismissal of director or group of top managers;
- withdrawal of a major funder/s;
- unusual staff turnover of core professional staff;
- unusual fall in membership;
- unusual fall in volunteers.

There still remain some questions to be asked. What, for example, can be considered as 'unusual'? Although it is difficult to give precise figures, different agencies will have their own good sense of meanings to be attached to what is an unusual fall in staff, members or volunteers. Indeed raising the question may be a fruitful exercise. How, for example, does a particular fall in any group of stakeholders compare with the past history of the agency? How does the fall compare with other similar agencies? What is the expected position next year? A starting description of 'unusual' might be a fall in a group of stakeholders that is higher than previously experienced by the agency, is higher than that experienced by similar agencies and that is expected to continue.

A state of crisis can be illustrated by a brief account of the position in one welfare agency in Cleveland, Ohio. The agency was heading for a merger driven by several influential private sector Chief Executive Officers (CEO) on the Management Committee or Board. Further analysis employing the five-systems model reveals the extent and depth of the tensions. (*a*) *Explanatory System*: the agency faced a dilemma with regard to its operational policy. The law had changed in 1985, the public system had become heavily involved in the agency's area of work: 'the question is what is our niche?' (*b*) *Governance System*: 'the Board is in disarray ... there are no long range plans, things get shelved'. (*c*) *Human Resource System*: 'there is resentment amongst the staff. Communication is bad and trust is bad'. (*d*) *Funding System*: this too was the subject of some confusion despite the very healthy position. The policy with regard to bequests and legacies, and the consequent rapid growth of the endowment fund, was the source of friction. (*e*) *Internal Accountability System*: here there were deep differences between the Board and staff regarding the appropriate principle of organisation. 'This place is run by consensus, by teams. All the staff meet once a month. The CEOs on the Board would be happier with a strong manager as is the position in other outfits'.

It was not only in the Accountability and Human Resource Systems that there were *cross-system* tensions. As was noted, the funding system was the cause of substantial friction between staff and board: it was said that 'programme people say it is obscene to sit on so much money'. There was uncertainty and differences of opinion amongst board, staff and volunteers regarding who should be responsible for the agency's core work – the state or the agency. There were deep rifts between the Explanatory, Governance and Human Resource Systems.

In exploring why these severe tensions had emerged it was revealed that the agency contained board members with very different backgrounds and approaches to the provision of services. The composition of the board had changed radically in the past nine years. Most of the group that had 'been here forever', were supplanted by businessmen and young women who had started large fundraising events. Unlike the 'early days', only about 25 per cent of the board of 45 were relatives of past or present clients. The gap between mission and board was graphically described by the CEO who explained that they 'had become heavily involved in fundraising; but not in programmes'. It was this group of board members who saw in a competing agency the sort of managerial hierarchical structures and approaches that they knew well and appreciated. They were opposed by parents on the board and a large number of people on the advisory committees, all of whom were parents, siblings or who had disabilities.

In summary therefore, there were severe tensions and contradictions within and between the systems which could not be explained by theories focusing on resources. These do not explain a situation in which there was a strong possibility that the agency would lose its individual identity despite the fact that there were $6 million in endowment funds, a wide range of self-generated and sympathetic income sources, and no pressure from government.

Conclusions

There are questions which have intrinsic value in themselves, and asking them can imply that things may not be as they appear on the surface. This chapter has attempted to broaden the range of questions which need to be asked when analysing the current life and future survival of voluntary agencies. Thoughtful respondents are impelled to give consideration to previously unconsidered issues. Further questions follow: perhaps questions that might previously have been thought too sensitive or awkward to ask. On those occasions when the question: 'Who cares whether your organisation survives?' has been put, it has inevitably generated lively discussion. Initial answers tend to list the obvious organisational 'stakeholders' (committee, staff, users, volunteers, funders, and so on). As the discussion proceeds, further questions follow previous answers. Differences of perception arise within the same agency about the role and relative importance of different stakeholders. How much do we really matter to the local authority or a specific funder? How committed are our staff, committee, volunteers? What is the basis of their commitment? Are we providing anything distinctive to our users, members, clients? If we closed down tomorrow, after the immediate shock, what would be the impact?

In approaching these issues this chapter has presented a model of a *set of systems* which embraces not only resources and stakeholders but also policies and structures. It has demonstrated that voluntary agencies are complex social institutions in which all these variables interact in an intricate fashion. We might just emphasise that an important guiding line for the development of the model has been its potential utility for those in the voluntary agencies themselves. What can they change?

In the main I have therefore eschewed including 'environmental' factors which lie outside the possible control of agency leaders. I have preferred to regard the environment as capable of permeating and influencing any of the systems in ways which are essentially outside agency control. For some agencies this is a simplified picture. They may well be powerful enough to influence specific elements of what we crudely regard as the environment. However, for this paper the image is less complex. It is of an agency that can be capable of controlling its own destiny through its planned response to the environment; rather than by changing that environment.

That is not to say that 'control' of the five systems is easy; it can demand a vast expenditure of energy, but it can be done. Governance Systems can be changed. So too can the Human Resources System. Policies can be added, changed and abandoned. New structures of accountability can be introduced. And – probably the most controversial element – money does not have to be taken.

These are turbulent times for the voluntary sector. The pace of change, the need for thoughtful decision-making, and the possible hazards of any failure in strategic analysis have all increased. David Wilson (this volume) in arguing for a collaborative strategy, makes a similar point when he stresses the need for managers to be sensitive if agencies are going to survive in current conditions. At the level of the individual agency the model is intended to provide a practical tool for analysis and strategic planning. It is one possible piece of armoury in the fight against the wider problem of 'sliding into change'. I have not argued that change and agency survival is, or is not, desirable, either at the level of the agency itself, or indeed at a wider societal level. That is another sort of discussion. What I have suggested is that whether or not change takes place is largely in the hands of the agencies themselves – providing that agencies have a better understanding of how mission, policies and activities develop and interact.

And here I would like to earmark one final implication of this discussion for those in, and concerned with, the voluntary sector. Although it was not the main purpose of this paper, I hope that I have helped to demonstrate that voluntary organisations that employ paid staff operate in a very different fashion from organisations in other sectors. The systems themselves, and the nature of the interactions between them, are fundamentally different in ways that deserve further research attention. I suggest that failure to develop theories that distinguish the basic and different characteristics of the sectors is likely to lead to the total domination of market theories. We shall then truly be faced with a question of survival.

References

Aldrich, H. (1976) 'Resource dependence and interorganizational relations', *Administration and Society*, 4(7).

Bennis, W.G., K.D. Benne and R. Chin (1970) *The Planning of Change*, 2nd edn, Holt, Rinehart and Winston, London.

Billis, D. (1984) *Welfare Bureaucracies: Their Design and Change in Response to Social Problems*, Heinemann, London.

Billis, D. (1989) *A Theory of the Voluntary Sector: Implications for Policy and Practice*, Working Paper no. 5, Centre for Voluntary Organisation, London School of Economics, London.

Billis, D. (1991) 'The roots of voluntary agencies: a question of choice' *Nonprofit and Voluntary Sector Quarterly*, 20(1): 57–70.

Billis, D. (1993) 'Organizational change and crisis in nonprofits', paper prepared for presentation at the Annual Conference of ARNOVA at York University, Toronto, October.

Billis, D. and M. Harris (1992) 'Taking the strain of change: UK local voluntary agencies enter the post-Thatcher period', *Nonprofit and Voluntary Sector Quarterly*, 21(4).

Billis, D., J. Ashby, A. Ewart and C. Rochester (1994) *Taking Stock: Exploring the Shifting Foundations of Governance and Strategy in Housing Associations* Working Paper no. 16, Centre for Voluntary Organisation, London School of Economics, London.

Brophy, J. (1994) 'Parent management committees and pre-school playgroups: the partnership model and future management policy', *Journal of Social Policy*, 23(2): 161–94.

Common, R. and N. Flynn (1992) *Contracting for Care*, Joseph Rowntree Foundation, York.

DiMaggio, P.J. (1983) 'State expansion and organizational fields' in R. H. Hall and R.E. Quinn (eds) *Organizational Theory and Public Policy*, Sage, London.

DiMaggio, P.J. and W.W. Powell (1983) 'The Iron Cage Revisited', *American Sociological Review*, 82.

Glennerster, H. (1992) *Paying for Welfare*, Harvester Wheatsheaf, London.

Gronbjerg, K.A. (1993) *Understanding Nonprofit Funding*, Jossey-Bass, San Francisco.

Hage, J. (1980) *Theories of Organizations*, John Wiley and Sons, New York.

Hall, R.H. (1987) *Organizations: Structures, Processes and Outcomes*, 4th edn, Prentice-Hall, Englewood Cliffs, NJ.

Harris, M. (1993) 'Exploring the role of boards using total activities analysis', *Nonprofit Management and Leadership*, 3(3): 269–81.

Jaques, E. (1976) *A General Theory of Bureaucracy*, Heinemann, London.

Kimberly, J.R., R.H. Miles *et al.* (1980) *The Organizational Life Cycle*, Jossey-Bass, San Francisco.

Kramer, R. (1990) 'Change and continuity in British voluntary organisations, 1976 to 1978', *Voluntas*, 1(2): 33–60.

Leat, D. (1988) *Voluntary Organisations and Accountability*, NCVO, London.

Levine, S. and P.E. White (1961) 'Exchange as a conceptual framework for the study of interorganizational relationships', *Administrative Science Quarterly*, 6.

Lewis, J. (1993) 'Developing the mixed economy of care: emerging issues for voluntary organisations', *Journal of Social Policy*, 22(2): 173–92.

March, J. and H.A. Simon (1993) *Organizations*, 2nd edn, Blackwell, Cambridge, Ma.

McCarthy, J.D. and M.N. Zald (1977) 'Resource mobilization and social movements: a partial theory', *American Journal of Sociology*, 82, 6 May.

Pfeffer, J. and G.R. Salancik (1978) *The External Control of Organizations*, Harper & Row, New York.

Powell, W.W. and R. Friedkin (1987) 'Organizational change in nonprofit organizations' in W.W. Powell (ed.) *The Nonprofit Sector: A Research Handbook*, Yale University Press, New Haven, CT.

Powell, W.W. and P.J. DiMaggio (eds) (1991) *The New Institutionalism in Organizational Analysis*, University of Chicago Press, Chicago.

Quinn, R.E. and K.S. Cameron (1983) 'Organizational life cycles and shifting criteria of effectiveness: some preliminary evidence,' *Management Science*, 29(1): 33–51.

Rowbottom, R. (1977) *Social Analysis: A Collaborative Method of Gaining Scientific Knowledge of Social Institutions*, Heinemann, London.

Skinner, J. (1994) 'Who cares whether your organisation survives?' – a practitioner's comments', paper presented to 15th Anniversary Conference, Centre for Voluntary Organisation, London School of Economics, London, March.

Smith, S.R. and M. Lipsky (1993) *Nonprofits for Hire: The Welfare State in the Age of Contracting*, Harvard University Press, Cambridge, Ma.

Stinchombe, A.L. (1965) 'Social structure and organizations', in J.G. March (ed.) *Handbook of Organizations*, Rand McNally, Chicago.

Weisbrod, B.A. (1988) *The Nonprofit Economy*, Harvard University Press, Harvard.

Weitzel, W. and E. Jonsson (1989) 'Decline in organizations: a literature integration and extension', *Administrative Science Quarterly*, 34: 91–109.

Wilson, D.C. (1992) 'The strategic challenges of co-operation and competition in British voluntary organizations: towards the next century', *Nonprofit Management and Leadership*, 3(2): 239–54.

Young, D.R. (1985) *Casebook of Management for Nonprofit Organizations: Entrepreneurship and Organizational Change in the Human Sevices*, Haworth Press, New York.

Young, D.R. (1989) 'Local autonomy in a franchise age: structural change in national voluntary associations', *Nonprofit and Voluntary Sector Quarterly*, 18(2): 101–17.

15

Conclusion: Emerging Challenges for Research and Practice

Margaret Harris and David Billis

This book provides a unique record of current understanding of the organisational challenges facing the voluntary sector. Not only have the authors addressed 'real world' questions, they have also had their findings and arguments scrutinised by a group of experienced voluntary sector managers. As a result, this volume provides a substantial bridge between theory and practice. Its publication also reflects the major developments in research and in interest about the voluntary sector which have been made since the early days of the Centre for Voluntary Organisation fifteen years ago.

In addition to analysing some of the key issues currently facing voluntary sector practitioners, the book provides a further contribution. For when the chapters are considered together, broader themes which cut across individual essays are discernible. These themes encompass a number of challenges for future voluntary sector practitioners and researchers. The themes and challenges are the focus of this concluding chapter and we consider them under four headings: organisational knowledge; distinctive features of management and leadership; the organisational environment; and the authenticity of the sector.

Organisational knowledge

A key challenge which emerges from this book is to develop and
use concepts and theories in ways which reflect the dynamic and
flexible nature of voluntary sector organisation. Several of our contributors have argued that living with change, paradox and ambiguity is a distinguishing feature of voluntary sector management
and leadership (Billis, Davis Smith, Kay). There are unlikely to be
single 'best', or once-and-for-all, answers to voluntary sector organisational problems (Paton, Wilson). The most useful organisational tools will be those which offer explanations and models which
respond to current issues, but which can also be revisited as agency
circumstances and purposes change (Billis, Harris, Paton). Deakin's
chapter illustrates the point: in tackling a question about the impact
of contracting, he uses concepts developed long before the advent
of contracts – consumerism and citizenship – to throw light on a
new problem.

A second challenge is identified in Wilson's chapter: to develop
a 'culture' in which learning within and about voluntary organisations becomes an accepted activity. Such 'organisational learning'
entails going beyond the latest management fashions. It means understanding the way in which current problems, and choices for future
action, are rooted in the past history of an organisation (Billis, Harris,
Wilson). It means understanding underlying systems and organisational needs (Billis, Osborne). It also means making links between
the experiences of individual organisations so that common problems can be tackled, where appropriate, in a strategic rather than an
ad hoc fashion (Osborne, Wilson). Above all, as will be discussed
in the following section, organisational learning in a voluntary sector context involves understanding, and responding to, the sector's
distinctive features and organisational problems.

A third challenge is to tackle the large gaps in our knowledge of
the sector which remain despite the major developments in the last
fifteen years in research on voluntary sector organisation. For example,
lack of descriptive data is impeding attempts to answer some of the
key questions (see, for example, Knapp, Leat, Lewis) and a long-
term commitment of resources will be required for the necessary
'intelligence gathering'. Substantial financial, intellectual and institutional resources will also be required to tackle fundamental puz-
zles of voluntary sector organisation. The chapters in this volume

demonstrate that many of these have deep roots in, for example, public policy, legal regulations, cultural history, or organisational structure.

If the necessary data-gathering and problem-solving is to be achieved, there will be a need in the future for at least a proportion of voluntary sector researchers to be located within research centres which can provide sufficient continuity of resources and collegiate interchange to enable substantial pieces of work to be carried out. Institutional bases of this kind can also provide a framework within which researchers can carry out their work in an independent fashion, without feeling under pressure from powerful funders (Gray, 1990; Van Til, 1989).

Distinctive features

To what extent is it appropriate to apply to voluntary agencies the managerial solutions and practices developed for other sectors? It is clear from this volume that this key question remains as it did when the CVO was established fifteen years ago. Taylor, for example, expresses concern about the reluctance of governmental funders and policy-makers to take this question seriously. Several other contributors counsel caution about the application of general organisational theory and management solutions to the voluntary sector. Fundamentally, this theme is about the extent to which voluntary agencies are, or are not, like other kinds of organisations.

As we described in the Introduction, the establishment of the Centre for Voluntary Organisation was driven in part by awareness that people who worked in certain kinds of organisations – nongovernmental and non-profit-seeking – felt a commonality of interest and organisational experience. Groupings and institutions of this 'voluntary sector' had a number of distinctive features and those who worked in them experienced a number of distinctive organisational problems.

During the 1980s, researchers and practitioners in North America started writing along similar lines. Despite the difficulties in defining the sector, despite the blurred boundaries of the sector and despite the heterogeneity that exists *within* the sector, they also concluded that the 'voluntary', 'nonprofit' or 'third' sector has organisational features which pose special challenges for both researchers and practitioners (Mason, 1984; O'Neill and Young, 1988). The chapters in this book confirm and amplify this earlier conclusion and carry forward the debate.

Thus the special difficulties of being 'accountable' in the voluntary sector are addressed specifically in Leat's paper but are also referred to by several other contributors including Deakin, Lewis and Taylor. The nature of voluntary sector governance is considered specifically by Harris but is also referred to by Billis, Kay and Leat. The difficulties of taking into account the different viewpoints and interests of a voluntary agency's varied 'constituencies' or 'stakeholders' is a theme pursued by several authors (including Billis, Kay, Knapp, Leat, Paton and Taylor). In addition to these three 'problem areas' – difficulties surrounding accountability, governance and stakeholders – which are now widely accepted and debated amongst researchers and practitioners of the voluntary sector, further distinctive features are examined in this volume.

Paton, for example, provides tentative explanations of why it is that values are more likely to be a source of conflict in voluntary agencies and shows how such conflicts are different from those which arise in other kinds of organisations. Kay looks at the special challenges and tensions of leadership in the sector. Both he and Leat point to the way in which a voluntary sector 'culture' can exacerbate, or differentiate, problems which arise in some way in all sectors. Billis and Wilson both consider what is different about organisational change in the sector. And the challenges of managing staff in the sector are considered from a number of perspectives: Billis and Osborne look at the special context of the work of voluntary sector staff; Davis Smith considers the position of both volunteers and 'paid volunteers'; and Harris and Leat consider the relationship between staff and their governing bodies.

Wilson argues that the competitive strategies recommended for companies pursuing 'excellence' in the business sector are not suited to the contextual contingencies and organisational structures found in the voluntary sector. He, like Taylor, suggests that co-operation is a generally more effective and appropriate strategy for voluntary agencies. Similarly, Paton argues that 'general management thinking' does not provide appropriate responses to the value conflicts of the voluntary sector, where goals are often not well-defined and where means–ends relationships are often not well-understood. In similar vein, Davis Smith searches for a way of managing volunteers which is not only 'appropriate', but which also takes into account the heterogeneity of volunteers as a grouping. And Osborne points out that there is a distrust within the sector of training which does not acknowledge differing needs and which offers skills and values which are 'alien'.

Thus there appears to be an emerging consensus about features and problems of the voluntary sector. The challenge now is to build on this work; to apply and adapt general management literature in circumstances where it is appropriate, whilst simultaneously continuing the quest for specialist organisational tools.

The organisational environment

The chapters of this book, then, confirm and amplify earlier initial findings about the distinctive features of voluntary sector organisation and management. They also point to the implications for those very features of the rapidly changing environment within which the sector operates. The need to understand the way in which environments impact upon the organisation of voluntary agencies is a third emerging broad theme of this volume.

One environmental factor which is currently important was anticipated in the previous section: the pressure to be 'business-like' and to adopt the principles and operating practices of the for-profit sector. The chapters by Leat, Knapp and Wilson are examples of how researchers can provide a basis for informed discussion about the applicability of popular concepts to the circumstances of voluntary sector management.

Another environmental factor which is currently causing concern is the introduction of the 'contract culture'. Here again, this volume shows how research can tease out the complex interplay of influences on voluntary sector organisation and help practitioners to understand, respond to, and even control their environment. The two authors who specifically address this topic (Deakin and Lewis) were generally pessimistic; they suggest that the governmental agenda can overwhelm voluntary agencies in a climate in which the voluntary sector is seen more as an instrument of government policy than as valuable in its own right (a point also made in Marshall's chapter). Davis Smith argues similarly that contracting is likely to increase pressures for 'managerialism' and reduce support for volunteering.

Knapp considers that it is the simultaneous promotion of competition which should be seen as more threatening to the voluntary sector than contracting itself.

The 'contract culture' and the pressure to be 'businesslike' are not only significant features in their own right in the environment of many voluntary agencies; they can also be seen as part of an important broader shift in public policy (Davis Smith, Knapp, Lewis, Taylor). This shift entails an expectation by governmental agencies that voluntary agencies will expand their role in the provision of welfare services of all kinds. It includes a move away from a grant-aid relationship between governmental funders and voluntary agencies (Lewis); a demand that voluntary agencies demonstrate greater public accountability (Leat, Osborne); and reluctance to accept that voluntary agencies do not necessarily operate in quite the same way as public sector bureaucracies or commercial businesses (Harris, Taylor). Deakin suggests that a long-term trend could be an erosion of the traditional role of voluntary agencies in assessing and identifying social needs, with public sector purchasers consulting directly with end-users.

A host of other important environmental factors which need to be taken into account by those who work in and with the voluntary sector are identified by authors: demographic and technological changes which give rise to changed expectations of voluntary agencies (Taylor, Wilson); new ideas about equal opportunities and vocational training (Osborne); rise in demand for services combined with concurrent decrease in available resources (Deakin, Taylor, Wilson); changed expectations from service consumers (Deakin, Leat); and the 'Europeanisation of British society' (Osborne).

What, then, are the implications for voluntary agencies of these environmental factors? Several authors explore this. Billis demonstrates how one change can trigger a range of other changes in the five 'systems' which constitute a voluntary agency. Harris shows how statutory sector staff who do not appreciate the special nature of voluntary sector governance can aggravate the difficulties experienced by voluntary management committees. Taylor suggests that, as their environment changes, voluntary agencies have to reposition themselves in relation to each other to ensure that diversity of broad provision is maintained. And Lewis distinguishes from her research to date three major areas in which the impact of contracting is felt in voluntary agencies. She considers that goals and governance patterns can be subject to important changes and that there is a concurrent tendency to formalisation and professionalisation.

Knapp points out how complex these links between voluntary agencies and their environments are, suggesting that he would need a hologram to portray diagrammatically the way in which voluntary sector providers, key actors, and environmental pressures are interrelated. Billis, more optimistically, suggests that voluntary agencies can control their organisational destinies by making planned responses to change. They need not necessarily be helpless victims of their environments.

Yet, in the face of a rapidly changing environment, the question arises: how far can voluntary agencies retain their distinctive organisational features? Grappling with this point is the fourth and final broad theme of this concluding chapter.

The authenticity of the voluntary sector

The fourth emerging broad theme, which might also serve as a concluding message for this volume, concerns the 'essence', or 'authentic core', of voluntary agencies and the voluntary sector. It is expressed in these chapters in numerous ways, but it is seen most clearly, perhaps, in Marshall's work. He attempts to find a path through the accumulated earlier debates about what constitutes the voluntary sector; rejecting definitions which define the sector in terms of what it is not, whilst also seeking a definition which responds adequately to its evident diversity. Marshall argues that there are, in practice, many voluntary *sectors*. Drawing on theories of democracy, he contends that the common characteristic of these sectors is that they mediate between individual citizens and the large public and private organisations in society. This echoes the views of Deakin, Leat and Knapp, about the importance of voluntary agencies as vehicles of empowerment.

Other contributors also explore 'the essence' of the sector and, in so doing, signal concern about threats to its organisational integrity. Thus Harris rejects the viewpoint that regards voluntary governing bodies as inefficient and pointless. Lewis is concerned that, as a corollary of being seen primarily as service providers, voluntary agencies may be pressurised into divorcing their advocacy role from their providing one. She and Davis Smith speculate about the possibly negative implications for volunteering of the contract culture. All of these authors imply that they are discussing features – voluntary governing bodies, advocacy, volunteering – which constitute the 'authentic core' or 'soul' of the sector and that its continued legitimacy is predicated on their preservation.

Several contributors echo this general viewpoint. Osborne's paper demonstrates how answering practical questions – in this case what training is needed – demands a prior understanding about the organisational nature of the sector. Billis, Knapp, Leat and Taylor question whether the voluntary sector agenda should be set by reference to the norms and explanations of other sectors.

Previous research indicates that, in responding to the agenda of other sectors, voluntary agencies undergo important organisational changes. These changes can entail the loss of valued organisational features such as informality, responsiveness, particularism and advocacy work (Billis and Harris, 1992; Gronbjerg, 1993; Kramer *et al.*, 1993). They can become instruments through which other sectors can achieve *their* goals, rather than expressions of the values and visions of the philanthropists, social activists, local residents or oppressed people who started them and whose voluntary commitment has maintained them.

In these circumstances, it is becoming increasingly difficult for voluntary agencies to maintain their identity; to know where they stand and to defend their organisational integrity. The difficulties are compounded by two other trends.

First, there is the fact that a range of organisations that could once be unequivocally located in the governmental sector have apparently moved to inhabit the boundaries of the voluntary sector – NHS hospitals, local schools, social housing and so on. Some private sector agencies are making similar moves: for example, residential care homes may claim the characteristics of altruism and particularism traditionally associated with the voluntary sector (Challis and Bartlett, 1987).

Second, as several contributors point out, there appears to be increasing diversity and complexity within the voluntary sector itself; for example a growing gap between large and small agencies (Wilson), and between endowed charities and service-providing agencies (Leat).

In the face of these trends – threats to valued features of voluntary agencies, pressure to take on the agenda of other sectors, uncertain sector boundaries, and increasing diversity within the sector – constant reconsideration of what constitutes the core of the voluntary sector remains as a key challenge for both practitioners and researchers.

As this volume demonstrates, enormous strides in the development of knowledge about the sector have been made in the last fifteen years. We believe that the material brought together here can provide a foundation on which further knowledge can be built in the future.

References

Billis, D. and M. Harris (1992) 'Taking the strain of change: UK local voluntary agencies enter the post-Thatcher period', *Nonprofit and Voluntary Sector Quarterly*, 21(3): 211–25.

Challis, L. and H. Bartlett (1987) *Old and Ill: Private Nursing Homes for Elderly People*, Age Concern England, Surrey.

Gray, B. (1990) 'Commentary on Van Til's "independence of research": of disclosure and diversity,' *Nonprofit and Voluntary Sector Quarterly*, 19(1): 73–8.

Gronbjerg, K. (1993) *Understanding Nonprofit Funding*, Jossey Bass, San Francisco.

Kramer, R., H. Lorentzen, W. Melief and S. Pasquinelli (1993) *Privatization in Four European Countries: Comparative Studies in Government-Third Sector Relationships*, M.E. Sharpe, New York.

Mason, D. (1984) *Voluntary Nonprofit Enterprise Management*, Plenum Press, New York.

O'Neill, M. and D. Young (1988) *Educating Managers of Nonprofit Organizations*, Praeger, New York.

Van Til, J. (1989) 'On the independence of research on nonprofit organizations and voluntary action', *Nonprofit and Voluntary Sector Quarterly* 18(2): 95–9.

Index